First Edition

First published in 2018 by Pannasastra University of Cambodia,
South Campus, No. 184 Preah Norodom Blvd, Phnom Penh
Reprinted 2018

Distributed in Southeast Asia and United Kingdom by
Talisman Publishing Pte Ltd
52 Genting Lane #06-05
Ruby Land Complex 1
Singapore 349560
talisman@apdsing.com
www.talismanpublishing.com

Distributed in Australia by
Dennis Jones & Associates Pty Ltd / Port Campbell Press
1/10 Melrich Road Bayswater, Victoria 3153

Bibliography

ISBN-13: 978-99963-41076

Hunt, Luke 1962 --
1. War, 2. Media, 3. International Relations, 3. History,
4. Pham, An Xuan, 5. Vietnam, 6. Cambodia

A catalogue record for this book is available
at the National Library of Cambodia

Printed in Cambodia by Digital Advertising

PUNJI TRAP

PHAM XUAN AN:

THE SPY WHO DIDN'T LOVE US

BY

LUKE HUNT

Pannasastra University of Cambodia

For Lance Corporal John Gillespie

CONTENTS

ACKNOWLEDGMENTS

MOST BOOKS covering the Vietnam War were written with a focus on American involvement. Those that stand by Hanoi's view of events can carry the official approval of the Vietnamese government, which remains Communist, authoritarian and is often tempestuous towards anybody who strays from its official line, in particular—outsiders. This book appeases neither the hardliners of the politburo, nor those who subscribe to the many and varied academic theories surrounding United States action in Vietnam, or those who find common ground in Indochinese history. Instead, it seeks solely to relay a story, which carries its own significance, as told by those who were there.

My involvement dates back to 1989 when I began happening across the principle characters while completing an undergraduate degree in journalism. What began as a final undergraduate thesis for Deakin University in Australia progressed much further than I would have dared imagine at that time. Since then age and in some cases harsh living has caught up with some of the people interviewed for this story and their passing has allowed me to take what was initially off the record and spell it out for history's sake. This was also the deal struck with the man who forms the focus of this story, Pham Xuan An. Those interviewed who have since died include Gen. Tran Van Tra, Pham Ngoc Dinh—a generous man and a staunch believer in the noble truth—Tran Kim Tuyen, Peter Smark, Stanley Karnow, Billy Powis, Hu van Es, Morley Safer, Kate Webb and Denis and Peg Warner. It should also be pointed out that information An shared with the author, during many interviews spanning a decade, was to remain off the record until after his death. He died on September 20, 2006.

Since the initial round of interviews were conducted in Vietnam in 1992, with the official approval of Hanoi, scattered evidence concerning this book has appeared on the record and much has been confirmed through secondary sources. Throughout, rough drafts have been reworked and for that process the following people deserve far more than a vote of thanks on this page. They are Bill Charney and Shannon Gillies—for whom the author owes an expensive dinner—Peter Maguire and Josie Taylor. Others, like Karl Wilson, Paul Ruffini, Michael Hayes, Hurley Scroggins, Wilson da Silva and Ray Leos, Robert Carmichael, Mike Dunn, Nathan Green, John O'Callaghan, and Dave Potter helped this author at various times with their advice.

In particular the author wishes to single out Ginny and Joel McCormick whose editing did rein in a sometimes wayward writer with their eye for detail, and a touch of sensitivity that is difficult to find in the publishing trade. The coverage afforded the Vietnam War in newspapers, magazines, film and in non-fiction academic books, memoirs and other publications has been immense. As such it is impossible to single out every author and publication for mention in the actual text. Nevertheless, every effort has been made to attribute other people's work wherever appropriate. Given that much of the information that formed the basis of this narrative was obtained through exclusive one-on-one interviews, the author has opted primarily for explanatory notes for each chapter at the back of the book, as opposed to numbered citations and a reference list. This, alongside a standard bibliography, should add clarity and context for the reader in regards to sourcing. Small SEO Tools, *https://smallseotools.com/plagiarism-checker/* was used. Thanks also to Winifred Hunt, Laura Reinwald, Lisa Hunt, Wendy Lucas, Suzanne Reinwald and Peter Starr.

All figures are in U.S. dollars unless stated otherwise.

Many students of war, for good reason, loathe to compare conflicts but parallels are inevitable and lessons learned must be applied in future where necessary. Of the great atrocities committed by man on man—Japanese barbarity in China, Nazi extermination of the Jews, auto-genocide by the Khmer Rouge in Cambodia, Rwanda, and in more recent times Islamic State or Daesh—in all, independent journalists were made absent. A rigorous media inside a conflict zone tends to limit excesses in the field by ensuring the facts register on the conscience of the outside world and local journalists working hand in glove with foreign correspondents are a formidable force to be reckoned with. Local journalists also have to tend with local issues. This was the case in the Vietnam of the 1960s and 70s as it was in Afghanistan, Iraq and Syria during the first decades of the 21st century. The brave and true deserve their pedestal, the dishonest need to explain.

FOREWORD

*'Both the North and the South saw the conflict as "a war of national
survival". Editors and correspondents on both sides were,
therefore, willing propagandists for their cause, often adding
to the inaccuracy of the published reports of the war.'*
– from *War and the Media: A Random Searchlight,*
a reference to press behavior in the American Civil War
by Miles Hudson and John Stanier

HALF WAY DOWN Ly Chinh Thang Street at number 214/A in District
3 in the suburbs of Ho Chi Minh City, great secrets lie closeted in the
memories of an ailing old man. But Pham Xuan An is content with the
thought that history will remember him as a great war correspondent and
leave matters there.

Of this, An (pronounced 'Arn') seems sure. How he became privy to
history's judgment we will probably never know—and challenging it here
would only give An's fascinating story away before the telling of it.

Besides, there is ample evidence supporting it. Conflict, whether moral
or physical, whether communal or personal, held little fear for him. His
high-profile work at the Reuters news agency, and later at *Time* magazine,
gave An ready access to power brokers on both sides of the 17th parallel
that divided his very divided country. And in the tradition of power brokers
and journalists of stature, his highly placed political friends grew suspicious
of An at different times for different reasons.

The great war correspondent also developed, as high-profile journalists often do, something close to an entourage, or at least a circle of admirers, although few of his contemporaries ever really knew Pham Xuan An underneath his very polished surface.

Like many journalists with claims to greatness An was also detained by the authorities. This included a stint in a Communist re-education camp and later, under what was for all intents and purposes house arrest, imposed periodically throughout the late 1970s and early 1980s.

Visitors were rare in his early days of house arrest. But as tensions subsided after the war, more of them came by, nearly always heralded by Mr. Chin, a short, pot-bellied man with a watchman's scowl.

Happily, Mr. Chin's scowl would vanish if the visitor came armed with a sense of humor. The slightest remark unzipped Mr. Chin's lips, revealing a very wide and warm smile—and wonderfully straight white teeth, which in this country towards the end of the Cold War almost certainly signals stature.

Mr. Chin, indeed, was the man in charge of the government press office in Ho Chi Minh City. The office was located downtown in District 1, just a short distance from Independence Palace at the end of Le Duan Street, and it was from here that he kept tabs on foreign journalists.

Although its original purpose was to guard against visiting journalists engaging in serious probing or otherwise undermining the Communist regime, the office had assumed a more prosaic mission as the years rolled by—essentially, talking up the moribund economy and organizing press tours of the country's woefully inefficient state factories.

One might assume this less fraught agenda made Mr. Chin's job easier, but the truth of it was many of his visitors came for rest and recreation cures in old Saigon's bars and brothels, not wide-eyed tales of Soviet-style economic development.

The exceptions, even more problematic, were journalists who came neither for bar nor factory tours, but to revisit the past along Ly Chinh Thang Street. Mr. Chin had to be especially alert in these cases, always being sure to arrive outside the rusting blue wrought iron gates of An's large villa ahead of scheduled visitors.

And so, again, one day in March 1992, the tremendous bark from the German Shepherd echoed down the driveway, announcing Mr. Chin's presence. Moments later, An appeared from behind the building's entrance and shuffled toward the gate as Mr. Chin peered between the bars and down the concrete path to where the old white Renault had been left rusting for years.

Mr. Chin continued to be impressed by the old man. His height and wrinkled face, now partially obscured by thick black-rimmed glasses, still exuded authority, and certainly wisdom.

The dog continued barking, a bruising exercise for a shepherd deep in the tropics. But An repeatedly brushed his hand against the animal's tail, coaxing the tension out of the animal and, finally, it sat and started panting again, draining more sweat from its system.

An reached into the pocket of his cotton shirt, retrieved a cigarette, lit it and parked it in the corner of his mouth. He smoked one cigarette, then another and another, the fiery ash casting intermittent sparks of light on the past.

Like many of his celebrated peers in the press, An got himself an American college education and had gone from there to cover one of the great stories of his generation, the Vietnam War and its defining battles—Ap Bac in 1963, the Tet offensive of 1968 and finally, the fall of Saigon in April 1975. But he got into places his peers never could. As a foreign-educated local working for prestigious global news organizations, he had the credentials to gain access to the highest levels of government and traded on a nearly continuous flow of inside information to advance his career and expand his influence.

An's rise in the news business couldn't have happened at a more crucial time. As Stanley Karnow once remarked, Vietnam was the world's first television war. Daily, the TV networks served up more horror and atrocity than Americans could ever have contemplated. Prosecution of this horrible adventure wasn't forever going to be left to backroom boys inside the Beltway, to use a Washington term unknown at the time. Americans at large would be the ones to stop this terrible waste—that is, if antiwar sentiment could be cultivated and spread.

As one bloody year rolled into the next, news organizations delivered an ever worsening picture—yet An, backed by an informer network that reached into Vietnam's most mysterious places, always had new details to paint and that made the picture even worse.

The images never got better, only worse, even as the U.S.-led allies were gaining the upper hand. And eventually, of course, Americans did turn against the war—and President Richard Nixon did order the withdrawal of American troops from Vietnam. An, through his journalism, certainly contributed to this chain of events, as did other journalists through theirs. Like mice performing in some imaginary Marshall McLuhan experiment in communications theory, they proved that the medium is the message:

That the images of war and their shocking impact on the American public at home really determined the outcome, not battlefield action in Vietnam. But were these journalists who did McLuhan's work all disinterested observers, or did some have hidden agendas to follow? The answer to that gets to the heart of this story.

* * * * *

AS THE YEARS PASSED, it was more the legend than his presence that impressed Mr. Chin. By the 1990s, An was a sickly and frail-looking old man, even if his mind was still agile. At five-foot-nine, he made an unusually tall Vietnamese. Senior government officials were said to grow irritable having to crook their necks back to look him in the eye. But now the years were taking their toll. An was all aching joints and migraines. His eyes had sunk deep over the years and his teeth stood as an indictment to decades of smoking 40 a day, usually Luckies or Pall Mall. His long, pencil-thin fingers were like his teeth, they too were permanently stained from decades of smoking.

On this visit, Mr. Chin held out a message on a small piece of paper. The note was from Pham Ngoc Dinh, a former Reuters correspondent who had fled Vietnam a decade earlier. Dinh was now living in Sydney with his new family—not counting his other children in California and his mother, still in Ho Chi Minh City. Now, it transpired, An's onetime cocksure student wanted to meet up with his old mentor.

The prospect made An uncomfortable, just as other visits from the past haunted him. There were Pulitzer prize-winners Neil Sheehan, Stanley Karnow, Peter Arnett, Malcolm Browne, David Halberstam and Horst Faas. But there were others, also icons of journalism, who along with the Vietnamese, followed the wars of Indochina from 1945 to 1975—Americans, Australians, British, Canadians, French and Koreans. An had his favorites, among them, the late Bob Shaplen, Jim Pringle and Morley Safer—and John Cantwell, who died on the job, and Neil Davis, who died on assignment in a different conflict more than 10 years after hostilities in Vietnam had come to a close.

One by one, names of friends from the past drifted into the HCMC press office, each visitor application daring Mr. Chin to provide access to An. Some got it, sometimes arriving with gaps in half-finished books and other works in progress. Some of them tried to pry information from him in an effort to link An with all his storied contacts in hopes of piecing together another Vietnam mystery. But they never knew enough to ask about a phantom called Hai Trung, his closest contact of all. An enjoyed these visits but only up to a point, for this was dangerous ground visitors were treading on.

PART ONE:
1850-1960

1. CHILDREN OF DIFFERENT GODS

*'I had never visited Indochina, nor did I understand
or appreciate its history, language, culture or values.
The same must be said, to varying degrees, about President Kennedy,
Secretary of State Dean Rusk, National Security Adviser McGeorge
Bundy, military adviser Maxwell Taylor, and many others.
When it came to Vietnam, we found ourselves setting
a policy for a region that was terra incognita.'*
– Robert McNamara, former U.S. Secretary of Defense

FOREIGN INVASIONS run through the history of Vietnam, but its modern-day plight began with the French conquest of Indochina and the first missions organized by the Society of Jesus. During the 18th century, French missionaries arrived along the coastal plains of the South China Sea to establish a foothold and offer salvation. A variety of highly developed indigenous cultures, in fact, were well entrenched after 2,000 years of evolution and revolution with an emperor, whose power was often challenged from within the royal courts of Hue. For more than a millennium they had to some extent put their ethnic differences aside and when they were not fighting among each other the Vietnamese united in the north to fight Chinese aggression and occupation. Although the country hardly knew more than a few decades of peace, the Jesuits came at a time of relative calm.

Initially, the outposts were insignificant, but with the opening of trade routes and colonization of nearby countries by rival Britain, France started to pay closer attention to her missions. By the late 1850s they had become important trading centers, and the French moved to protect their interests by annexing Indochinese territory through a series of swift, brutal military exercises. Although Laos and Cambodia were easily vanquished, Vietnam had maintained a competent army and it withstood the onslaught for nearly three decades. But, heavily outgunned, the Vietnamese were slowly worn down. They finally capitulated in 1886 and the country fell completely under French domination. With Napoleonic zeal for organization, the new masters formally carved the territory into three administrative regions, drawing two parallels running from the South China Sea to the spine of the central highlands. Following Jesuit nomenclature, the north, bordering China, was officially called Tonkin; the central region, Annam; and the southern bloc, Cochin China.

This was the backdrop for the 20th-century struggle to end Vietnam's subjugation—a struggle that defined many people, but two men in particular.

* * * * *

LITTLE IS known about the early childhood of Nguyen Sinh Cung. Born in northern Annam on May 19, 1890, he was the youngest of three children and quickly proved a handful. His rebellious streak seemed to be in the blood. His teacher father, Nguyen Sinh Sac, was said to have quit the imperial court for refusing to toe the line. Sac was a genuine scholar of his day, and had risen through the academic ranks after beginning life as the son of an impoverished farmer. When Cung turned 11, his father assigned him the name Nguyen Tat Thanh, or, "he who will succeed". But young Thanh was quickly marked as a troublemaker at his own school and expelled at 13 on police orders after taking part in anti-French protests.

For the next seven years, he passed from one job to the next, his movements still confined to the central provinces. Occasionally, we see him flailing at authority—showing up at tax revolts, for instance—but Thanh's personal rebellion really didn't find direction until he decided to leave Vietnam.

In 1911, as Sun Yat-sen was preparing his vision for a republic in China, Thanh signed on as a cook on a freighter bound for Europe, now a hive of growing intellectual and political agitation. He set his sights on France, understandably enough, given his desire to understand the colonialists who occupied his country. But he only made a stop long enough to catch the attention of police in Marseilles ("Appearance awkward—mouth half opened", they noted in his dossier*). His voyages would prove long and arduous, taking in Africa, the United States and Europe. Eventually he fetched up in London, where he took work as a street sweeper, an inconsequential Asian eking out a living, before finding a job as a kitchen hand.

The romance of travel may have seemed a hoax, but Thanh got an introduction to politics through the Chinese Overseas Workers Association, one of many self-help organizations formed by impoverished workers. Thanh was beginning to see social and political action groups as the key to change—anything outside the established colonial or religious framework—even if he must have seemed the odd man out in this group. Most Asians in London came from India and Burma down the Malay Peninsula to Singapore. Indochinese like Thanh gravitated to France as a rule.

Thanh went to Paris towards the end of World War I, his mild distaste for Catholics, Buddhists and the Chinese brand of Confucianism soon to be overtaken by a hatred for France's ruling classes, although he found French people in France far more convivial than those who occupied Indochina. There he found a job as a photographer's assistant retouching black and white photos with color. By this time, the war effort had consumed 80,000 Vietnamese either as enlistees in the army or as factory workers.

Determined to make a political name for himself, Thanh took the name Nguyen Ai Quoc. Nguyen was the Smith of Vietnamese surnames; Ai Quoc translated as patriot. France, of course was under siege, and Thanh, living in a down market apartment in Montmartre, was starting to see Vietnam's imperial rulers in a very revealing light. Reports were rife of French units mutinying and that Vietnamese military police had been used to put them down—a clear sign of cracks in the colonial order. The notion that Europeans were the betters of Vietnamese was coming unstuck.

As, indeed, was France's political order. As the Great War drew to an end, the French Socialist movement, splintered though it was, had been growing as never before, giving hope to subject peoples in France's colonies. Notions of independence in those colonies were buoyed by Vietnamese support for France in its years of dire need.

The people of Indochina—with their own ancient histories, cultures and sense of national identities—rallied and proved themselves able allies, worthy of recognition that they belonged to their own sovereign country.

---

* For further reading see *Ho Chi Minh* by William Duiker and *Ho Chi Minh on Revolution*, edited by Bernard Fall.

Those calling for independence had hoped that such service to France would deliver a sympathetic ear from political moderates who held the power to grant the Vietnamese what Quoc cherished most, the freedom to determine their own destiny among the brotherhood of nations.

But the Socialists were at this point the only political group prepared to grant indigenous people in the colonies the right of self-determination. According to entrenched government policy, which survives to this day, offshore possessions were considered overseas departments of metropolitan France—part and parcel of the republic.

Such attitudes, for Quoc and independent minded Vietnamese, were galling.

Far removed from his mediocre beginnings at home, Quoc rose through party ranks, high enough to convince the leadership to put his nationalist objectives for Vietnam on the agenda. Initially Quoc was awkward and shy and he found public speaking difficult. The historian Boris Souvarine once described him as "a timid, almost humble young man, very gentle, avid for learning". His quiet nature earned him a nickname, "the Mute of Montmartre". This started to change when friends urged him to speak at public meetings organised by chapters of the Socialist Party. In time, his confidence grew.

But the party had become deeply divided between left and far left—with Quoc leaning to the latter. In December, 1920 at the 18th Congress of the Socialist Party at Tours in central France, a majority led by Marcel Cachin, Gaston Monmousseau, Paul Vaillant Couturier and others, voted to form the French Communist Party (FCP), leaving only a rump affiliated to the Second Socialist International.

The splinter group eventually recovered and became the Parti Socialiste Francais. With these deep divisions in the background, Quoc managed to consolidate his own position within the FCP. In just a few short years, he had become the voice of Vietnam, indeed all of Indochina, in the political circles that counted in France—despite a dizzying fixation with his name and image. Amid the factional brawling of the left, Quoc established the Association of Annamite Patriots, an umbrella organization founded to represent some 50,000 Vietnamese who were living in France by the end of the war.

Quoc put forward the case for Vietnamese independence at the World War I peace talks at Versailles in 1919. His eight-point memorandum included a list of French abuses in Vietnam, but it was all too much for U.S. President Woodrow Wilson. Wilson wouldn't abide discussion of the petition and rejected it out of hand, as did the French. That rejection was troubling for its hypocrisy, because it was Wilson who led the call of self-determination for all peoples but the political realities, that France was important and the colonies of Indochina were not, served as a potent lesson for the future. The petition circulated around the streets of Hanoi and succeeded in frightening the French who zealously guarded their colonial interests. Police soon identified Quoc as Nguyen Tat Thanh, son of the scholar Nguyen Sinh Sac, the young man who had been blacklisted from school because as a child, he was a trouble maker. Quoc was placed under surveillance, but he moved and agitated around Paris for the next four years, baiting the authorities with routine appearances at Socialist congresses and with aggressive articles published in the left-wing French press.

Quoc's audacity at the peace talks had won him admirers but his supporters had gently pointed out that his knowledge of Marxist/Leninist theory was wanting and as a revolutionary he stood at the start of a steep learning curve. He hadn't read Marx's *Das Kapital.*

Quoc sought to remedy his shortcomings and became a regular visitor to the national library but it was the publication of Lenin's famous "Theses on the National and Colonial Questions" that, according to historian William J. Duiker, had electrified Quoc. The Russian's argument that Western Communists should support nationalists movements in colonial Asia and Africa proved pivotal and Quoc's views began to shift to the more extreme side of the far-left. By the end of 1921, Quoc had begun writing under another pen name, Nguyen O Phap, or, "Nguyen who detests the French". The change reflected his hardening stance that armed insurrection was required to evict the French from Indochina but this idea had not won broad support, either among the French Socialists, or Vietnamese living in France from whom Quoc relied on while playing a cat and mouse game with the authorities.

As he studied, he wrote for publications including *Le Matin, Le Humanite, Le Populaire* and *Le Paris.* According to Duiker: "There was nothing fancy about his style. He had learned the importance of simple and direct writing style by reading Leo Tolstoy." Within that style he prophetically theorized that the Soviet Union would in future lend support to China and he noted that East Asian countries were increasingly at the mercy of Japanese capital. In early 1922 he founded *Le Paria,* or, "the pariah". Subscriptions peaked at 300 and anybody caught reading the journal faced automatic arrest. It was smuggled into Indochina where Quoc's father, Sac, was saddened to learn of his son's extreme agitation.

His close friend at that time, Tran Tien Nam, doubted his extreme political outlook, and noted that Quoc's views were not always shared and others argued that French influence in Indochina was required at least for the time being. This theory was expunged from the thought that peasants, with no education or experience with the outside world, needed a gradual exposure to the West before they would be able to cope with Socialism.

The wily Quoc countered, noting there were more French jails in Indochina than schools, he pointed to Siam and Japan which enjoyed full rank and status alongside sovereign nations and he singled out Confucian culture as being far closer to the principles of socialism than the French cornerstones of liberty, equality and fraternity.

He echoed those views during an official tour by the Vietnamese Emperor Khai Dinh in mid-1922 when Quoc used his by now well-honed journalistic parlance to ridicule the emperor as a mere colonial showcase for Paris while his people grovelled.

Throughout the early 1920s, Quoc had been ably assisted by Phan Chu Trinh. Trinh backed his friend with supportive editorials during the emperor's visit but the pair were split on how best to attain independence for Indochina. Trinh felt Quoc was wasting his time by delivering hard-line speeches to the Socialist Party faithful and that his message was not being received by those who mattered—the Indochinese people. He urged his colleague, also dubbed the "fiery stallion", to return home and agitate but Quoc, frustrated by dominant opinions held even by the most ardent European Socialists—that Asians were backward and not ready—turned his sights towards Moscow, and eventually China. Campaigning in Paris attracted the attention of Dmitry Manuilsky, a Ukrainian delegate in the Comintern. He invited the young revolutionary to study in Russia. In June 1923, Quoc announced he was leaving the French capital for a three week holiday in the south of France.

The trip was a ruse which he used to smuggle himself as an Asian merchant into Germany. He then traveled through Berlin to Hamburg where he boarded a ship to Petrograd with the prospect of meeting his hero Vladimir Lenin. But Lenin was ill and died in January the following year and Petrograd was renamed in his honor. Quoc attended the funeral.

Initially, Russia was kind to Quoc, he had arrived as Russia was attempting to consolidate after the Bolshevik revolution. Stalinist purges lay ahead and for the time being the fledgling Soviet Union still enjoyed comparative freedoms including cultural and multi-political assertions, and capitalism.

But he would face the same problems he encountered in France. Quoc continued to push the peasantry in colonial Asia and Africa as a foundation for establishing a global Communist system. In October he addressed the International Peasant Congress. He spoke in French and told the conference of the plight of rural people in Asia and was warmly rewarded with the establishment of an International Peasant Council where Quoc was elected to an 11-member presidium. It appeared a victory. However, as the months rolled by he realized that Communist backing for nationalist causes in colonial Indochina was far from being a priority. Lenin, who made it a priority, was dead, and Joseph Stalin was engaged in a power struggle for control of the Kremlin and there was a common theme that Asians were of no concern to European workers. Requests for an interview with the Comintern secretary general, Grigory Zinoviev, were ignored. According to Duiker, the American historian, Zinoviev was bored by the issue, Quoc's sponsor Manuilsky was more concerned with the Balkans and this had prompted Quoc to remark to a friend that he was a "voice in the wilderness".

As Indochina's voice in the Communist arena, Quoc had always intended to return to the Far East and while in Russia held meetings with comrade Zhou Enlai, future prime minister of China, and Chiang Kai-shek, then military advisor to Sun Yat-sen.

But getting out of Russia with a Comintern mandate to expand his revolutionary activities had become bogged down by bureaucracy and a lack of interest and finances. Persistence, which had proved a Quoc hallmark, prevailed and eventually he received permission from the Comintern to return to East Asia to carry out his work, however, Quoc would have to operate out of China illegally and fund himself. The latter was resolved after a deal was struck with the Soviet news agency ROSTA for which he would write stories from China in return for a small stipend.

In October 1924, Quoc boarded a train in Moscow and departed for the Far East. He arrived in Vladivostok the following month where he boarded a train for Canton and linked-up with the Communist Party of China (CPC) which had been established four years earlier amid social convulsions and the reign of war lords.

In a bid to shore-up his presidency and halt the disintegration of China, Sun Yat-sen sought to unify factions by moving the Kuomintang to the left and establishing formal relations with the CPC. Such relations were extended to Russia which did not endear the Chinese leader to Western governments. But an environment had been created that would allow Quoc to thrive for the next two decades. He immediately made contact with the Comintern mission in Canton and assumed a false identity under the name of Ly Thuy while he wrote for the ROSTA news agency under the pen name Nilosvki. It was a means to an ends: The backbone of Quoc's existence remained his long term agenda, to ferment a Communist revolution and achieve a unified independence for Cochin China, Annam, Tonkin, Laos and Cambodia.

* * * * *

CHINESE ASTROLOGY has adherents across Asia and is based on a 12-year lunar cycle, each year represented by an animal and its associated traits and linked with one of five elements; metal, wood, water, fire or earth. Astrologically, 1927 was a propitious year. Pham Xuan An was born in the Year of the Cat, its element fire. The omens generally favored cats, despite their tendency towards mood swings and over-sensitivity. Believers hold that fire empowers cats with psychic strengths, and for An's Confucian family this mattered.

His father, Vien, was a Mandarin descendent from the royal courts in the north-central provinces. He followed the zodiac but never let it overshadow his practical side, nurtured at school in Hue and at university in Hanoi, where he obtained an engineering degree. Soon after graduation, Vien traveled south, married a local girl in the province of Bien Hoa in Cochin China, and settled in My Tho, about 70 kilometers southwest of Saigon on the northern rim of the Mekong Delta, where the couple raised four children.

An was close to his mother in his early years but eventually warmed to his disciplinarian father, who introduced his son to sports, swimming and boxing in particular. Tennis was fun, if frivolous, hunting manly. An learned how to survive in the bush and in the nearly impenetrable forests of the surrounding districts. The gift of a puppy when he was five sparked an enduring passion for animals.

An's father worked daily to instil in his children respect for family, country and humanity. Family overrode everything else and the siblings grew very close, becoming model students of Confucian philosophy. As the eldest, An came second in the family pecking order after his dad. Hard-working and frugal, Vien taught him to abhor corruption and the abuse of power. In high school, the boy became fluent in French and earned top marks in mathematics. He helped the younger children with homework and earned extra money from tutoring. Pham Xuan An, in short, was a son a father would be proud of.

In his spare time he read adventure stories about hunters stalking tigers with the Montagnard hill tribes. But this was a family, comparatively well-off though it was, that never confused fiction with the realities of colonial life under the French. Vien, ever the pragmatist, knew that publicly voicing any anti-government sentiments he harbored, for example, would cost him the permits he needed for his engineering work. Immediate economic priorities held sway even though he knew in his bones Indochina was heading for upheaval.

As the children were growing up, the mysterious Nguyen Ai Quoc was vigorously laying down his Communist agenda. The prescription was straightforward: Overthrow French imperialism, feudalism and the local capitalist classes to make way for an independent Indochina uniting the French colonies. A popular government would be formed from the ranks of the army and the peasantry. The banks and capitalist enterprises, being extensions of French interests, would be confiscated and nationalized. Plantations and property belonging to the French capitalists would be redistributed among the peasants.

In Canton, Quoc had made a fundamental shift from independence and Communist advocate to logistics. Effectively, he began planting the revolutionary seeds by establishing the Revolutionary Youth League, and traveling across Asia to build a network of Communist parties. This culminated in the formation of the Indochinese Communist Party (ICP) in 1930, a triumph made after Quoc boarded a boat and sailed the murky waters of the Pearl River to the British trading port of Hong Kong where a meeting of nationalistic cadres had been organized to resolve factional differences. But it was through the Revolutionary Youth League that infiltration of Cochin China, Annam and Tonkin initially began, forming the embryonic cells that would later evolve into the Viet Minh.* He also found favor in Thailand where a ruling monarchy shared his distaste for French colonialists who were challenging their borders.

Students were recruited from Confucian ranks south of the Chinese border to Canton where they were trained under Quoc's stewardship at the Special Political Institute for the Vietnamese Revolution which was partly funded by the CPC. While stressing the role of the peasantry, Quoc's teach-

---

* This type of cell structure was emulated by Osama bin Laden when building his al-Qaeda network.

ers tutored their classes on Marx and Lenin, coached students in public speaking, taught the Chinese language and exposed students to an indoctrinated and highly imaginative version of Vietnam, within a world context. Zhou Enlai was one of many Communist luminaries who visited the school as a guest lecturer.

By the time An was a toddler, his provincial town of My Tho had become one focal point for the fledgling Communist movement which probably held no more than several hundred cadres broken-up into cells of between two and four people. It was a tiny start but with a Communist charter gift-wrapped in an independence agenda, the movement was embarking on its mission during a period of historic economic turmoil. The stock market crash of 1929 had struck at the heart of global capitalism triggering fortuitous fears of a great depression that would pit workers against employers en-masse throughout much of the 1930s. Armed with an alternative political philosophy, the proponents of communism found themselves in an opportunistic time.

Quoc would return to Moscow and study, where he received solid support for his plans in Southeast Asia and then traveled across the continent drumming-up support. He was arrested in Hong Kong but found a sympathetic ear among the British elite and the authorities who didn't mind outsiders meddling in French affairs.

But it was the outbreak of World War II and the Chinese Civil War that would harness his enigmatic personality, firmly placing his nationalistic agenda in the box seat and reinvigorate the ICP.

Quoc and his colleagues did not foresee Vichy France cooperating with Tokyo after Japan began its military incursions into Indochina in 1940, even though the puppet regime and nominal government of unoccupied 'Free Zone' France was collaborating with Germany, Japan's axis partner 10,000 miles away. Through an uneasy alliance, the Japanese allowed the French to keep their middle and lower ranking jobs in the bureaucracy and administer the day-to-day operations of the Indochinese colonies. At first, most Vietnamese were pleased to see the Japanese smash the Europeans and walk over their colonial regimes. But as the Japanese spread their own brand of cruelty, ordering mothers and daughters to work as "comfort women" in army brothels and dispatching their men to labor camps, attitudes quickly changed. Certainly, any lingering doubts about Japanese intentions dissipated in 1943 when famine devastated the region. An, like everyone else, could only watch helplessly as the Japanese confiscated millions of tons of desperately needed rice to use as fuel to keep troop and supply trains moving from China through Indochina and down through Malaya to Singapore.

Japan's barbarity spawned an unlikely partnership. It began in February, 1941, when Nguyen Ai Quoc, adopted another pseudonym—Ho Chi Minh, or "he the enlightened one"—and crossed the border from his base in southern China into northern Tonkin where he established an operations camp at Pac Bo. With him was Vo Nguyen Giap and Le Duan, three men who held a united purpose, to fight French and Japanese alike. Together they organized the Viet Nam Doc Lap Dong Minh Hoi, which translated as the League for the Independence of Vietnam but would be popularized by its abbreviated form, the Viet Minh; a coalition of Communists and nationalist groups, and a small, ill-equipped army. Ho Chi Minh had succeeded in recruiting enough peasants to the cause to form an alliance with the British and Allied forces.

For middle-class boys like An, ousting the French and confiscating their wealth all looked highly improbable. But Ho's call for an eight-hour workday and abolition of poll taxes and other levies squeezing the poor seemed plausible and An began to listen. He liked the sound of the Socialist agenda with its demands for universal education, equality for women and freedom for the masses. Universal education struck An as a prerequisite for solving Vietnam's political and economic woes—and a cause worth fighting for.

Armed with the ignorance of his youth, An did not feel his middle-class lifestyle was threatened by Ho's disdain for locals who wormed their way into the colonial establishment. Ho's broad agenda for equality fitted too neatly within his homespun family-country-humanity credo for the boy to be swayed by any unsavory particulars. In 1943, An signed up with the National Youth Association after being introduced by a school friend, Cao Minh Tuong. Tuong's family were dedicated Communists with links to the Revolutionary Youth League that had begun in Canton under Ho, and An became what the French would call an agent provocateur.

Ho, by now, had considerable drawing power: His name often featured in the flyers and posters An passed out in the steamy streets of My Tho, which had been heavily infiltrated by the Viet Minh through the Revolutionary Youth League more than a decade earlier, during the early months of 1944. And he was drawing power from the oddest corners of local society. As American and Allied military aid increased, even the disenfranchised mandarin class fell in behind him.

As the Viet Minh's legend grew, Japanese casualties grew. The Viet Minh and Ho Chi Minh's peasant irregulars were proving a lethal combination. But with no political alignment between Allied forces and the Viet Minh, the partisans fought largely alone—and if that said anything, it said the different people of Ho's Vietnam could fight[*]. The immediate goal may have been defeating the Japanese, but the ultimate one was ridding Indochina of all occupiers, whatever their imperial stripe. Where French occupation once seemed immutable, ousting the French had by 1945 become a real, if still distant, prospect.

* * * * *

THE AMERICAN political humorist P.J. O'Rourke once argued that young revolutionaries were often born not out of political idealism, but boredom: "Picking up a gun and showing off in front of chicks is, after all, far more fun than hoeing a rice field." Along with his idealism, An was no less attracted to the prospect of being a hero than anyone else his age. Many of his classmates joined the National Youth Association (NYA); it had become the thing to do. There were girls and dances, political workshops, and fundraisers on Sunday afternoons—all good reasons to get together and strut a little.

In late 1944, An's chief concerns remained with the NYA propaganda platoon. At that point rumors of a Japanese retreat were rife. An spent weekdays canvassing for new NYA members and making the case for unification and independence for Tonkin, Annam, Cochin China, Cambodia and Laos. He handed out flyers advertising public meetings and circulated protest messages from one branch to another—all activities that were banned so there was a nicely clandestine feel to participating in these blitzes.

The youth movement had ambition but little stature in the nationalist political structure. It sat on the bottom rung alongside the Liberation Farmers' Association and the Liberation Women's Association. All three were answerable to the local village party chapter, which answered in turn to the local district party committee, which reported to the provincial party committee, which reported to the inter-provincial party committee. While

---

* Scholars have argued that the China-centric narrative regarding Ho is a bit tired and that Ho's revolutionary origins exhibited a more regional cant. He left Canton in 1927 and transited Hong Kong, Shanghai, Vladivostok, Moscow and Paris and ended up back in Thailand in 1928. He returned to Hong Kong in late 1929 where he formed the Communist Party of Annam changing the name to ICP in 1930. The Siamese were just as happy as the Brits in Hong Kong for Ho to undermine the French in neighboring Indochina.

each committee level sought to mobilize the civilian population against the colonial establishment, they typically operated at arm's length from the Indochinese Communist Party and the growing Viet Minh army.

In early 1945, the NYA got an assignment some members were looking for. Betting the Japanese would withdraw completely and trigger a popular uprising that might conceivably oust the severely depleted French, Viet Minh and Communist Party officials decided to arm the propaganda platoons and use them as guerrilla fighting units. In their propaganda role, the platoons had worked in teams of 30 or so to build up relationships with local villages. Now the Viet Minh wanted to take advantage of those relationships: It charged each platoon with enlisting grassroots support to arrest French, Japanese and anyone else who opposed the Communist-backed Viet Minh. An formerly accepted a military posting on March 9, which meant transferring from Can Tho near the center of the Delta to a Viet Minh training base hidden outside his hometown of My Tho, allowing him regular contact with his family.

An was starting to feel easier about the local brand of communism. The party's decision years earlier to drop Stalinist-style fire-and-brimstone preaching and some of its ultra-left extravagances made visions of a free, united and independent Indochina more plausible. It was a decision made all the easier by the moderate appeal of the Viet Minh during World War II, made possible by an uneasy alliance between Ho's radical ICP and various non-Communist nationalist groups.

The lack of alternative organizations also helped, for the ICP would eventually appropriate the nationalist debate and inextricably link ideals of nationalism with Marxism. In time, the party made it virtually impossible to be a nationalist without attaching oneself to the ICP.

At 18, An was tall, almost gangly, but good-looking, with well-defined features sheathed in clear, amber skin. Immaculately groomed, he was a stark contrast to the ragged, calcium-deficient rotten-toothed illiterates usually recruited by the Viet Minh. Like An, most preferred the adventure of freedom fighting to the ennui of normal living, which in their case was farming.

Not surprisingly, An did not fit, cutting a prissy figure in the Viet Minh's crowd of ragamuffins. But as middle-class and fresh-faced as he was, he earned points for his vociferous condemnation of the existing political structure. The secret bush camp near My Tho was dry and dusty when An arrived in the heat of summer wearing his shiny shoes, pressed short sleeve cotton shirt and neat trousers. He was handed a pair of black pyjamas and told to take his shoes off.

Catering for 20 recruits, the camp was indistinguishable from any small hamlet; several barracks constructed of local timber with thatched roofs dotted the clearing. Training Viet Minh-style was primitive, archaic, sometimes ludicrous. Each morning before drill, the trainee guerrillas were fed a breakfast of rice cakes, soup and Chinese tea. They were handed guns and taught how to fire them. They practiced throwing fake hand-grenades made of clay. In the afternoon new inductees would line up side by side and repeat the process of holding a grenade, pulling the pin out with their teeth and lobbing the clay replica into a make-believe bivouac of legionnaires.

Target practice was followed by lessons in how to stalk animals and survive off the land. The trainees learned hand-to-hand combat, a skill in which An, who much earlier was taught boxing, excelled. Recruits were told to obey orders without question and were constantly reminded that this was a job for life. Like other fresh recruits, An was told his death would matter little and that he should expect it. Every Viet Minh soldier was replaceable and death was treated more as an inconvenience than a pathway to martyrdom. For An, some parts of the new-boy drill were harder to take than others, but he stayed the course—and it would be a long one. The struggle for independence would last for as long as it took, recruits were told, whether that meant 20, 30 or 50 years.

Training lasted eight weeks, and over this period An impressed his military instructors with his common sense and intellect. He was fluent in French and could manage a few words of English: He had a knack for organization and was extremely fit. Each day he swam five kilometers in the rivers of the Delta, as he had done since childhood. Fellow recruits began to like and respect him. His local knowledge was also sound and his hometown, nearby, had developed into a nationalist stronghold. Bien Hoa formed the tip of a northern triangular zone flanked by the villages Thu Dau Mot and Thu Duc. Another friendly zone, which became known as the Saigon Triangle, was formed 100 kilometers to the south between Saigon, Tay Ninh and Loc Ninh.

An's superiors made him a platoon leader, the equivalent of lieutenant. With more than 30 men under his command, he was ordered to patrol the Mekong Delta through the Saigon Triangle and then move further south towards the Gulf of Siam.

Just before heading south, tragedy struck and it would haunt An in a blackly comic way for the rest of his life. A young man just out of high school had arrived at the secret base for training. An never knew his name or where he came from, but he handed the budding revolutionary a French-made World War One six-shooter and instructed him to point the gun in front of him and squeeze the trigger. The thought of firing his first gun charged the rookie with adrenaline. A quick tempered lad, he pointed, tightened his face and prepared his eardrums for the loud bang that was supposed to follow. The gun simply clicked. Nothing happened—the Viet Minh's home-made bullets often didn't work. Cartridges were reused and reloaded with powder and lead, often with mixed results. He pointed again and fired and again it didn't work. It failed him a third time and he lost his temper, stomping around the Viet Minh's secret rifle range and cursing the useless weapon. "Why won't you work?" he screamed down the barrel, playing with the trigger. The inevitable happened. He blew his face apart, an unwitting player in a game of Russian roulette. On the dry turf of the summer delta moments before their first mission, a recruit lay dead in his own blood never learning that each chamber in the cylinder held a bullet. It was the first time An watched someone die by one.

An's mission was to round up remnants of the Vichy regime, colonialists looking to reestablish the prewar order once the Japanese left. As platoon leader, he was entitled to his own French World War One rifle with a clip of three rounds. Each time he fired, the discharged cartridge had to be retrieved for reloading at their makeshift munitions works at the end of the mission. The rest of the platoon shared firearms, often three or four men to one. They also carried crossbows and spears.

Patrolling was difficult, the heat exhausting, intelligence poor. An was almost as much a novice as those he was leading, but the Japanese had sapped French resources and morale. They were surprised by the unwillingness of the French to fight. By mid-June, the Japanese had virtually given up any hope of holding Indochina and were preparing to retreat and defend their country against the advancing Allies. The young rebels were starting to believe that total victory was assured—that the Japanese would leave and the remaining French could be evicted.

2. END OF ANOTHER WAR

*'... there is little doubt that Communist ideology had repelled
the vast majority of Vietnamese people.'*
– Peter M. Dunn, author of *The First Vietnam War*

BY MARCH 1945 the Japanese had six months left in their war with the
world. The Vietnamese knew it was almost over; so did Tokyo's French
collaborators who planned an uprising of their own. Getting wind of the
plan, Japanese leaders countered and moved swiftly. Tokyo's policy in Indochina reflected its position in occupied territories elsewhere in the Pacific
theater: Its military was expected to oppress and control the natives but
leave day-to-day running of government services to existing administrators,
thus avoiding disruptions of supply lines, in particular the rail link between
Saigon and Hanoi, by following established bureaucratic practices. Occupation was also costly and met by the Vichy French who were effectively
Tokyo's tax collectors, filling the war chest off Vietnamese backs. Such policies were becoming irrelevant and on March 9, under the command of
Japan's Supreme Commander for the Southern Region Gen. Hisaichi
Terauchi, senior officers orchestrated a coup designed to thwart Paris taking
advantage of its Vichy French administration in Indochina to restore the
pre-war colonial order. French bureaucrats and their cowered troops who
had acquiesced to Japanese rule were interned. The French strata of the
civil service was dismantled and the upper levels of the pre-war colonial
administration that had carried forth under occupation was replaced with
a staff of cooperative locals.

Then, two days later amid mounting pressure from advancing Allied forces, the Japanese military hierarchy allowed Emperor Bao Dai to declare Vietnamese independence—hoping to limit any Vietnamese attacks on a retreating Japanese army. The monarch sent an emotional message to Free France leader Gen. Charles de Gaulle, asserting his country's independence and pointing out that French domination had ended six years earlier. The old colonialists would not be welcomed back, and that included Cambodia and Laos too.

As a symbolic ruler with some public support, Bao Dai and the Imperial Court in Hue had always held a nostalgic place in the hearts of the Vietnamese people, particularly among the urban middle classes and especially in central Vietnam. His letter was enough to stir the public's imagination. The puppet position of French governor general, as the Japanese defined it, was abolished.

It was a bold assertion and as with other messages that challenged French traditions in the colonies de Gaulle found this disagreeable. He dismissed Bao Dai's claim, but wasn't blind to the situation. Knowing the French hold on Indochina was slipping, de Gaulle pushed for a charter loosely granting autonomy to the area under a federal framework. In Vietnam, the pitch was ignored. Independence beckoned.

* * * * *

INSPIRED, AN had signed-up with the Communists on the same day that Bao Dai declared independence. The Japanese had backed the emperor by canceling the French administration and interning civil servants and troops. French forces of legionnaires and army regulars in Indochina at the outbreak of World War II were no match for their Japanese counterparts and numbered between 5,000 and 10,000 men. The British considered them useless as a fighting force and as potential allies. Following the March 9 orders, more than 5,000 French troops escaped into China while others escaped to the relative safety of Laos. The leftovers were stuck in the south and those who could avoided arrest and fanned out across Cochin China hoping to bide their time ahead of a return to French rule.

Those remnants were An's military target. But as the monsoon rains set in, turning the Mekong Delta into a quagmire of mud and flooded plains, his troops grew tired of soldiering and he had his moments keeping them together as a fighting unit. A few had been wounded in sporadic attacks.

During those skirmishes it was not unusual for the platoon to find itself on the defensive, at which point it was each man for himself. Later An would regroup with his men in the nearest sympathetic hamlet.

More than once, An outwitted the colonial troops. Villagers were a prime source of intelligence and could pinpoint their movements, helping An play energy-draining cat-and-mouse games on them. Once informed of their whereabouts, they would act. In one isolated incident he rigged up a megaphone on a tree and played a taped message on a stolen recorder calling on the people to rise up and defeat the enemy. He would leave enough blank tape to spool off ahead of the message, giving him and his deputy enough time to leave the immediate vicinity. By the time they reached a safe distance, the loudspeaker would start playing calls to the people to rise up and revolt. Moments later bursts of gunfire would be heard, followed by a grenade, as happened with the forces under Gen. Jacques-Philippe Leclerc. They, too, would claim another enemy "kill"—a two-dollar megaphone. If there was sufficient ammunition, An's platoon would attack from behind, catching the French by surprise and inflicting at least a few casualties. The tactic was hit and run, moving in and out before the legionnaires could regroup and counterattack.

Another tactic involved the punji trap. The technique was simple, the results excruciating. The trails across the Mekong that were commonly used by foreign forces could be found on any map in Saigon, and while the Viet Minh avoided them, the tracks provided easy ambush locations for the Communists. An's platoon, and hundreds like them, would dig a small hole, several feet wide and deep. Inside the hole, scores of razor-sharpened bamboo sticks were secured upright and then packed tightly with mud. The men would then generously paste human and animal excrement across the tips and cover the small dugout with twigs and leaves. The punji trap was cheap and highly efficient, as ignorant soldiers would discover after the bamboo had sliced their boots and pierced their soles with festering feces. One trap would incapacitate one man but require another two to carry him; the pace of the entire platoon would slow and the ceaseless cries of the injured would grind down morale—and often cut these military sorties short. If troops failed to make it back to base in time, a leg would be lost to gangrene. The simplicity and cunning of such tactics would frustrate almost a dozen foreign armies for decades to come.

An loved the freedom of roving through the bush, swimming each morning and chatting with villagers. It gave him a sense of identity and duty, and the thrill that often goes with risk-taking. During the day he and his men crossed the river system in sampans, which carried three to four men and one gun. At nightfall they would camp with friendly villagers and catch up on the latest news. As An's platoon headed north, information was relayed south through the networks of hamlets and villages. Each night, news of the day's events in Saigon became more staggering and convoluted.

Casualties were rare, but that near-spotless record was about to be bloodied as An turned his troops for home. The platoon had picked up a cache of hand-grenades and an opportunity to use them had suddenly presented itself—a mission that called for attacking a contingent of French soldiers busy rounding up known Viet Minh sympathizers.

The grenades differed from the mock clay bombs the troops had practised with on the Viet Minh's secret training grounds at My Tho. These had hammers released by thumb triggers jutting out from the neck; once the pin was pulled the trigger had to be pressed tight against the body of the grenade. Releasing it left only three seconds to discharge. There was no margin for fumbling or second-guessing targets, and certainly no timeouts for southpaws trying to cope with devices designed for right-handed troops.

On this day to remember, before dawn, each soldier was given his quota of grenades. Then the unit moved out and, as planned, proceeded to encircle the enemy as it plodded south. Right on cue, each man placed the pin of the grenade between his teeth and waited for An, a safe distance away, to give the order to lob the bombs at the unsuspecting colonial troops.

They did not know what the hammers were for.

Finally, An gave the order. A dozen pins from a dozen grenades were pulled—and nearly as quickly a dozen hammers on a dozen grenades sprang into action. And moments later a dozen of An's troops, their faces obliterated, suddenly lay dead.

The survivors fled.

* * * * *

THE OCCASIONAL firefights encountered by An's platoon were as his drill instructors had foretold—insignificant—especially when considered within the context of the political maneuverings being played-out in the capital cities among the Vietnamese Communists, nationalists loyal to Emperor Bao Dai, the exhausted French along with their native collaborators and depleted Japanese forces.

Throughout the final months of World War II the Japanese withdrew their troops from across East Asia and the Pacific, steadily towards home in anticipation of a final pitched battle against the advancing Allied armies who were approaching the doorsteps of Tokyo. Then, with a sudden and mighty blast, Hiroshima was obliterated by an atomic bomb on August 6. Nagasaki was next three days later and Japan's Emperor Hirohito declared an unconditional surrender on August 14; the war in the Pacific, and with that World War II, was declared over the following day.

According to the historian and author Peter Dunn there were only 5,000 Communists in Indochina at that point. "And there is little doubt that Communist ideology had repelled the vast majority of Vietnamese people. Hence the party's constant use of cover organizations, fronts, alliances and so on."

But it was enough. As news of Japan's surrender spread those heavily factionalized fronts coalesced to a point and launched their bid for power. While appreciating Bao Dai's March declaration of independence, the Communists as a whole refused to accept the monarch's Japanese-approved government and a power vacuum persisted in Hanoi, Hue and Saigon.

On August 13, the Indochinese Communist Party called for a general insurrection. Four days later, in Hanoi, the Viet Minh hijacked a mass rally and a show of support for Bao Dai. Then on August 19 the party initiated its own rally at Municipal Theatre Square where a new national anthem and flag were produced, and the insurrection moved into full swing with Viet Minh seizing control of government offices.

Across the country, the cell networks established by Ho Chi Minh in the 1930s and supported by the Viet Minh who had fought alongside the Allies were rising on a wave of nationalistic fervor and taking over government. In Hue, on August 23, two mandarins from the royal court were killed by the Communists as the Viet Minh delivered an ultimatum to Bao Dai. The Emperor abdicated, spelling an unceremonious end to Vietnam's royal rule and perhaps one of the few institutions which had consistently delivered a face of national unity amid decades of colonial divisions. It was, in fact, a coup.

Two days after the abdication the Viet Minh struck Saigon. Under Tran Van Giau, the ICP had seized control of the printing presses in Saigon. His men were veteran fighters who earned their experience with Allied and Chinese troops and the Japanese genuinely feared them. Quickly, Giau deployed his forces and occupied the offices of government and bureaucratic administration. His headquarters was established in Saigon's City Hall.

The Viet Minh now claimed complete control of Hanoi, Hue and Saigon and the time was ripe for Ho to make his move. On September 2, in Hanoi, the arch enemy of Paris, veteran Communist and upstart to boot, reared. Sporting a goatee beard that would become his trademark motif, one he had used while traveling incognito and one that would stick. Ho Chi Minh stood on a wooden podium in Ba Dinh Square and flanked by minders in white suits he announced Vietnamese independence—through a familiar declaration: All men are created equal. They are endowed by their Creator with certain inalienable rights, among these are life, liberty and the pursuit of happiness. Looking on were Americans from the Deer Mission, set-up by the Office of Strategic Service (OSS), forerunner of today's Central Intelligence Agency (CIA), to train a guerrilla force to fight against the Japanese.

The Democratic Republic of Vietnam had been formed and as Ho put it the "double yoke of the French and the Japanese" had been removed. Unification of Cochin China with Tonkin and Annam had been achieved. Cambodia and Laos could wait. And in the eyes of the half-a-million people who had turned out to hear him speak, for the first time since the French Jesuits began carving up Indochina, Vietnam was united. Ho and the Communists had stolen the nationalist agenda, filled the political power vacuum and captured many a heart. Bao Dai had, after all, ruled under the whims of the French and Japanese.

Now they had all been removed.

Blood spilled in the streets of Saigon the same day. A mass demonstration in support of a united approach to independence went awry. Despite their best attempts, the Viet Minh were unable to control splinter groups and criminal elements. A riot erupted and five Europeans, including a pro-Viet Minh priest, were fatally shot outside the Catholic cathedral in the center of Saigon's business district. The violence incited looting and ransacking of shops and houses; French business owners were taken prisoner.

Tran Van Giau was embarrassed and the fracas prompted the Viet Minh to later release the recently jailed French prisoners in a desperate goodwill gesture. Those rounded up by forces like An's platoon in preceding months remained incarcerated. But appeals for calm did not work. Trotskyites denounced their comrades as soft but the Communists were suffering in the south where non-Communist nationalist groups held more sway and Vietnamese society was far less homogenous. The French were only more terrified.

Events in Vietnam stunned the Allies. Ho Chi Minh and his Viet Minh had seized the initiative and control before the Allies could arrive and restore the pre-war colonial order. For military operational purposes, the

Allies had assigned China the northern half of Vietnam but in reality this was a move designed to appease Chiang Kai-shek and it would be the Americans who would call the shots ahead of a mandated French return. The south fell under a British mandate led by Lord Louis Mountbatten who charged Maj. Gen. Douglas Gracey with occupying Saigon, maintaining public order and restoring French responsibility for the civil administration.

A massive fly-in was arranged for September 12 and 13 with 1,203 men and 37 tons of equipment flown into Saigon's Tan Son Nhut Airport. POWs were evacuated on the return leg to Bangkok. More would follow. Gracey was widely regarded as an affable and liberal chap, a methodical man who held an intense dislike for needless casualties. He arrived in Saigon on the 13th, his contingent made up of British and French troops, the 20th Indian Division from Burma along with a detachment of Gurkhas. Further orders included the disarming of what was left of Japanese Field-Marshal Hisaichi Terauchi's troops, and to free any Allied POWs and jailed civilians. Under the terms of Tokyo's surrender, however, the Japanese with an estimated 71,000 troops still in Indochina would share responsibility for maintaining law and order. French troops began returning in smaller numbers and immediately re-activated their former units.

The August revolt had not been viewed by Allied Command within the same context as those who supported it. As far as Gracey was concerned anarchy had won out and this had to be resolved. Furthermore, this would prove baffling to the Viet Minh, who after years of soldiering in the same military theaters as the Allies, expected recognition and support in their efforts to obtain self-rule. Expecting the West to support independence, locals strung up Union Jacks along the road from Tan Son Nhut to Saigon.

Quiet had returned. The Viet Minh claimed control of essential services like garbage collection and public transport and ran the newspaper presses and Saigon Radio, but everyday necessities remained in short supply. A part-time police force existed but what little order that was maintained among Saigon's 150,000 citizens was largely due to efforts by the Allied forces. Japanese soldiers, left free, were orderly during the day and retreated to the bars and brothels of nearby Cholon at night.

Unable to distinguish its various religious, ethnic and political layers, Gracey found the place disorderly. According to Dunn: "As far as the eye could see, there were scattered groups of totally unconcerned Vietnamese around their cooking pots, which were bubbling over open flames and exuding thick smoke and pungent aromas. Half-naked urchins tumbled about the floor. The City Hall was little more than a squatters haven."

With little evidence of formal governance, Gracey initially decided on drawing up administrative arrangements with the Viet Minh. But first, he wanted to create the perception that he was in charge and capable of enforcing the law through a court system. The general saw it as the responsibility of the Japanese to supervise law enforcement until his full complement of troops and back-up staff arrived, and instructed Terauchi to take charge.

Gracey's mandate did not include holding Indochina until the French could regain control, although Britain still recognized France's sovereignty. His orders were only to disarm the Japanese and establish temporary control, and carrying them out would effectively reintroduce pre-war conditions in Indochina.

Hard-line Trotskyites and disaffected Cao Dai religious students were proving a handful and stirring-up rumors that Britain would hand Vietnam back to the French. The scurrilous loose-talk was inflamed by reports on Saigon Radio and would prove fateful, and the Viet Minh upped the ante by leading protests calling for general strikes that threatened food and medical supplies. Gracey retaliated on the 19th, shutting down the printing presses and Saigon Radio. From that point he refused to deal with the Viet Minh, ordering all Vietnamese to be disarmed. Viet Minh police were systematically relieved of their guns. Their worst suspicions were confirmed when Gracey declared martial law on September 21, banning demonstrations, public meetings and the carrying of arms—including sticks and bamboo poles that could be used as spears. He implemented a curfew between 9:30 p.m. and 5:30 a.m. The Viet Minh responded with more strikes, shutting down transport, postal, telephone, telegraph and medical services. The shutdown spread to shops and businesses till Saigon basically stopped. Events in the southern capital were shaping-up for a tumultuous showdown.

Enter Col. Jean Cedile—an able and ambitious Frenchman—who offered Gracey a means of restoring French authority and in doing so the British a fast track out of Indochina. Cedile held an intense distaste for the Vichy French and had been anointed the next governor of Cochin China by de Gaulle. He had parachuted into Vietnam almost a month earlier and his relationship with Gracey was convivial. Gracey had no wish to bog his troops down in a quintessential French affair and agreed to Cedile's offer to wrest back control of Saigon and *Notre Indochine* through a coup d'etat. The British general agreed to rearm 1,400 of Cedile's militia, composed of both soldiers and civilians.

With precision Gracey's men, in this instance primarily Gurkhas, took control of the police stations and banks, the treasury, post and communications. Then in the early hours of Sunday, September 23, Cedile set out with a compliment of 300 hand-picked French troops. As reporters of the day noted, a coup d'etat was beginning and Saigon would soon become French again.[*]

An heard that morning that the *tricouleur* had been hoisted and the Viet Minh driven out of their headquarters at Saigon City Hall. Unsubstantiated rumors told of scores of Viet Minh being killed, of many more being shackled and beaten and of leaders being jailed while the British turned a blind eye to French concepts of revenge. Elements of the Viet Minh soon retaliated. On the night of the 24th and 25th as many as 150 Eurasian and European civilians were massacred in Cité Heriault, Saigon's expat dormitory suburb. Many were tortured, their bodies mutilated. Investigations would later lay blame on the Trotskyists but in the meantime Gracey held the Viet Minh, as he knew it, totally responsible.

By now Gracey was convinced a civil war was in the making and feared the entire French community was in mortal danger. He saw no choice but to support the full reinstatement of French authority. In an extraordinary move, he went a step further. Japanese troops charged with sharing the burden of maintaining law and order had not been disarmed and Cedile would charge that some of Tokyo's men had Viet Minh sympathies and allowed the Communists into Cité Heriault to carry out the massacre. Gracey then ordered Japanese troops to fight alongside British and French soldiers in a bid to quash the Viet Minh. For the Vietnamese this was the ultimate betrayal. The bid for independence was lost and An was disgusted. The initial hallmarks of the First Indochina War had emerged.[†]

---

[*] Dunn notes in *The First Vietnam War*, p200, that acrimony between the military and the press, mainly American and Australian, escalated over the rearming of the Japanese and that Gracey, confronted by a "ghastly" press conference was "given hell" by journalists of the day.

[†] The importance of this period and the impact that events would have on the shape and nature of the civil wars to come is often overlooked. In early October, the French Navy delivered the first 1,000 troop contingent of the French Fifth Colonial Regiment and the last British soldier had been evacuated by March 1946. The rapid usurpation of power by the French in the south stood in stark contrast to the situation in northern Vietnam. There the Chinese dithered until the spring of 1946, never allowing the French to regain a clear upper hand over the Viet Minh, forcing the rebels into an uncomfortable coalition with other non-Communist Vietnamese nationalist groups.

3. THE FIRST INDOCHINA WAR
1946-1954

'The French usually bombed us twice a day—mornings and afternoons.'
– Pham Ngoc Dinh

BORN IN 1936, Pham Ngoc Dinh spent his childhood in famine-ravished areas of Quang Nam province in Vietnam's Annam central region. His village sat on the edge of paddy fields against a backdrop of forests and steep mountains. With the Japanese finally smashed in 1945, coalition Viet Minh forces were the heroes in this part of the world. The locals had armed, clothed and fed them with food and the latest intelligence—and for all intents and purposes were a natural extension of the same fledgling guerrilla army.

Dinh's parents backed the Viet Minh, too, but not out of any idealism. As rice-producing landowners, they hated the Japanese for confiscating the family's desperately short grain stores. Dinh's father, Van, had no Communist leanings, but Viet Minh socialist policies aimed at improving educational opportunities appealed to his sense of justice. In this sense, Van's aspirations for his family were much the same as those of Pham Xuan An's father.

When the Japanese left Quang Nam province and withdrew north, the Communists re-emerged to fill a vacuum. The Viet Minh immediately threw out the exclusive boys schools of the French regime and implemented a basic form of universal education offering math and Vietnamese reading and writing to everyone.

Returning French didn't make distinctions. Farmers, nationalists, Communists were all the same ugly animal to them. Three times Van watched as French soldiers burned his home because it was a suspected Communist safe haven. He rebuilt again and again. Fifty years later, Dinh would vividly recall, as if the horror had just revisited him, how in 1948, when he was 12, his father was ambushed and shot in the head, neck and chest.

Following Van's death, Dinh's grandmother took over as head of the family and sent Dinh and his older brother into the Communist-ruled Ashau Valley for schooling. Pedagogical methods were crude. On one occasion, Dinh and 50 classmates were led to a nearby lane where they took turns punching and kicking a French soldier who had been tied up—lessons devised to vividly establish who the enemy was and how to treat him.

Dinh remembers hesitating at first; next to his small frame the Frenchman was a giant. But after some coaxing from friends and a reassuring smile from the guard, Dinh joined the assault with gusto.

Communist curriculum concentrated on areas previously neglected. Unlike An, Dinh studied French history and politics from a Communist perspective. He also studied the history of another traditional enemy, China. But there was certainly nothing privileged about his school days, as Dinh was to recall.

The Ashau was a valley and a Viet Minh area—no-one else came in. One of the first things we did was build our own bomb shelters. We would dig down and then across [underground]. The shelter itself was shaped like the letter 'L' and when the French bombed us, each of us would dive down our own hole and lie horizontally at the bottom of the shaft. The French usually bombed us twice a day—mornings and afternoons.

I was living with my aunty and I was always up very early. At six in the morning I would go down to the river and fill up the water barrels, drag them back up the hill and fill the tanks connected to the house. School began at eight and lasted till five, and because I was at primary level our studies were more general. We did not have any paper or pens; instead we used banana leaves and a toothpick. The Communists pushed independence. My father had been killed by the French and the Communist propaganda about liberation was brilliant—they made me angry, very angry.

We were always hungry. Once we ate an entire banana tree as opposed to just the bananas. There was never any real food; usually it was rice mixed with sweet potato—real slop. I was hungry, really hungry—you would go to school with nothing in your belly. But the teachers tried to treat us kids well. When we were hungry they would explain to us the need to sacrifice for our country. The food was for the soldiers in the battlefield. But Ho Chi Minh was always saying the children must be looked after for they are the men of tomorrow—the workforce, the soldiers—and even though we were always hungry there was a feeling of common purpose, of camaraderie.

There was never really any meat at all. Sometimes we might catch a fish in the river and on special occasions—like a wedding or birthday—a chicken would be killed and shared among 20 or 30 people. To keep our minds off our bellies we played soccer, volleyball, ping pong or tennis, and naturally we went to class, where I hated mathematics and loved to write stories. I was always number one at writing.

The school was opposite a Viet Minh military hospital and often I would go and see the soldiers who had returned from battle. I wanted to know who they were and what they had done, to see them fight. I already wanted to be a reporter.

It was always late before we went to bed. There were Communist seminars and meetings to attend. People would sit around and sing songs dedicated to the cause—liberation. I believed in it at the time, I believed it all. I believed if we could win the war then there would be no more poor people and everybody would have somewhere to live. Like Marx says, like Lenin says, like Mao says, then Ho Chi Minh says: "You work if you can work. If you can't then the party will look after you and everybody will be equal and everybody will be protected."

In just 12 years Dinh and Pham Xuan An would cross paths as they launched on journalism careers like few others. For the time being, young Dinh attended class and bomb drills. An, meanwhile, settled into a stretch of relative obscurity after being discharged from the Viet Minh, grateful to emerge from the fighting unscathed with a home and family to return to.

At 19, he was a veteran of a world war and a failed revolution, and the complexities of Vietnam's situation remained a Machiavellian puzzle to him. Vietnam was still three states instead of one and an Indochina federation uniting it with Cambodia and Laos was as elusive as ever. The British proved to be traitors who had rearmed the Japanese and allowed the French collaborators to snatch back his country. In the musical chairs of postwar alliances, the Communists once again counted the Cao Dai and Hoa Hao religious sects as enemies, like the Binh Xuyen crime ring. Catholics were nationalists but could not be trusted. The promise of America with its long-held opposition to colonialism only diminished as the country grew larger on the international stage. It seemed content to ignore the plight of Indochina and unwilling to compromise British efforts to build NATO bases on French soil. Paris was resisting moves by Washington and London to form a Western military bloc that would incorporate West Germany as a bulwark against Soviet expansionism. Instead, French foreign policy was attempting to steer the country on a hopeless course that would allow Paris to establish itself as a bridge between West and East. That strategy, like French policies in Indochina, were at best misguided arrogance. And Washington was warned. On September 26, 1945 Lt. Col. Peter Dewey, a former correspondent with the *Chicago Daily News*, was ambushed and killed by the Viet Minh while traveling near Saigon becoming the first American casualty in Vietnam, although his death was not classified as a Vietnam War casualty. The Viet Minh would later claim the killing was a mistake, and Dewey's legacy was far greater than an historical statistic. He was attached to the OSS and shortly before his death the 28-year-old Dewey had prepared a report that was ominous in its conclusions: "Cochin China is burning, the French and British are fnished here and we (the United States) ought to clear out of Southeast Asia."*

Throughout the following year returning French troops replaced the withdrawing Allied and Chinese forces and engaged in hit and run battles with the Viet Minh while Paris entered drawn-out negotiations with Ho Chi Minh. Truces were made and broken as both sides sought to avert an all out war while refusing to yield on their stated positions. France attempted to make some concessions in recognizing Vietnam as a free state with its own parliament, army and finances but only as part of an Indochinese federation and the French Union. Ho was under no illusions and in October, with Vo Nguyen Giap beside him, began secret preparations for an all out war which would require the Viet Minh to retreat to the countryside and substantially build upon its ranks from the peasantry before initiating a campaign of surprise strikes and later a series of country-wide, furious, assaults. Such a process would take years, not months, and its delicate beginnings were imminent in December, 1946 after peace talks at the Fontainebleau Conference, in France, proved worthless.

Shortly after eight o'clock on the evening of the 19th of December an attack was launched on the Hanoi power station and the city plunged into

---

* Lt. Col. Peter Dewey's report and subsequent death have been well-documented. The most recent was by Claude G. Berube and can be found online in HISTORYNET, entitled Vietnam Point of View, Vietnam War, published October 6, 2009.

darkness. French targets were attacked across the capital as the Viet Minh forces signalled the beginning of the First Indochina War with a bloody and violent pull-out to the country-side that left dead about 100 French troops and more than 40 European civilians.

* * * * *

THE ADJUSTMENT from battlefield platoon commander to civilian was difficult. After returning to My Tho in late 1945, once the Mekong floods had begun to recede, An decided to fill in the gaps in his political knowledge. He began by reading the illegal literature circulated by the Viet Minh proclaiming the rights of nationalists and Communists alike. He would later begin learning English through American-sponsored programs but by this point his exposure to U.S. troops had been restricted to the post-World War II mop-up. The war against the French was mild when compared with Japanese occupation and the events of 1945 and by the late 1940s were having little impact on home life.

But just as his life was falling into place, his health began to deteriorate. Diseases like meningitis, smallpox, cholera, dysentery and diphtheria dropped into the tropics as easily as the common cold, so An wasn't shocked when the doctor told him he had come down with malaria. The mosquitoes that transmitted the disease were rampant in the waters of the Mekong, where he'd spent most of his fighting days.

In 1947, the one known effective drug for treating malaria was quinine, though doctors had difficulties with An's particular diagnosis because he seemed to be carrying more than one type of infection and quinine had only a marginal effect.

Although it would be a few more years before penicillin was readily available in Indochina, its use as an anti-malarial agent was already known in 1941. In the early trial days doctors in Cochin China were wary of prescribing it. Still, An was desperate to contain the pain of recurring fevers and obtained some on the black market, jabbing his thighs with hybrid doses of quinine and penicillin.

An's disease, at times life-threatening, stayed with him for five long years. Extreme attacks of fever culminated in severe vomiting, paralysis came and went, but as time passed the periods of relief gradually grew longer. The chills and depression continued, but An's self-medication—his concoction of quinine and penicillin—allowed him to cope with the pain. Slowly, the malaria worked its way out of his system.

Throughout 1947 he studied for his baccalaureate in My Tho and would make trips to Saigon where he would take part in anti-French student demonstrations. Then later that year, An's father moved the family from rural My Tho to Saigon, where there were better medical facilities—he had come down with TB. Tuberculosis was not considered an automatic death sentence anymore, but he was no longer in his prime when it struck.

The Cochin China capital also offered new opportunities for the children, and the rest of the family arrived a year later. An enrolled in English classes organized by the United States, took the baccalaureate examination and with his malaria subsiding he eased himself back into the workforce. Each morning he would rise before dawn and report for work at the Caltex service station in District 3, where he kept the books and occasionally pumped petrol into the Peugeots and Renaults that putted so ubiquitously around the city. The job was part time, ending late morning. He spent most afternoons resting, but as his health picked up he took on extra work to help with family finances. An started private tutoring in math and French, which included regular part-time classes at a local grammar school. Then he took a third job—in the evenings, he pedaled a cyclo taxi, allowing him to earn, besides the usual crumbs, extra cash as a translator and fixer. Fixing usually entailed pimping and ferrying expats to favored brothels. Demeaning though the work could be, the exercise gave him back the physique he had before marching off to fight the French and further fuelled his distaste for the colonialists, leading An into the Tran Van On Movement. On was a local student activist whose protests focused on the periodic closure of schools deemed as problematic by the French. He was shot dead on January 9, 1950, during a demonstration and his death triggered wider protests.

Still, it was a mundane existence which lasted until mid-1951 when An's luck apparently changed. His studies had paid off and he successfully applied for a job as a clerk at Customs House on the Saigon waterfront. Besides filling the usual import/export clearing functions, the department ran communications and foreign currency exchange services and enforced colonial regulations for Cochin China. It also provided a cablegram service by which foreign correspondents would file their copy. This simple back office would provide An with his first exposure to the international press corps.

An's new position also grabbed the attention of Dr. Pham Ngoc Thach who headed a regional committee for the Communist Party in Cochin

China. After checking on An's background, highlighted by his recent involvement in the Tran Van On Movement, Thach immediately set about co-opting An and the pair met secretly during the Tet New Year Festival in early 1952.

Thach was part of the cell structure sowed by Ho Chi Minh in the 1930s, that had blossomed in World War II and he had risen through the Communist ranks via the youth movements. According to Duiker, Thach had also grabbed the attention of U.S. diplomats during Ho Chi Minh's attempt to negotiate independence and they considered him "a man of intelligence and very considerable energy". He had gone underground after the British restored the pre-war colonial order. Now the Communists were reemerging and Thach wanted An to work for Viet Minh strategic intelligence but, according to official Vietnamese records published more than half a century later, An was not at all pleased:

Being influenced by family tradition, what I hated most was the jobs relating to intelligence, secret service or police. When I was a child, I had been arrested by the police several times for protesting. When taking part in demonstrations, I witnessed the police's suppression and beating of people. So when I was asked to undertake the job, I was not very happy, How can I assume the job of … hunting dogs or preying on birds.

An was, however, a proven hunter and Thach was patient and reminded An of the purpose of the revolution. In fact, what followed was reminiscent of the lectures An received when the Communists decided to arm the propaganda platoons seven years earlier. According to the official record, Thach told An that once a person had joined the revolution, he or she had to be ready to undertake any task and go anywhere that the revolution required, even if it meant sacrificing one's life. Thach also gave long-winded explanations about strategic intelligence and spying, matters of political security and secret service affairs saying: "Senior leaders have entrusted you with the job because they firmly believe that you will do the job well. You will learn much in the process."

Thach had made it impossible for An to reject the order and he was placed under the authority of Duong Minh Son and Nguyen Vu. Decades later An would credit these two for teaching him the basics about intelligence but in the meantime it was imperative that An kept his job at Customs House as this would enable him to carry out Thach's instructions and monitor and report the rising shipments of U.S. military arms to the French administration and, where he could, the deployment of French troops. U.S. involvement was beginning to weigh heavily on the minds of the Viet Minh leadership. It had begun on September 17th in 1950 when, without ceremony, 128 members of the Military Assistance and Advisory Group (MAAG) were secretly dispatched to supervise the use of U.S. military equipment. But by the time Thach and An met during the Lunar New Year holiday period of 1952 this quiet assistance was proving effective against Viet Minh cadres in the field and spies inside Customs House were a perfect clandestine way of monitoring the dispatching of military hardware. An had been press-ganged back into the Viet Minh's ranks.

But he also had more immediate problems at home.

TB had forced his father, Vien, to retire from the building business in 1952. Fortunately, An's new job lifted the family income enough to compensate for that and allow An to resume smoking. Three years later he would switch to Lucky Strikes,* smoking up to 40 a day—in the manner of the chain-smoking Ho Chi Minh, who also patronized the brand.

But just as family finances were coming comfortably into balance, he contracted TB himself. Unlike his father, unfortunately, he had lived at close quarters with a TB carrier and had been hit by malaria, a combination that lowered his resistance to TB still further.

By late 1952 An's TB was fully developed, his lungs inflamed, his cough bloody and his body riven with fever. He opted to skip the expensive streptomycin treatments doctors recommended and decided on a simpler course of fresh air, a healthy diet and isolation—essentially sitting the disease out and studying English to fight boredom. And slowly An recovered, enough for doctors to lift the quarantine and allow him to return to light duties at Customs House, and subsequently the Viet Minh.

* * * * *

THE SAIGON waterfront was filled with the buzz of hustlers, and the Customs House was at the center of it all. Here An monitored the daily traffic of people, goods and services moving in and out of Cochin China. His duties also included checking newspaper copy cabled by the handful of

---

* Author of *Perfect Spy*, Larry Berman, says it was American advisors who introduced An to Lucky Strikes and taught him how to inhale in 1955.

foreign correspondents operating out of Saigon. He had been instructed to pay especially close attention to a British correspondent, Graham Greene, whose leftist views caused French officials and their Vietnamese underlings considerable worry—though Greene usually avoided offence by saving his most damning observations for his novels published after leaving the country in question.

Apart from Greene, who worked for British intelligence*, and at various times wrote for *Life* magazine, *The Times* of London and *Paris Match*, the most prominent reporters on An's watch list were the American Bob Shaplen of *The New Yorker* and the Australian Denis Warner, who worked for the Australian Associated Press and Melbourne *Herald*, among other publications. Their careers stretched back to World War II.

It was the enigmatic Greene who first switched the Custom Department's factotum on to journalism. An's English had improved markedly on the job and in no time at all he was second-guessing Greene's copy. Like a seasoned editor working with the same correspondents, he could easily pick out the Englishman's style from the cablegrams submitted by Shaplen or Warner.

An liked Greene's writing for its raw simplicity, and he started to think he might be destined for a career in journalism. He continued to improve his English and remained, despite his increasingly anti-French sentiments, a voracious reader of classical French literature, a habit easily pursued in a French colony. His favorite was *Cyrano de Bergerac,* but his areas of interest were decidedly eclectic, ranging from the revolution and Napoleon to French cuisine.

While his work for the Viet Minh was also hampered by illness, he had impressed and in February 1953, An—who at that point was still a member of the lowly rated National Youth Association—was made a full member of the Communist Party of Vietnam at a ceremony held in Ca Mau province, and in the presence of party's southern chief Le Duc Tho who heaped advice upon the young spy. The presence of Tho—a close confidant of Ho Chi Minh—underscored the faith and importance the Communists were placing in An.

"Peace will eventually come," Tho said, according to official records. "But for the coming period, the situation will change. We will conduct a long war against them. You have to take advantage of the peaceful time to learn,"

---

* Graham Greene's career in espionage can be traced back to Sierra Leone in 1941, according to Keith Jeffery, author of *MI6: The History of the Secret Intelligence Service 1909-1949.* p479. Other writers and correspondents who also worked in intelligence included Somerset Maugham.

he told An. Thach, also had important advise for An: "Avoid being conscripted. If you are, try to be a battalion commander."

An's interest in the media and the political affairs of home heightened with three quite separate events; a terrorist act, a ticking-off at work and, two years later, publication of a Graham Greene classic. Shortly after his elevation to full party membership, An was strolling home from work when a bomb exploded nearby on the popular Rue Catinat in the middle of a military parade. The blast killed several soldiers and French officials immediately blamed the Viet Minh.

When An queried his handlers—Son and Vu—he was told the Communists had no knowledge of the bombing. It was not them. They said it was the work of agents provocateurs, a ruse perpetrated by colonial officials to land the Viet Minh in trouble.

Just about the same time, An's pro-French superiors at Customs House reprimanded him for getting too close to Greene. An had talked openly about how he found Greene likable, and he dismissed the reproach as a petty overreaction—until *The Quiet American* came out in 1955. In Saigon, Greene's blockbuster was an immediate talking point. Most of the characters were inspired by real people, although Greene made the standard denials. The novel's principal character, an economic attaché named Pyle, was often said to be modeled on the CIA's Col. Edward Lansdale, who would eventually help to maneuver Ngo Dinh Diem into power as South Vietnam's first president.[*]

The Quiet American exposed an incident involving bicycle bombs and American-instigated attacks in Saigon, which killed and maimed civilians, many of them women and children. A journalist reporting an explosion was one thing, identifying those responsible was quite another, and An believed his handlers, and knew the political machinations behind these deaths were also true. Bicycle bombs, a novel idea at the time, were made by inserting plastic explosives into standard pumps held in the cross bars of bikes; operatives went around substituting real pumps for deadly ones on bikes jammed into street corner parking jungles. When unsuspecting civilians pedalled home after work or school, the pumps were exploded by transmitter.

Greene was horrified by the carnage, prompting him to tread the dangerous boundaries of journalist and advocate; and he liked the Viet Minh

---

[*] The current consensus is that Pyle was modeled on either Robert Blum, the head of the U.S. economic mission in Saigon at the time, or his deputy Leo Hochstetter, both mentioned in Robert Shaplen's *The Lost Revolution*.

cause. *The Quiet American* told how U.S. economic programs were a front for anti-Communist activities; these included attacks on the French military, staged in the hope of undermining Communist sympathy. Americans and their agents simply blew people up in the expectation Communists could be blamed.

Son and Vu confirmed to An that what Greene put forward as fiction was very real. In the early 1950s, local cadres were blamed for every anti-government attack from Tonkin to Cambodia. The situation was confused, and complex: Domestic Vietnamese politics was bound up in France's increasingly desperate bid to shore up its prewar colonial hold on the region—just as the United States was emerging as the dominant Western power and extending its influence over Indochina.

There had already been loud hints that the French and Americans were engaged in bloody tit-for-tat politics and this fed the enormous rumor mill around Rue Catinat, to the point where the fashionable street was dubbed Radio Catinat. One rumor accused French agents of murdering a group of American secret servicemen in Saigon and that this was also designed to look like a Viet Minh plot. The agents, or so the rumors assumed, hoped spreading U.S. fear of Viet Minh attacks on American interests would dissuade Washington from further involvement in Indochina. Some in the French colonial administration viewed American support as a means of encroachment on their territory, and with much the same suspicion that Gracey faced when the British first arrived. Despite American discomfort with France's thinly-veiled colonial revanchist project in Indochina, Washington resigned itself to continue its military support of the French expeditionary mission in Vietnam partly in exchange for Paris' cooperation with the collective defense in Europe, but mostly because the only alternative to supporting the French was a Communist Viet Minh victory.

* * * * *

AN'S DISTASTE for the French-controlled local Vietnamese armed forces was as natural as his wayward attraction to the Viet Minh, and the prospect of being drafted was drawing ever closer. Between 1950 and 1954 he dodged several draft orders by producing a doctor's certificate citing his malaria, tuberculosis and weak lungs, and each time he received a waiver. Thach's advice rang thick in his ears. But by early 1954, Vietnamese manpower had fallen to a new low. With more border skirmishes and an escalation of fighting at Dien Bien Phu in the far northwest of Tonkin, the French had to lower standards and sign up even An with his congested lungs and shortness of breath.

Dien Bien Phu became a juggernaut that added thousands to the recruitment list. But An really had no stomach for fighting fellow Vietnamese battling for independence and decided to pre-empt the authorities. He got his cousin to engineer a job for him in the Western-backed military: That effort got him a spot in the Joint General Staff (JGS), which accepted him, reckoning his customs experience and language abilities might be useful. An was made a secretary in the Psychological Warfare Department, also known as G-5, working as an assistant and staff secretary to his cousin Capt. Pham Xuan Giai, who headed the unit.

By "volunteering" for JGS work, An had reduced the risk of becoming a front-line foot soldier and increased his chances of a better job with better pay. He also drew two salaries; because a soldier's pay was notoriously small, at the JGS as anywhere else, An was allowed to keep his job at Customs House where he continued to draw the same pay even though he rarely turned up for work.

At G-5, An helped with translation and the preparation of psywar materials, like pamphlets and the accoutrements of propaganda, indoctrination, and disinformation. But it was also at G-5 where An first encountered Edward Lansdale whose efforts underwrote and assisted much of Giai's work product. An eventually arranged a transfer from G-5, out of the Vietnamese government to the affiliated but separate Training Relations & Instruction Mission (TRIM), carved out of MAAG and staffed by both U.S. and French officers and at the time still under the command of the top French military official in Indochina, Gen. Paul Ely.

TRIM's primary role was to provide advice and to assist the upper echelon of French-trained Vietnamese officers leading the nascent Vietnamese National Army in the herculean task of transforming their forces from a colonial auxiliary into a modern, capable, and self-sufficient army. TRIM was not CIA, but the Saigon Military Mission led by Lansdale was, and TRIM had by 1955 been subsumed and placed under Lansdale's aegis by U.S. Ambassador Lawton Collins.

Both groups, Collins recognized, shared intertwined objectives in terms of grooming Vietnam's future military and political leaders to fill the leadership vacuum opened in the wake of the country's partition. Their task amounted to, essentially, Nation-Building 101—to cobble together a non-Communist regime in the south that could compete with Hanoi for the hearts and minds of the Vietnamese population. But for An specifically, his role in TRIM provided him not only access to the top U.S. and French advisory personnel, but proximity to the most senior caste of the Vietnamese general officer class. In 1956, TRIM became CATO (the Combined Arms Training Organization) and An ended up responsible for the vetting and documentation of senior Vietnamese officers chosen to travel to the United States for command training at U.S. military establishments, further enhancing An's connections to the top rung of Vietnamese leadership.

An's relationship with Lansdale cultivated at TRIM would play a crucial role in An eventually securing a scholarship to study journalism in the United States. When An turned down Lansdale's offer to assist him to gain a spot at the School of Intelligence and Psychological Warfare explaining that he'd prefer to study journalism, it was Lansdale who steered An to the Asia Foundation and offered to sponsor him.

* * * * *

BY 1950, American foreign policy had become preoccupied with the Domino Theory, the theory being that states and territories from Burma to Indonesia could fall like dominoes to communism if effective action weren't taken. That May, Truman's Secretary of State, Dean Acheson, denounced Communist influence in Indochina and pledged military and economic aid to France—as a means of "restoring stability and permitting these states to pursue their peaceful and democratic development".

But the sun was already setting on this part of the French empire. The Viet Minh in the south with Ho Chi Minh in the north had sharply escalated guerrilla operations in the early 1950s culminating in the battle of Dien Bien Phu. Worn out from years of fighting, France's 17 battalions and 10 companies of 16,000 troops capitulated at the tiny outpost, following a siege that lasted from March 13 to May 7, 1954. This lead to the negotiation and signing of the Geneva Accords, which divided Tonkin, Annam and Cochin China into North and South Vietnam.

The key clause in the accords was a proviso requiring elections in the South no later than July 1956 to decide the future of South Vietnam. In the meantime, Ho Chi Minh would rule the North from Hanoi with his territory bordered by China in the north, Laos in the west, the South China Sea in the east and the 17th parallel in the south. Catholics and other anti-Communist groups were relocated to South Vietnam and Viet Minh sympathizers in the south were supposed to migrate north.

4. PLEDGES OF ALLEGIANCE
1954-1960

NGO DINH KHOI WAS one of the two mandarins who were brutally slain by the Communists when the Viet Minh delivered their abdication ultimatum to Bao Dai during the heady days of August 1945. And given the scale of political turmoil and bloody conflict that punctuated the next nine years, the relegation of his name to a mere footnote in Vietnamese history would not seem improper—save for his family connections. Khoi had five surviving brothers; among them Diem and Nhu. As children the siblings were close and raised as devout Roman Catholics through the French education system. Aristocratic in upbringing the family could trace their lineage to the 17th century when their ancestors had converted to Christianity. Diem had served in Bao Dai's administration before World War II then, when the Japanese made it possible to oppose the French; he did. But traditional enmity between Catholics and Communists meant a partnership between Diem, Nhu and Ho Chi Minh was never a realistic prospect; the murder of their brother made it impossible and Diem rejected an offer from Ho to serve in his brief post-war administration. Diem hated Communists.

Instead, Diem went into exile in the United States with his younger brother who served him as an advisor and the aspiring pair worked Vietnam's American connections, particularly influential Catholics that included John F. Kennedy and his family. The French thought Diem was crazy. By the time the Geneva Accords were signed pledging elections by July 1956, Khoi's surviving brothers had been fast-tracked by Washington into the corridors of power and Diem was named South Vietnam's first President but his position had to be—in the eyes of the Americans—legitimized

and an election was held in October 1955. The poll gave South Vietnamese a choice between the ousted monarch Bao Dai and Diem as leader,
the winner would then challenge Ho at the U.N. mandated elections which
would have unified the country under a single administration be it Communist or otherwise. But due process in the South Vietnamese ballot was
corrupted from the start. Col. Edward Lansdale opted for two types of
ballot papers, red which signifies good luck was allocated to Diem, green—
the color of misfortune—signaled a vote for the former emperor. Diem
claimed victory with 98.2 percent of the vote counted in his favor amid
reports that people who had attempted to cast a vote for Bao Dai were beaten,
and had witnessed their ballots being stuffed into rubbish bins. The Americans were incensed and urged Diem to declare victory with a more believable
figure of 70 percent. Diem refused.

The U.S. also had repositioned its military foray in South Vietnam on
November 1955 with a restructuring of MAAG operations which enabled
all U.S. military aid to be funneled directly from MAAG Vietnam directly
into the Vietnamese National Army and no longer through French military
command. Its mission now was to assist a fledgling South Vietnam.

Vietnam was split in two, but Cambodia and Laos remained intact, giving some hope in the West that Communist ambitions could be contained
in the northeast corner of Indochina—North Vietnam. As rewarding as it
must have felt to give the French a good thrashing, Ho's dream of an independent Indochina federation had come up decidedly short. The Communists had won control of only the relatively poor northern provinces of
what he called Vietnam.

But Ho never abandoned his designs on the south, or elsewhere of course,
and he ordered Viet Minh forces to remain there, in part to monitor activities in the run-up to the elections. To meet Hanoi's obligations under the
Geneva Accords, more than 50,000 Viet Minh headed north; but estimates
put the number of "stay behinds", as they were later called, at up to 15,000.
At the same time about 850,000 people fled the North for South Vietnam.
Of those, 600,000 were Catholics who, with the maneuvering of the CIA
and Col. Lansdale, would form the political power base of the new South
Vietnamese state under Diem. But thousands more among the southward
bound were Communists sent to support clandestine operations below the
17th parallel.

French troops were to remain in the south until after the elections of
1956. But the newly installed South Vietnamese president, Ngo Dinh

Diem* had no intention of holding elections—and nor did he intend to allow the French to stay. President Diem proved adept at exploiting America's ever increasing fears of communism. He played on this and enticed Washington into South Vietnam.

With that unremarkable, almost casual, turn, the First Indochina War was over, the second had begun. It was a low-key start to an extraordinary conflict. The Gulf of Tonkin incident, which would erupt ahead of a sharp escalation of the war, was still eight years away.

Among Diem and the anti-Communists, chief targets for arrest included the mercurial Le Duan, the man Ho Chi Minh assigned to run underground Communist Party activities in the south. Duan was proving hard to keep up with, even for Ho. He had ignored Hanoi's orders for everyone to lay low and restarted guerrilla activity in the south from an area that would become known as War Zone D. An himself knew little of the man from his own fighting days, limited as they were to the Mekong Delta, and he learned little at JGS. Sick much of the time, he hardly got close to Dr. Tran Kim Tuyen's secret police whose job it was to hunt down and remove Duan from the political equation.

The 1954 Geneva Accords called for resettling religious and Communist minorities, more or less as Partition on the subcontinent seven years earlier called for Muslims to go west into the newly-created Islamic Pakistan, and Hindus to head east into a shrunken, Hindu-dominated India. Possibly due to that bloodbath—in addition to a natural disinclination to leave home —many Communists in the south refused to resettle in the north. But these so-called stay-behinds were no happier for that; on one hand, they felt alienated by Hanoi, on the other, aggrieved that South Vietnam had somehow been shortchanged by the Accords.

Duan, like most of his ilk, refused to recognize a divided Vietnam, and by 1955 he and his partisans had devised a strategy to force Hanoi to redirect weapons and supplies to the stay-behinds, who would effectively ignite the Second Indochina War.

Ho had been reluctant to start another fight, hoping that South Vietnamese President Ngo Dinh Diem would proceed with elections, as provided for by the Accords, and allow the polls to determine a future head of state and whether the two Vietnams would be united.

---

* Elections were always unlikely. Fearing electoral fraud, the U.S. and South Vietnam insisted on U.N. supervision of the poll. However, the North Vietnamese, backed by the Soviet Union, refused.

By early 1956, Duan lurked in the background as a 'Diem versus Ho' contest grew into a hotly anticipated fight at the ballot box. President Diem was the recognized interim leader of South Vietnam, with the blessing of the United Nations and the United States. But Diem's yearning for power rose to the fore almost immediately after he was installed.* Popular though Diem turned out to be, the possibility of being defeated at the polls hung over him and his interest in holding elections waned accordingly.

Politics in the south were polarized over issues like land reform and re-settlement. Duan had bargained correctly that President Diem would simply let the July 1956 poll deadline lapse. As the year progressed, Duan plotted. He wanted to stage a terrorist response but knew it would be impossible to unleash a successful insurrection without the North's help. In the end, he opted to reactivate small-scale terrorist activities in the South, deliberately without the approval of Hanoi.

Dr. Tuyen and President Diem initially viewed Duan's ad-hoc attacks as minor brush fires orchestrated by a few renegades. What they didn't realize was that Duan had embarked on the exercises to embarrass Hanoi into lending its support. As frustrations heightened, so did public sympathy for Duan. Border skirmishes erupted around the 17th parallel and soon escalated, with Duan narrowly escaping several attempts to capture him. Ho Chi Minh was annoyed by the audacious Duan, and all the more because his tactics were working.

It was here that several mysterious characters emerged. Viet Minh military intelligence in the south was putting together an informer network from their base in Tay Ninh, near the Cambodian border, with hundreds of recruits, and Dr. Tuyen was their nemesis.

The Viet Minh relied heavily on spies—people who lived double lives where the routine of day job and family life proceeded so naturally that no one would suspect for a moment the possibility of a second life. By 1975, they would number around 20,000. At this, Pham Ngoc Thao proved a highly accomplished practitioner—at least for a time.

In public, Thao was a tireless staff member of the South's propaganda department (and an active member of his church). Dr. Tuyen, South Vietnam's spy chief, was more than his boss. Thao's deception was so complete that Tuyen dropped easily into the role of friend and mentor. They were

---

* Arguments have persisted that Diem was installed by the CIA but this still isn't clear. He was initially picked by Bao Dai despite protests from the outgoing French.

both Roman Catholics, and it's important to note—and often discounted today, that religion played an important part in political networking in the 1950s and 1960s. Dr. Tuyen had studied for the priesthood, his beliefs as unshakable as those of President Diem, himself a product of a New Jersey seminary. Communism was anathema to these God-fearing men.

Rattled by the escalation of conflicts near the Cambodian border, Diem turned to Dr. Tuyen to address the problem. He immediately put Pham Ngoc Thao on the case. Since Thao was playing both sides of the fence, it took him no effort to locate Duan's hideout, though much was later made of his heroic detective skills. Slipping briefly into spy mode, Thao of course alerted his Communist boss, Maj. Gen. Dang Tran Duc. He also worked for Tuyen, and was a double agent like Thao and An and was known within the Communist hierarchy by the code name Ba Quoc.

Dr. Tuyen was told of Duan's whereabouts—leaving enough time for the bandit to move out and evade capture. Sure enough, the secret police arrived at the camp exactly one hour too late. The coffee was still warm, but more importantly for Thao, there was enough evidence of Duan's recent occupation to earn Dr. Tuyen's unwavering faith.

Thao became a capable double agent, sending Maj. Gen. Duc information on troop deployments and even the agendas of President Diem and his secret police chief. Although Thao had officially earned his Communist stripes arranging the Duan escape, his true leftist leanings were long held. Unbeknownst to his superiors at the Joint General Staff, Thao never accepted the Church or its faith—these were strictly vehicles for ingratiating himself with the South Vietnamese establishment.

Before long, Thao made it into the presidential circle. Shortly after Diem returned from the United States to assume control over the South, his brother Nhu sent a message to JGS requesting a security guard and a valet. JGS sent two men, one of them Thao—an appropriate choice, given his presumed Catholic background and perceived enthusiasm for Americans. Throughout his life, Thao always rated America "number one!" as he liked to put it. Unfortunately, Nhu took an instant disliking to Thao and made him the valet, as opposed to giving him the more useful role of security guard.

Diem's brother took particular exception to Thao's appearance, especially his eyes. In fairness, they were disconcerting. As *Time* correspondent Robert Sam Anson once noted, Thao would sit in front of a person and hold a conversation with one eye trained on him while the other eye remained fixed on the ceiling. As a palace valet, Thao spent much of his time tending to Nhu's baggage and travel requirements, but he was still high enough in the hierarchy to obtain confidential information.

* * * * *

DESPITE THE frustrations of those pushing for elections, President Diem had managed to gain support from large sections of the population, to the point where Thao concluded that assassination—nearly always under consideration—would prove counterproductive. In the early days, Diem proved an avid mixer with the people, cementing his popularity by traveling throughout the countryside, where he tucked into the local fare, often fish soaked in *nuoc mam* (fish sauce) with rice. He mixed easily with villagers who were usually more concerned with feeding their families than debating the merits of a union with the north.

Thao got himself assigned to go on one country tour and told Viet Minh intelligence of the plan. They agreed any attempt on the president's life could not be justified. But they did decide on a plan designed to raise Thao's stature in the South Vietnamese establishment. As Diem and his entourage weaved their way through the countryside, a planted stooge suddenly appeared from nowhere and threw a grenade that landed at the feet of President Diem. Assuming the grenade was about to explode, the intruder dropped to the ground. Everyone scattered and Diem himself thought for sure he was about to die. And thus the stage was set: Knowing the grenade was a dummy, Thao immediately flung the dud grenade far out of the way and shot the unfortunate stooge dead.

The charade was an enormous success. Thao became a trusted hero of the president and the Viet Minh had succeeded to the point of having a spy within the highest echelons of government. From that day forward, Thao's career as a South Vietnamese up-and-comer was assured. He was promoted to captain, then major and finally colonel. In the process, he became provincial chief of Ben Tre, an area known for Viet Minh hostilities. Once Tay Ninh knew of Thao's appointment, the Communists shifted hostilities out of the province and Thao was again decorated by the president for achieving the impossible—ridding Ben Tre of the troublesome cadres.

Thao was so successful that Diem's suspicions were raised. When Thao's short tenure—about six months—was coming to end, Diem summoned Thao's successor as province chief to the palace. Diem cryptically asked Tran Ngoc Chau if he had "formed any opinions" about Thao, and instructed

Chau to surreptitiously survey opinions of other provincial officials. Chau found opinions of Thao among his colleagues to be predominantly positive and warm—and told as much to Diem—but several priests did question Thao's loyalty to Saigon. And one lieutenant colonial launched into a harangue, exclaiming that Thao "was a Communist, an agent for the North!"

Chau ignored the skeptics. He simply assumed their opinions were due to jealousy or guilt by association given that one of Thao's brothers had remained with the Viet Minh and had even been named as Hanoi's ambassador to East Germany. That was not unusual. In Vietnam thousands of families had been divided by the 17th parallel, a fact that was more tragic than damning.

Duan, too, came out a hero—and the accolades were as undeserved as those heaped on Thao. He never knew how his escape (ultimately to Hanoi) was engineered, except that "someone" with Viet Minh contacts and probably well placed in the South Vietnamese government was behind it. But Duan's apparent dashing and his outsmarting Diem's henchmen won him both notoriety and respect among the peasantry. And once in Hanoi he used this support to convince Ho Chi Minh to rearm the Viet Minh.

As the deadline for the poll approached it had become obvious elections would not take place, so Ho capitalized on Duan's popularity, giving him a leading role within the Communist Party and formally putting him in charge of the terror campaign in the south. By October 1957, 37 armed companies had been deployed into the Mekong Delta—and about 400 South Vietnamese officials were marked and assassinated. Over the next two years a further 600 were abducted for ransom. Diem's presidency was becoming untenable.

Although it would be two years before the first Americans were killed in this war and five years before the Communists would lead a successful major attack against U.S.-sponsored forces, the fighting proved an ominous sign to locals. Another war appeared as certain as Duan's ability to disrupt the lives and infrastructure in South Vietnam's northern provinces.

Dr. Tuyen's sense of justice was swift and without mercy. An would be away for the next two years in California, when 5,000 Communists were slaughtered and more than 180,000 suspected Viet Minh arrested. More than twice that number were injured. Many of the details of the arrests and executions were never revealed. Certainly, Vietnam was growing into a big news story.

Maj. Gen. Duc never doubted his Number One man—Pham Ngoc

Thao. But there was a second agent in the shadows, still known by only a few. He was called Hai Trung, a name that would come to be revered within the inner sanctum of the Communist intelligence network.

* * * * *

AN REPORTED to the chief of psychological warfare, the well-connected Dr. Tran Kim Tuyen who acted as head of political research, essentially a CIA front within the information ministry. Like most people, An was struck by Dr. Tuyen's diminutive stature; he towered over his new four-foot-nine boss but it wasn't till his Reuters days, years later, that they became genuine friends. An also met others who would play leading parts in his own unfolding story: Pham Ngoc Thao—and Nguyen Ngoc Phach, who like An himself, would wear two hats and surprise a lot of people.

An and Thao worked as press agents, interpreters and information gatherers. In the propaganda department they would script leaflets and broadcast anti-Communist tirades following a vague plan aimed at encouraging Communist defections. Hyperbole was never in short supply. The Communists were portrayed as sons of the Antichrist and as men who fathered bastard children. An also got out of the office and worked on the CIA's pacification projects in the countryside, although he doubted his meetings with villagers would sway anyone. When it came time for the mission to file its report, An contributed a section arguing for land reform and a spending program aimed at raising living standards.

Had French or American officials known of An's history of fighting with the Viet Minh against the French, he would have been quickly exiled to the north—as his sister had effectively been after she married a known Communist sympathizer. Thach, An's regional chief of intelligence for the Viet Minh also moved north after receiving orders from Ho Chi Minh. In Hanoi, he would serve as Minister of Health while in the south he was replaced by Tran Quoc Huong who was also known as Muoi Huong.

Huong and An's other minders knew their spy in the JGS ranks was positioned well. One Vietnamese journalist would later note: "After the signing of the Geneva Accords, he (An) had better chances to penetrate deeply into the enemy's confidence." But An didn't see it like that. Having formal—if secret—contacts with the Viet Minh, former colleagues in the war against the French, was not out of the ordinary given the turmoil which had afflicted his country over the previous decade.

At JGS, An impressed the Americans with his abilities as a translator. And they impressed him. He went to work for the American Combined Army Training Organization (CATO)—the successor to TRIM—where, despite some initial reservations, An found them refreshing compared to the French—and a lot different than the characters in *The Quiet American*.

Conditions in Saigon were improving generally. The South was becoming awash with money from the American influx. More importantly, fighting was limited, and while disputes lingered, there was still hope that a political solution could be found.

With the assistance of the Asia Foundation and Dr. Elon Hildreth, who was simultaneously the head of USOM's education division as well as a senior advisor to the South Vietnamese government on education policy, An applied for a government scholarship to study journalism in the United States. Fully cognizant of the potential benefits An's training could bring to his propaganda department, Dr. Tuyen approved his request to travel abroad after he won a scholarship through the United States Overseas Mission (USOM) to study at Columbia University. The problem was getting an exit visa, which was repeatedly denied. Senior government officials often did this to scholarship winners to redirect the awards to friends and relatives; they were part of the currency traded for political favors.

Officially, the palace through the Overseas Study Council vetoed An's eligibility because he didn't have a high school diploma and argued there was no urgent national requirement for foreign trained journalists. However, Hildreth admitted to An that it was nepotism inside the Vietnamese government that was behind the rejection and he intervened on An's behalf.

In the end, An gave up the scholarship route and decided to go abroad as a fee-paying student. On that basis, exit visas were obtainable. So he approached an American contact who put him in touch with Dr. Basil Peterson, the president of Costa Mesa's Orange Coast College in California, which had a heavy emphasis on adult education and accepted him. One deciding factor for An was that the fees were made all the more affordable thanks to the generous exchange rate arranged by colleagues at Customs House.

An had received clearance from the Communist Party to pursue his studies in the U.S. In fact they urged him to spend between four and six years studying for a PhD, which upon his return would have served the revolution well. The Communist Party would later claim that senior leaders had ordered An to retire from JGS to pursue his education in the U.S. for up to six years "so that he could improve his education, broaden his knowledge and gain a deep understanding of the U.S.".

The reality was An, who had always harbored academic designs, had planned his own future and one that just so happened married well with Viet Minh intelligence. An's plan suited the cunning threesome—Huong, Son and Vu—who kept watch over him. A further Communist line would claim that An was encouraged to study journalism because through this he would establish important relations "so that he could fulfill his revolutionary tasks" and at the same time earn a living. Again, this appears more as an improbable afterthought, one that attempts to place An in an American university at the behest of Vietnamese Communists.

An was a solid student who knew his own mind and the idea of a university education in California was his ambition, which was supported by the Communist hierarchy, not the other way around. An was happy to put some distance between himself and the party.

Such historical arguments were meaningless as An was packing his bags in September 1957. His departure for America approached as his father's tuberculosis was closing in for the kill. "Don't be gone too long, you have a family to look after," the dying Vien told his grieving son. On October 10, 1957, An boarded his flight to the United States. Eleven days later Capt. Harry Cramer, Jr., became the first U.S. casualty to die in what would become the Vietnam War, killed during a munitions handling accident.

The Hanoi Exhibition, a world's fair, was held in late 1902 and early 1903 at the local racecourse and in the Palais d'exposition, an exhibition hall destroyed in WWII.

Compagnie Aérienne de Transports Indochinois (CATI) was an airline founded by Roger Colin, the Indochina representative of Aigle-Azur, a private French airline set up in 1946. CATI became known as Air-Outre-Mer in 1953.

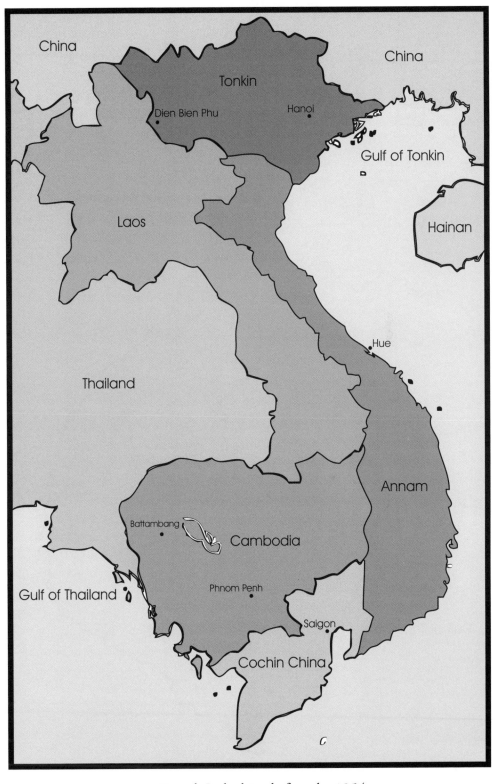

French Indochina before the 1954
Geneva Accords were signed.

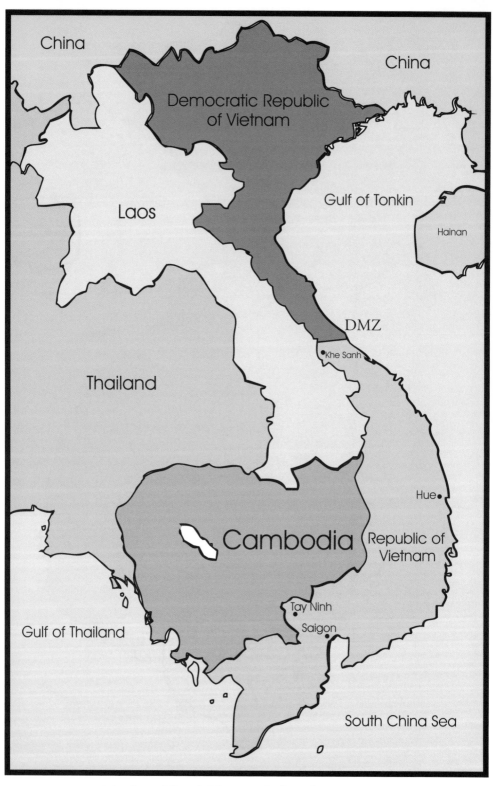

North and South Vietnam before they were
formally united in July 1976.

Top Left (1): Nhan, the future wife of Pham Xuan An, poses shortly before her wedding; *Top Right (2):* Pham Xuan An in the Reuters office in the early 1960s, following his return from the United States; *Below (3):* South Vietnamese Prime Minister Ngo Dinh Diem in Saigon.

Top (4): Pham Xuan An and Nhan on their wedding day; *Below (5):* South Vietnamese Prime Minister Ngo Dinh Diem in Saigon.

Top Right (6): Australian journalist Peter Smark asks a question during a Saigon press conference. Pham Xuan An is seated to his left; *Left (7):* Pham Ngoc Dinh after he was recommended by Pham Xuan An for a job at Reuters where he initially fetched the coffee.

Above (8): Peter Smark, seated on the bumper, chats with his wife Jan and Pham Xuan An during a road block caused by a heavy firefight up ahead in the South Vietnamese countryside.

Top Left (9): Reporter Jim Pringle carries a sick child near a battlefield on the Thai-Cambodia border; *Top Right (10):* Combat cameraman Neil Davis at the Grand Prix, his favorite bar in Bangkok, shortly before his death; *Above (11):* The Cao Dai citadel at Tay Ninh in southwest Vietnam near the Cambodian border. They were notoriously anti-Communist and Pham Xuan An was told by his chiefs to stop dating a local girl because of her father's political affiliations.

Top Left (12): Hanoi remained a poor, grim city well into the 1990s; *Below Left (13):* Michael Caine with correspondent Jim Pringle on the set of the movie *The Quiet American*; *Below Right (14):* Welsh photographer Philip Jones Griffiths.

Top (15): Pham Xuan An with Canadian scholar Bill Charney; *Right (16):* Jim Pringle reporting on refugees in South Vietnam.

Left (17): The Foreign Correspondents Club in Hong Kong has provided a haven for journalists working abroad for decades, including those covering the Vietnam War.

Top (18): Pham Xuan An in the driveway of his home, the Renault parked beside him. By 1992 his health had improved slightly, although he was still monitored closely by the authorities; *Below (20):* Pham Xuan An in 2002 with a treasured songbird. He often told friends he'd like to come back in another life as a songbird.

Above (19): Bui Tin, who accepted the unconditional surrender of South Vietnam, chats with Pham Xuan An (right) during a meeting of the Communist Party faithful. Both men are dressed in their military uniforms.

Top (21): Pol Pot's trusted former head of state for the Khmer Rouge Khieu Samphan seen here at his home in Pailin. Pham Xuan An warned the Vietnamese hierarchy not to invade Cambodia in late 1978 saying the costs would be too great.

Above (22): Khieu Samphan on trial for crimes against humanity and a genocide, which ended with the Vietnamese invasion.

Left (23): Pham Xuan An at home.

PART TWO:
1960-1968

5. CALIFORNIA DATELINE

*'I couldn't even find it on the map. A few years later it was
on the front page of every newspaper across the country
and I always wondered what happened to An.'*
– Earl Gustkey, Orange Coast College, Class of '58

LOS ANGELES was the antithesis of Saigon. For an alien like An, the
atmosphere was humbling, the opulence and contentment on the Orange
Coast campus in Costa Mesa overwhelming. In 1958, Orange Coast College (OCC) was a small junior college with about 7,000 students and a
short history. It was founded 10 years earlier by Basil Peterson who remained president and had organized An's enrolment. An paid the $600
airfare—a princely sum in those days—and $40-a-month in dorm fees
out of his own pocket. There were two male dorms and another for women,
and in all 71 buildings on 243 acres of land which once served as an air
base. The school colors were scarlet, black and white.

"He never put his hand up. He sat quietly and rarely bothered anyone,"
remembered former student Earl Gustkey[*], who went on to a journalism
career himself at the *Los Angeles Times*. Like Ho Chi Minh trying to make
ends meet in a Paris photoshop, An's existence was meagre and inconsequential. In decades to come, however, An's byline—and story—would jolt
Gustkey's memory back to college days, if only because An's abilities had
seemed so unremarkable. Combat correspondent for *Time* was a huge men-

---

[*] Earl Gustkey became a celebrated sportswriter with a career spanning 30 years at the *LA Times*.
He died in 2009 aged 69.

tal leap for former classmates, who took some solace in the thought that Orange Coast, not just Ivy League schools, produced *Time* material.

For the Class of '58, and their no-nonsense journalism teacher Phyllis Jackson, insurrections in Vietnam were as off the track as football scores from Australia. "I doubt if I had heard of Vietnam at the time. I couldn't even find it on the map," Gustkey, then 18, later recalled. "A few years later it was on the front page of every newspaper across the country and I always wondered what happened to An ... and all I remember is An never asked a question and was kind of a loner—he kind of blundered in."

In fact, An was just being an average Asian student. Respectful of authority, happy if reserved. He was naturally shy, but his silence in Phyllis Jackson's class did not reflect a lack of drive or interest. Locals could be eager, even brash, but to an Asian, conspicuous behavior was distasteful, certainly in the less globalized 1950s. An's flawed English only deepened his natural shyness. But he worked on the eight-page campus weekly, *The Barnacle*, which focused on typical collegiate fare for the times—sports, campus politics and local issues. It would be years before student editors would write acid-dipped editorials aimed at Dow Chemical and the military-industrial complex. The United States and Soviets were posturing their way through the nuclear stand-off and Bertrand Russell did lead the first peace protest in 1958, but the next decade would have to get going before campuses would be overturned by student papers.

Like Gustkey, most students in An's class were between 18 and 20—about 10 years younger than An, though the visitor still passed for 21. Classmates assumed he was, like them, a recent high school graduate. An never mentioned he fought the Japanese in World War II, took part in a failed Communist revolution, or spent two years working in military intelligence. Who would believe him anyway? He did not mention his long history of illness, even when the occasional bout of malaria recurred. He simply studied hard, took notes and watched as the world evolved around California. In his spare time he visited Disneyland and Santa Cruz. He wandered amid the tumbleweed—through ghost towns in the nearby deserts and as his command of English grew he started taking Spanish lessons.

An, in fact, did better at Orange Coast than anyone would have given him credit for. The Asia Foundation in San Francisco thought well enough of him to help him win an internship on *The Sacramento Bee*. The foundation was established in 1954 as a private grant-making organization, its chosen mission to "encourage Asian-Pacific efforts to strengthen institutions concerned with representative government, effective legal systems, human rights, market economies, and independent and responsible media".

At *The Bee*, An learned the mechanics of newspapers, like copy flow, deadlines and layout. A svelte blonde named Lee Meyer edited his work and she became an object of his desires. Meyer may have suspected but An, as always, kept his feelings to himself, including a passionate love for his boss. His mission was also spelt out by his editors in his copy. On June 2, 1959, *The Sacramento Bee* published a story by An, his impressions of an American institution—the county fair—and an editor introduced readers to the young man with his job description:

Pham Xuan An of Saigon, South Viet Nam, is in Sacramento for a three month period of observation and study of The Bee. The on the job training for the student of The Bee is sponsored by the Asia Foundation. Upon completion of the training and a tour of the eastern United States he will return to Saigon to seek employment on a newspaper. Here is his story on his reactions to the county fair, an American institution.

The Asia Foundation was an outgrowth of the Committee for a Free Asia. Both were initially funded by the CIA and assigned the codename Project DTPILLAR. Effectively, CIA money was being used to fund overseas scholarship programs at that time.

An was impressed by the Sacramento County Fair. It was a very hot day, the national anthem—the Star Spangled Banner—was played and An showed a keen interest in the local livestock which was of a much higher quality than the local beef served-up in Vietnam. Overall the story revealed a rare insight into what An was thinking at the time. He wrote:

"The High quality of agricultural products, beef and dairy cattle, poultry, rabbits, swine, horses and sheep does not surprise me because they are well known all over the world through books, magazines and movies.

"The strong impression I have is that this livestock is raised by youngsters between 12 and 20 years of age. They certainly will be successful future farmers of America."

His thoughts were expressed simplistically but local newspapers everywhere indulge themselves in the praise of outsiders, and An had plenty on offer. He was also impressed by the traditional dances performed by native

Americans and suggested that U.S. cultural missions abroad make better use of "the beautiful handiwork of the Navajo Indians and the magnificent and majestic dances of the Sioux". However, his reportage of mini-bumper cars—driven "by the dynamic and talented youth of California" at the fair —must have proved a source of amusement for his editors: "How can the Vietnamese people imagine children from 4 to 10 years racing in their one quarter midget cars." This skill had quite an impact on An, who throughout his life, in war and in peacetime, had readily distinguished between people raised in the countryside and the urban elite: "The members of 4H clubs have exhibited not only their skill in raising livestock but also in art at their talent show. I cannot distinguish whether they belong to farming families or business families because the ways of living between city residents and those who live on the farm are not so sharply contrasted as in underdeveloped countries."

There was one additional paragraph, a comparison of gun cultures that might have grabbed the attention of editors at *The Bee* had they been aware of An's former affiliations: "In contributing to the visitors' interest, the armed forces, police department, fire department, coast guard and others have displayed their equipment to protect American citizens. These exhibitions are not unusual in comparison with any fairs in Vietnam except for more advanced and complicated gadgets."

This story* was the first of three pieces concerning An to appear in *The Bee* during his three month stay. The second was written about An and published on July 5 without a byline and touched on issues of a far grander scale. The intro is self-evident and was written under the headline:

VIETNAM JOURNALIST AIMS TO FIGHT RED PROPAGANDA

The urgency of the fight against Red propaganda in the Republic of Vietnam was the main factor which influenced Pham Xuan An, 32, of Saigon to embrace journalism as a career.

Pham, who recently graduated from the Orange Coast College in Costa Mesa, Orange County, will spend three months at the Sacramento Bee studying American newspaper operations and learning the practical aspects of his college course.

---

* Vietnamese Takes Look At County Fair Art – Likes It, detailed An's first trip to the Sacramento Country Fair and was published by the *Sacramento Bee* on June 2, 1959.

The story then offered basic background on An's family and then:

Pham was employed by the psychological warfare department of Vietnam during the 1954 campaign against the Communist military attack which divided the country.

He explains the success of that campaign by the fact the Red leaders never preached open Communism at the time but branded their movement a nationalist fight against the French who were ruling Indochina.

This fact made him decide, he said, that the best way to help his country would be to become a journalist so he could explain to the public the real goals and methods of Communism.

He said the Vietnamese government now maintains tight censorship on all newspapers as a matter of necessity because otherwise the Reds would have a field day in spreading their ideas throughout the country.

There are nine daily newspapers in Saigon. Among them there are six Vietnamese publications, one French, one English and one Chinese.

All have a rather small circulation, he said, because few people can afford to buy them every day. But he added it is common to rent or swap newspapers.

"Our people are poor," he concluded, "but they are eager to learn, from the students to the rickshaw men."

He said he plans to join the staff of one of the Vietnamese dailies when he returns to Saigon.

An was showing signs of distancing himself from his Communist past without breaking the umbilical cord. He implies government censorship is desirable because the Communists carry a hidden agenda, but he declines to argue for or against that agenda, or explain what it is. He also had access to international wire services and other newspapers and magazines—and could watch for copy from Graham Greene, Bob Shaplen and Denis Warner. There was the occasional story with a Saigon dateline in the wire queue, and he noticed a new byline starting to routinely appear—Bruce Russell. Wires were interesting because they often seemed less biased than the gung-ho stories of some newspaper correspondents, and this impression came at a timely moment. An was turning his thoughts to a career with Vietnam Press (VP) in Saigon, originally established as a local affiliate of Paris-based Agence France-Presse (AFP). A job among others in the big league, with Reuters, Associated Press (AP), or perhaps United Press International (UPI) was also on his mind. An's perspectives were changing. Only rarely did papers report on Vietnam and when they did, U.S. media gave the copy a decidedly pro-South Vietnamese slant. When President Diem visited the United States, he was heralded as a vanguard against Communism. But the real story of Vietnam's wretchedness, the injustices, the suffering, the deaths, hardly made more than fillers in local dailies. And the thing of it was, he knew how big the original stories were, watching them come over the teletype machines in *The Bee*'s wire room. A 400-word lead story would be reduced to two paragraphs with little thought to how the significant portions might be mangled in the process. And events were turning nasty towards the Communists in South Vietnam during the final years of the 1950s. An concluded many Americans were naïve, realizing that news only matters if it has a home market.

He began to understand how to sell a news story and this became obvious when he tackled a subject dear to his heart for *The Sacramento Bee*. It was a rare indulgence and appeared on August 16, 1959, under An's byline and the headline:

HOW UGLY IS THE AMERICAN? —
HOW U.S. DIPLOMATS LOOK THROUGH VIET NAM EYES

It opens with: "The novel, *The Ugly American*, has raised a great deal of controversy in official circles as well as with the general public."

An identified with arguments put forward by the authors Eugene Burdick and William Lederer aimed at combating the spread of Communism. Burdick and Lederer contended that Americans had to forge much closer alliances with the people of other countries, to fully comprehend their cultures and understand their languages.

What followed in *The Bee* was a discourse that An had applied four years earlier when Greene released *The Quiet American*. Only this time An published what he thought, and he wrote with authority: "Even though *The Ugly American* is fiction, it contains actual facts which have been and will be happening in Southeast Asia where the Americans are stationed."

An argued that cultural differences were causing inevitable misunderstandings and conflicts.* "This difference of culture," he wrote, "can be un-

---

* Decades later An would continue to argue diplomatic postings, usually covering a two-to-three-year period, were far too short and this had contributed to deep misunderstandings in the West and diplomatic community in regards to Vietnam. He often said he could not understand why governments refused to change this policy.

derstood only when the Americans really eat and act like the natives, speak their languages and live with them as long as possible."

He applauded the individual efforts of Americans who had opened orphanages and were carrying out humanitarian efforts in his native Vietnam but he singled out a common problem: that those, and at this point it was a very small number, who were working in Vietnam were restricted to one or two-year postings or tours-of-duty. This was simply not enough time to become accustomed to the machinations of Vietnamese culture where the Americans were fearing and shaping up for a battle with the Communists. It was to be a battle of great differences, as An saw it, the freedoms in the West could not be compared with the enforced disciplines imposed by the Communists.

"… the difference of cultures is the most difficult problem. The Americans are taught to 'think for themselves'. Their philosophy of life is individuality. They cannot be forced to do what their government, political leaders, sociologists want them to do. They cannot be compared with the Communist cadres because the Communist members have sworn to sacrifice their lives. If the Communists do not follow what their leaders expect they would be punished and excluded systematically.

"The stories, facts and solutions proposed by the authors of The Ugly American *are unquestionably valuable but to carry out the authors' proposed solution realistically and quickly is another question."*

The quiet man with perfect manners continued to make his mark. The Asia Foundation gave him a trip to New York where he watched the United Nations press corps at work. He worked as an intern at the U.N. and was introduced to people associated with the United States Operations Mission in Saigon. An was earning his stripes as a role model, an Asia Foundation success story. His confidence was also shaping-up. He drove across the U.S. and visited Niagara Falls in Canada.

USOM offered him a three-year scholarship to study political science at Columbia University—where he'd won the journalism scholarship he was forced to give up—on condition he first undertake a one-year transition course. That was too much. Columbia seemed to be jinxed. Again, he had to pass up the opportunity of free study at one of the top schools in the United States. He concluded staying another four years in the States would be failing his father and breaking a promise to return home soon. With mixed feelings An opted to return home, where he would assume the role of family head—and just possibly find a job at Vietnam Press.

He took with him some souvenirs, one being a gold-handled coffee mug with the names of his Orange Coast classmates inscribed on it.* Viewed in the context of An's whole life, his two years in the United States amounted to no more than a snapshot with a California dateline. But it was a journey well worth the taking and An left with a great and genuine affection. In later years he would reflect: "Americans have taught me to view things objectively and evaluate oneself first. All American generations are taught to work hard and keep their feet on the ground. I hope that my children can be educated in America."

Upon his return, a subtle but highly important point was made. An had asked his mother to arrange for as many people as possible to meet him at the airport, to welcome him as he marched proudly through Saigon customs and onto his home soil. He was disturbed to find no-one was there.

---

* The coffee mug remained a permanent fixture on the coffee table in An's Saigon lounge room until his final days.

6. DOWN THE WIRE

'The decision was mine.'
- David Chipp, Reuters former head of Southeast Asia operations,
on hiring Pham Xuan An and Pham Ngoc Dinh

THE FOREIGN military presence in South Vietnam was small in 1960. Under the International Control Commission (ICC), overseer for the implementation of the Geneva Accords, about 1,000 Indians, 150 Canadians and 100 Poles were a part of the initial international contingent. Officially, among the Americans, there were 900 uniformed advisors but this did not include civilian advisors to monitor life below the 17th parallel.*

For most people life continued as much before. President Diem continued to nurture relations with the peasants, dispensing with the usual trappings of office on his regular tours of the countryside. As 'one of the people', he chatted easily with village elders discoursing on local issues.

Things were looking up. The economy was starting to grow with the injection of foreign aid and stability had become the order of the day, making it seem as if South Vietnam held unlimited new potential.†

---

* Scholars have noted the Canadians on the ICC were complicit in letting the U.S. bolster their advisory team in violation of the 1954 Accords by arguing that excess U.S. advisors were actually "replacing" French forces that had left Indochina since the accords were signed.

† The U.S. press certainly reinforced this perception of a rapid turnaround. In an April 1955 cover article on Diem, *Time* magazine portrayed the beleaguered leader's chances as dim—"the hour is late, the odds are long." Two years later, in May 1957, *Life* was celebrating Diem's consolidation of power calling him "the tough miracle man of Vietnam", who had "roused his country and routed the Reds".

* * * * *

IN FACT, understanding media developments in the background is essential to understanding An's story beyond this point. The presence of Western journalists reflected the demand for news from South Vietnam. In the early 1960s, there were no more than half a dozen foreign correspondents based in Saigon. This number would exceed 630 with the Tet offensive, when war peaked in 1968. More than 3,000 officially accredited reporters would pass through Saigon between 1965 and 1975.

Bob Shaplen, Denis Warner, Don Wise and Graham Greene were the best known, covering the region for newspapers in the United States, Australia and Britain. Warner and Shaplen were very tight. They first met at Guadalcanal during World War II and would become great friends. Warner worked for the Melbourne *Herald* and Shaplen for *Newsweek* before moving to *The New Yorker* in 1952. Soon after Warner quit *The Herald* to work as a freelance correspondent in the mid-1950s. Shaplen helped Warner in his bid for a Nieman Fellowship at Harvard University, which he completed in 1957. The Harvard credentials laid the ground for a successful career as a freelance journalist at the international level.

But news agency correspondents, not freelancers or journalists writing for individual publications, generated the bulk of international copy. The wires, then as always, also provided the bulk of foreign correspondents—either expatriates or locally hired reporters.

Essentially, wire services mostly started as cost-saving cooperatives owned by newspaper groups. Gradually, these co-ops developed into companies in their own right, employing as many as 2,000 journalists generating mountains of copy every day, allowing editors to pick and choose stories from hundreds of foreign dispatches which suited local interests. Major agencies could have as many as 8,000 newspapers subscribing to their services.

Shortly after World War II, Reuters needed cash to re-establish itself and internationalize operations rather than remain essentially a British-based news agency. Australian Associated Press (AAP) and the New Zealand Press Association (NZPA) became major shareholders. The new ownership arrangement provided for stories to run under joint AAP-Reuters credit in Australia and for Pacific correspondents to be appointed by AAP with Reuters approval. The inevitable happened—the influence of Australian and New Zealand journalists grew as Reuters grew. Australian and New Zealand journalists manned more and more bureaux, in large part because it was cheaper than sending staff out from London. Their copy reflected Domino Theory fears prevalent from Washington to Canberra—that allies such as Australia, Thailand or the Philippines would fall like dominoes and be overwhelmed by spreading communism if the West didn't rise up and crush it. The signs were everywhere; a divided Korea in the 1950s, and growing insurgencies in Indonesia, Malaysia, Burma and the Philippines in the 1960s. Amid a tense stand-off between North and South Korea, Communist China plunged into the madness of the Great Leap Forward, a practice run for the even madder Cultural Revolution. The 1960s were understandably unsettling times.

An had witnessed the rising concern and pre-occupation with the Communist East while in the United States although he did not attach much importance to Senator Joseph McCarthy and his blacklists identifying suspected Communists across America. He dismissed the campaigns as more political posturing than anything else.

In the event, he returned from the United States in late 1959 and used his connections with Dr. Tran Kim Tuyen and JGS to secure a reporter's job at Vietnam Press*, where he stayed long enough to grasp the difference between writing for newspapers and wires.

Wire and newspaper reporters answered different editorial needs. A major difference is that newspapers have one, or two depending upon editions, deadlines and a correspondent can monitor and use the wires, then write a comprehensive piece on the day's events while appearing to be in several places almost at the same time. By contrast, a wire reporter files each morsel of news that comes along and faces constant deadlines. He needs to meet demands and deadlines from newspapers all around the world. From Saigon, the first deadline of the day loomed around 3:00 p.m. when New Zealand newspapers were calling for last copy at around seven in the evening, their time. Two hours later and final demands were echoing from Australia, and so went on an endless 24-hour news cycle.

The first paragraph by a wire journalist must focus on the widest possible impact to provide for the widest possible audience, while a newspaper correspondent focuses on whatever angle is most likely to resonate with hometown readers.

---

* Vietnam Press (VP) acted as both a clearinghouse for 'official' regime opinion as well as a censor of foreign news feeds that could be reshaped for domestic distribution. VP wanted An because of his U.S. training and English language skills, while Dr. Tuyen wanted An inside VP to monitor its internal machinations.

Wire journalists would complain of having to serve too many masters, but it was just that burden that made for more objective copy. While newspaper correspondents were free to advance the political agendas of their publishers, wire reporters were prohibited from embellishing stories with political bias which risked alienating subscribing newspapers. Left-leaning or Communist newspapers would pay the same subscription fees to a wire as a right-wing publication.

That wire service discipline made agency correspondents attractive hires. Newspapers and magazines often poached journalists from the agencies they subscribed to. International wires such as Reuters, the Associated Press (AP), United Press International (UPI) or Agence France-Presse (AFP) in turn poached talent from local wires, such as AAP, NZPA, Press Association in Britain, Canadian Press or Vietnam Press.

So it was no surprise that Reuters Saigon bureau chief Bruce Russell, a New Zealander, was more than interested when he received a resume from Pham Xuan An of Vietnam Press in November 1959. He was so interested, in fact, that he contacted David Chipp, head of Reuters' Southeast Asia news operations. Chipp, then working out of Singapore, had covered Vietnam for Reuters between 1953 and 1955. He later recalled getting Russell's call. Russell wanted An taken on as a junior stringer and his boss agreed. "The decision was mine... all mine," Chipp acknowledged long after the dimensions of the deed became known.

As a stringer, An submitted regular local stories on a freelance basis, so his pay and benefits, such as they were, went up and down according to budgets and editors. But he quickly learned his way around the place and soon helped another local get on board—Pham Ngoc Dinh, a lad who was immediately impressed by Russell. "Bruce was tall, very tall, and I called him Sir," Dinh recalled later, remembering a man of intelligence and undeniable presence. "Every time he walked, he walked too fast and took huge strides."

Dinh's uncle, Dang Manh Chuan, had worked alongside An at Vietnam Press and kept an eye on Dinh after his father, Van, had been killed. It was Chuan who encouraged Dinh to pursue a career in journalism but, with vacancies reserved for aspiring journalists with relatives or friends in high places, he wasn't in a position to offer him work at Vietnam Press.

Chuan and An crossed paths just before Christmas in 1959 and Chuan asked if there were any jobs going at Reuters. Instead of asking about his nephew's aptitude for journalism, An first wanted to know if Dinh had ever been involved with the Communists. With a signal that strong, Chuan lied and said no, opting not to tell An about Dinh's Viet Minh tutors or about his many reasons for hating the French. Telling the truth would have killed off any possibilities on the spot. (Besides, Dinh himself had been disciplined in hiding his background from earlier days. His ever-vigilant grandmother used to whack him with bamboo simply for sharing cigarettes with farm workers, fearing even these gestures would betray Socialist leanings.)

As it happened, a vacancy had come up at Reuters. While fielding its own correspondents was the agency's main preoccupation, it also provided extra arms and legs to visiting journalists working for subscribing newspapers, helping them secure accreditation, visas, permits, drivers and the like; essentially the job of a fixer.

Chuan got down to his nephew's plusses, telling An the boy was "hard working, honest and forthright and talented". The hard facts included 11 years of village schooling by 1951, when he left home for Saigon and studied English. By 1954, with civil war breaking out and further undermining his family's already desperate finances, Dinh found coolie work. "Each morning I would go down to the banks and carry the loads," Dinh later recalled of sweaty days hauling fruit from the river market. "Then one day I got a copy of the *Times of Vietnam* and read it. I saw the stories and I saw the bylines and I thought, why not me?"

Soon after, Dinh started as a part-time delivery boy for the *Times of Vietnam* and quickly became friends with the managing editor, Le Trang. As Trang encouraged Dinh to absorb as much as he could, his uncle Chuan went to work arm-twisting An into opening doors at Reuters. An eventually had words with Russell and after a short interview, Reuters' Saigon boss put Dinh to work as an office boy fetching the coffee, cleaning the office car and doing the paperwork for staff and visiting journalists. And he soon proved a natural. He loved to talk and loved to pass on gossip, always careful not to betray his own background.

* * * * *

AN'S CONTACT book was a window on the times. It had many people in it, but three were especially important—Dr. Tran Kim Tuyen and Col. Pham Ngoc Thao at JGS and Bob Shaplen, with whom he shared too many cigarettes at the Givral coffee shop. Sometimes referred to as the Graham Greene Milk Bar, the Givral was fast becoming Saigon's "in" spot for people watching and being seen in the early 1960s. The tables outside marked the place, but regulars usually preferred something inside, especially during the hot season. Once an ice cream parlor, the Givral was the first building in the city to install air conditioning and offer some respite from the grinding heat. And it had novelty appeal among foreigners, who knew it as the place where Greene's *Quiet American* character Thomas Fowler watched American-sponsored bombs go off on the opposite side of Tu Do Street, outside the National Assembly. The Assembly building filled one end of a large square and from the Givral An could also observe comings and goings at the Continental Hotel to its left—and the Caravelle Hotel on its right.

Thao and An would often meet at the Givral—occasionally for lunch, often in the evenings—and they became people to be seen with. An would sit drinking bitter green tea with his German Shepherd at his side while Thao talked with one eye pointing skyward. Thao brought along a companion, too—a .45 holstered at the hip. As time went by, more chairs were sprinkled around the table, for Shaplen, Dinh and occasionally Warner, Wise and Dr. Tuyen.

These were the early days for Radio Catinat, the nickname given to the Tu Do Street rumor mill—a tag derived from the street's original name, Rue du Catinat—but it gained new importance with Thao's recently gained access to President Diem and Diem's brother Nhu.

An and Thao trusted each other up to a point. Thao certainly never mentioned his work for the Communists but that didn't make An any less suspicious. The colonel had an uncanny ability to predict events—and an ambitious journalist valued nothing more than a consistently reliable source of leaks. So from Dr. Tuyen, for example, An learned how the Pentagon—implementing one of its many counter-insurgency strategies—had tracker dogs deployed to sniff out Communist movements in the central and northern provinces. And from Thao, he learned how those same dogs had been trapped and cooked by enemy units desperate to improve on their meager rice rations—dog meat being a prized food in Vietnam's central highlands for centuries.

Peter Smark, who joined Reuters in Saigon in February 1961, later recalled how the dog chow incident was one of the first stories he filed. He estimated that perhaps 5,000 highly trained U.S. army dogs had been shipped to Vietnam, only to end up on Communist mess plates. The program was scrapped within 12 months. On learning of the debacle, Smark's belly ached from laughter: "You could just see the menu, dog burger, sauté dog." An, for his part, thought the episode was more stupid than funny.

Between Col. Thao's heroic rise in the South Vietnamese military and An's job performance at JGS, both men held the trust of the CIA in the person of Dr. Tuyen who routinely confided in them—even talking about botched operations in the North, and his own M.O.

Initially Dr. Tuyen's modus operandi was to extract information about the Communists through Vietnamese agents living abroad. The information was then compiled through embassies and consulates before being sent to JGS, where it was disseminated to the Americans and counterintelligence units at allied embassies. But a string of blunders had made the Americans nervous, and Dr. Tuyen was becoming worried for his own position. Too many South Vietnamese agents sent north had vanished—usually right after making first contact.

What seemed a worrying and unfathomable mystery at the time would be cleared up with the benefit of hindsight. Years later, long after the war had finished, Dr. Tuyen would concede that his agents were never given time to establish themselves. "We were too eager to get on with it," he recalled. "The agents should have simply done nothing and taken as much time as needed to settle into a local community before doing anything. Instead, they would transmit messages almost immediately from beyond the 17th parallel, essentially telling the enemy who and where they were. Some would go so far as to paint anti-Communist slogans on government buildings and ended up arrested and often shot. We didn't really know what we were doing and some of those exercises were stupid," Dr. Tuyen told this author.

But at the time, rumors of intrigue were rife. Thao said he'd heard that the Americans were deliberately circulating rumors that Dr. Tuyen was in fact a Communist spy, the idea being to undermine his position and get him removed. Repeated mission failures in the North and the continuing loss of agents, he said, were being used to justify the claim that Dr. Tuyen had used his position to benefit Hanoi. Soon the gossip had surged into the Givral and the word on Radio Catinat was that Dr. Tuyen was no longer trusted by the Americans.

Not surprisingly Dr. Tuyen was properly rattled by all of this and sought An's advice. An and Tuyen both acknowledged this to the author during a series of interviews in the early and mid-1990s. Hearing the rumors, An said they had been circulated by Americans who had grown very uncomfortable with Dr. Tuyen's easy access to President Diem's inner sanctum and were concerned their operations could be compromised. It seems unlikely that Col. Thao himself started the rumors, given that his position as a Communist plant was established successfully under the nose of the unsuspecting Dr. Tuyen; helping to get the spy boss removed would only risk his own position.

An had another theory and he told Dr. Tuyen about it. The reason the Americans might distrust him, he suggested, was that he always sounded suspicious—literally. An said that to Americans who were fluent in Vietnamese, his peasant vernacular, which did not match by any stretch his educated background, suggested links to the National Liberation Front, the Communist's political wing in South Vietnam.

After all, Ho Chi Minh deliberately spoke in peasant dialect to cozy up to the masses. The distinctions were obvious when he moved into English. Vernacular speakers often pronounce "n" as "l" so "Viet Nam" would be rendered as "Viet Lam"—as Dr. Tuyen himself did. An then set about tutoring Dr. Tuyen in an effort to clean up his Vietnamese.* He also tried to convince the American advisers that Dr. Tuyen posed no threat, recruiting *The New Yorker*'s Shaplen and others to help to get that message across. Foreign diplomatic missions were also helpful, but Shaplen—rated by An as his most trusted friend and colleague—was always the first contact.

Warner remembers well how the American's extraordinary connections often led to speculation that Shaplen was a CIA spy. "Bob was sometimes asked," Warner told me. "On one occasion he was asked straight out if he worked for the CIA, to which Shaplen replied: 'The CIA works for me.'"

The mystery remained locked in that little joke. But most journalists operating in the field got the spy tag at one time or other. At various times An, Dinh, Warner and Shaplen were all rumored to be on some nefarious payroll or other. Rumors often stemmed from petty rivalries; one journalist would scoop another, leading to unjustified claims that news-breaking journalists were getting inside information. With one or two exceptions, their stories were the fruit of years spent building up solid contacts and local knowledge, nothing more sinister than that. The rest was luck.

Despite the botched operations, Dr. Tuyen retained the support of President Diem and An succeeded in placating U.S. suspicions. Dr. Tuyen held onto his network of spies but shifted the focus from the North to the internal problems of South Vietnam. He kept tabs on Shaplen, a fitting irony, Warner (through An) and other expatriates. In the meantime, An's circle of

---

* Effective Language Learning ranks Vietnamese as among the most difficult of languages to learn.

interest and contacts was growing with the arrival of Australian business-men like Keith Hyland and Wilf Arthur, two newcomers who would prove highly useful sources.

Hyland had come to Vietnam to open a down processing operation and met Warner over a drink outside the Continental Hotel. Duck feathers were trading at a premium at the time. China, which once had a monopoly on duck down, had now firmly closed itself off from the outside world.

The down market was largely driven by military demand; armed forces used mountains of it to make winter garments and bedding. Hyland's first move was to rent a warehouse in suburban Cholon and he invited Warner along for a look. There was nothing appealing about the building, except that Warner noticed a large target, much like a dartboard, had been painted with a bull's-eye in the center of the floor.

Hyland set about covering the target with feathers and suddenly turned on the fan hanging right over it. In seconds, Warner was head to toe in duck feathers. Then the showman turned off the fan to explain the indus-trial principle revealed by the ferocious demonstration. Stunned and blin-king, like Big Bird after a difficult adventure, Warner silently listened.

"The feathers that landed farthest away from the bull's-eye are the lightest and best and will command the highest price," Hyland said with a knowing glint in his eye.

Indeed, keeping his eye on feather movements would earn Hyland mil-lions and make him one of the most influential businessman in South Vi-etnam. By 1975, he would account for a large portion of foreign currency earned in South Vietnam, excluding U.S. aid.

7. INCIDENTS AND RUMORS

FOREIGN JOURNALISTS covering Vietnam tended to fall into two categories: veterans who came and dug in—people like Bob Shaplen and Denis Warner—and the more temporary residents who did anything from the standard two-year stint to popping in and out in the space of a week. The short-timers outnumbered the old hands and this was especially true at the wire services, where the thinking was that reporters got stale staying too long in one place. As a result, most friendships struck up by Pham Xuan An tended to be brief encounters with people coming and going.

AAP writer Peter Smark and his wife Jan were among them. In February, 1961, only weeks after they were married, Peter was posted to Reuters Saigon. Seeing the AAP-Reuters news feeds every day in Melbourne, and briefed before heading into his new assignment, Peter arrived with some idea of the country he was about to cover. But all the attractive and much admired Jan knew about South Vietnam was that two brothers, Diem and Nhu, ran the country. It was a gap she resolved to fill: Shortly after arriving, she got part-time work teaching English—but more importantly, part-time work as a news reader at Radio Saigon.

Through Peter, she met An and turned to him for help editing her news bulletins. An readily agreed and the informal partnership proved timely. An explained the intricate web of relationships and events that set the scene for what would shortly be the first major military defeat of the South Vietnamese and their U.S. military advisors—at a village called Ap Bac. That pivotal battle would actually come right after the Smarks would head back to Australia—but their arrival timed well for the aftermath of an attempted coup, still fresh in everyone's mind.

On November 11, 1960, shortly before dawn, a telephone call roused Dr.

Tuyen. An, who was with Shaplen at the time, had heard gunfire and asked Dr. Tuyen if he had got word of a coup. He hadn't but that didn't stop him from calling his key informers to satisfy himself there was nothing in the rumor. Dismissing the random gunfire as nothing more than the noise of ill-disciplined troops, Dr. Tuyen got the shock of An's second call—confirming there had indeed been a coup attempt.

Dr. Tuyen had filled in the blanks by the time An and Shaplen arrived on his doorstep half an hour later. A paratroop contingent had made its way into the palace and was trying to oust the president. Dr. Tuyen responded by ordering troops to move into Saigon and quash the rebels. It was three days before the rebels were ousted but the coup attempt foreshadowed Dr. Tuyen's ultimate fate—and even worse for Diem.

It turned out the coup had been, in part at least, an attempt to cut the president's sister-in-law down to size. Madame Nhu, wife of the bachelor-president's brother, Ngo Dinh Nhu, was a power behind the scenes. She was "bright, forceful and beautiful", in the words of U.S. Secretary of Defense Robert McNamara, but also diabolical and scheming—a true sorceress.

The coup was the work of disgruntled military officers, South Vietnamese soldiers who were deeply upset by Diem's handling of the country and Madame Nhu's meddling*. And it must have been to the plotters' chagrin that the failure of the coup had only emboldened Madame Nhu and her commitment to steel her brother-in-law's regime against all enemies, within and without. She has even been credited with toughening up an unnerved Diem who had early in the coup drama toyed with capitulating to the rebels. In any event it was not a Communist plot. They were busy with an in-house restructuring orchestrated by Hanoi's leaders who had called the remnants of the Viet Minh together on December 20. They were to become the new core of the National Liberation Front (NLF), established to fight the Communist cause in South Vietnam. Diem's bureaucrats immediately dubbed the NLF the "Viet Cong", which meant Vietnamese Communists, and the name stuck.

* * * * *

---

* Demery, Monique Brinson, *Finding the Dragon Lady: The Mystery of Vietnam's Madame Nhu.* New York: Public Affairs, 2013. p114.

REUTERS NEWCOMER Peter Smark was picking up quickly on An's many sides. He had a lot of friends within Saigon's military and government network, that was clear. An also had his anti-American moments, as the occasional outbursts made clear, but Smark didn't really see much in it. Americanization of the city was very much underway, despite the occasional whiff of Gauloises culture, and you could see how it might get under the skin of a local. Coca-Cola, rock 'n' roll, clothing, beehive-helmeted women all fairly shouted, "Hey, Man!" So did the money. Alcohol, drugs and prostitutes were increasingly available in Saigon's bars and hotels. Prostitutes worked at all levels, servicing visitors and palace officials alike. They were becoming an important information source for Communist spies, government agents, reporters, anyone with a hunger for the latest word. And An knew them well.

Reuters was no exception in using this network, and if An got high marks at work, it was often for making good use of information the whores and pimps passed along.

An was also earning high marks from Jan Smark, the wife of the man who had since become his senior colleague at Reuters. The two had been driving through Cu Chi, about an hour from Saigon, when An's white Renault 203 broke down. An suspected a radiator leak had caused the engine to seize and told Jan to wait by the car while he went to fetch some water.

Evening was approaching and the area was controlled by the Viet Cong (VC), so this wasn't the best spot for a breakdown. The ingenious VC had secured all the surrounding villages through an intricate tunnel network—and were battling South Vietnamese troops less than a kilometer away. Jan became increasingly anxious—she could see the crimson trail of mortar/rocket fire getting closer. After a harrowing hour of noisier and noisier gunfire as the fighting edged within 200 meters, An reappeared with water and some tools.

An managed to nudge the car back to life and they sputtered back to Saigon in a reasonably short time, but it was the closest Jan Smark had been to the war, and didn't she let the world know about An's heroics behind enemy lines! Indeed, An had a way of surviving in places he shouldn't have been. In no time at all, Radio Catinat embellished the tale and his cameo role soon took on Hollywood dimensions as An was reported risking life and limb across enemy lines to snatch the beautiful princess from the jaws of death.

Then another incident came up, leaving no time to consider if An had really crossed enemy—or friendly—lines. This time, a Friday, October 20, 1961, An was on assignment with Peter Smark in the Mekong when they got word that an Australian farm manager had been kidnapped by the Viet Cong. He had been taken from the farm, located outside Saigon at Ben Cat, where it had been set up under the Colombo Plan, originally a Commonwealth initiative to help developing countries. This improbable project was sponsored by the Australian government, and well-intentioned though it may have been, cow's milk never figured in the Vietnamese diet. Wilfred Arthur, a World War II fighter ace, took over as manager in 1961, the latest in a string of managers who, but for him, all had a reputation for being critical of Vietnamese workers—an attitude Communist agitators didn't mind playing on. With 70 workers, this operation might have seemed overstaffed, but this was less of a conventional spread than an experimental farm and training facility—in a country where jobs were traditionally stretched and shared anyway. Fortunately for all concerned, Arthur broke the pattern and was popular with everyone.

His wife, Lucille, and their daughter lived in Saigon, where Arthur joined them on weekends—except this one. The Ben Cat farm had become important to local Communists. While Tay Ninh felt it was of little strategic importance, splinter elements of the NLF thought differently. Ben Cat cadres argued the location of the farm made it an essential part of local intelligence operations—and by autumn, the Communists had been working to establish control of the area. Believing the farm's economic largesse would undermine their efforts to win local support, they considered killing Arthur before opting to hold him for ransom and use the cash to restock needed supplies.

Kidnappings of Westerners were not uncommon and Arthur was usually careful to follow security procedures, leaving work promptly by 4 p.m. to reach Saigon by dusk. But on this Friday, he stayed later than usual to check out a problem with the milking equipment, a problem he suspected was the handiwork of Communists, possibly employed by the farm. Though he worked a little later that day, he'd planned to make it back to Saigon in time for a farewell party for the official Australian representative, Bill Forsyth, who was wrapping up his tour. Arthur never made it. But then Forsyth didn't leave as planned, either, after news of the kidnapping broke. Canberra told him to remain until Arthur's kidnapping had been resolved one way or another.

Arthur, it later transpired, had been taken to a tiny jungle village accessible only by foot—and parked for days in a steaming hut. In Saigon, Lucille sat up with the Smarks and An, anxiously waiting for Australian officials to react. The South Vietnamese government was doing little: Political kidnappings were not uncommon; indeed several French businessmen and attachés had been seized and murdered. Farmers, even Western ones, were not a high priority and Arthur was on his own.

An didn't know the Arthurs, but Lucille was a good friend of the Smarks, and he never missed an opportunity to play hero to Jan. He had developed an innocent crush on her and, eager to impress, cut the profile of a man of action. Jan watched as An called everyone from the police commissioner on down, urging authorities to get on Wilf Arthur's case. He reassured the women, then left, saying he had to get back to the office.

In truth, An's problem-solving abilities had been seriously undermined by events at the palace, where Dr. Tuyen's authority was being eroded by the scheming Madame Nhu. Had the kidnapping occurred several months earlier, he would have been in a better position to help. Still An left the women exuding confidence.

Later that evening, Arthur's driver materialized at the Australian mission with a ransom note demanding antibiotics, an Olivetti typewriter with a Vietnamese keyboard, and chemicals—which intelligence deduced were for bomb-making purposes. Unfortunately, the driver arrived at the mission just as Forsyth's farewell party was reaching a champagne climax. Forsyth, a man given to tirades during his difficult posting, needed time to regain his composure.

After several hours, he decided that an attaché to the Australian mission, Laurie Crozier, should go with an interpreter, Nguyen Ngoc Rao, to deliver the goods to the pre-arranged drop. They left around two-thirty the next afternoon without the chemicals, arriving at a roadside point near Ben Cat. From there they were escorted over difficult and muddy terrain to the hamlet, which they reached by early evening. Negotiations lasted nearly four days. The Communists aimed to win Rao over to the cause through a process called 'illumination'. If that failed, the interpreter would be executed. The Viet Cong worked on Rao between bargaining sessions over Arthur. The process involved a continuous barrage of heavy questioning interspersed with bursts of Communist doctrine. The Communists also wanted to know more about the dairy farm and, in particular, Australia's growing involvement in Vietnam.

Arthur's first fear was that the Viet Cong would mistake him for an American, which would have involved a bigger ransom demand and probably death, whether the ransom was paid or not—and his fears were certainly justified. When Arthur told his captors he was Australian, a Communist interpreter asked, "What's that?"

VC suspicions persisted until Crozier arrived. Crozier, a man given to seeing a larger-than-life figure in the mirror, arrived convinced he alone would win freedom for the captured Australian. Rao, more usefully, told the Viet Cong that Australia was an unimportant little island in the South Pacific, reducing Arthur's market price considerably. But more dangerously, Rao refused to be swayed by the illumination process and continually argued with his captors in Vietnamese, French and English.

Crozier thought Rao's reaction to the illumination effort was brave but foolish. As the arguing intensified, the Viet Cong decided to kill Rao; they blindfolded him and marched him through the scrub to a clearing. When they removed his blindfold, Rao realized he was standing at the foot of a freshly dug grave. The Communists raised their guns as Rao stood resolute, un-illuminated to the end.

Arthur and Crozier were told they were free to go—but just then, Rao walked in to say goodbye. The episode at the gravesite had been a tease. In any case, it would have been unusual for the Viet Cong to waste bullets in this situation, Rao being an easy candidate for bayoneting and drowning.

Arthur insisted the three be allowed to leave together. Crozier said it was better to just leave, advice Arthur ignored. The ace announced he wasn't leaving without Rao, not realizing he had the upper hand, in fact—it transpired that VC orders had come down that no harm was to be done to Arthur. The guerrillas of Ben Cat were suddenly in a predicament. There was little they could do except relent.

All three arrived safely back in Saigon, to champagne, beer and tears from Lucille. Jan was much relieved, too, of course—and Reuters got an exclusive.

* * * * *

An would soon be making his own news. He had been introduced to Thu Nhan by another journalist, Cao Giao, in a handicraft shop on Tu Do Street where she worked. Giao was also in the early stages of his career, and together with An and Nguyen Hung Vuong would figure prominently as part of a trio known as the Three Musketeers. An was smitten by the youthful lady, who was 10 years younger than himself. Although he didn't think she was much to look at, he was jumping to tell Jan about his bride to be.

"She's very plain," An told Jan.

"I don't care," Jan replied, dismissing the comment. "I'm happy for you."

Only once before had he fallen for a woman that he wanted to marry, the daughter of a doctor who was a member of the Cao Dai, a religious sect that combined Western fundamentalist religious zeal and Eastern mysticism. Their oddball pantheon of martyred saints included Jesus Christ, Sun Yat-sen and the poet Victor Hugo. Staunch nationalists holed up in their jungle citadel near Tay Ninh, the cult was bitterly opposed to communism but had little time for the regime governing South Vietnam. The group had built its own battle-hardened army with supplies secretly smuggled by the Americans, and had gained a fame of sorts after publication of *The Quiet American*. Graham Green argued, implausibly it had so far turned out, that the Cao Dai were a potential third force to be reckoned with in Indochina.

The Communists did not approve of that relationship and An ended it. This time, he seemed certain, except for one thing. He told Jan he had to see the astrologer.

"You must be kidding!" Jan shot back. She couldn't believe a man of his learning and background would seriously turn to a soothsayer for guidance on marriage, but she didn't push it and tagged along. The astrologer examined his charts and blessed the union.

Only after that would An introduce Nhan to Jan.

"An, you lied," Jan said. "I've never seen a more beautiful woman in my life."

* * * * *

As 1962 began to roll by, Reuters Saigon bureau chief Bruce Russell had left and New Zealander Nick Turner was coming to replace him, portending changes for An. Peter and Jan announced their time was up, too. But forever grateful for An's dedication, the couple paid for An and Nhan's wedding. Peter lent the groom his gold cufflinks and car for the honeymoon. Just before Tet, the traditional New Year, they were married in a Confucian ceremony in Nhan's family home.

The air was thick with incense as they stood before an altar beneath portraits of their ancestors. Jan stood alongside Cao Giao, the man who had introduced them, and Dr. Tuyen's wife, Jacky. After the couple exchanged vows becoming husband and wife, the room fell absolutely silent, eclipsing any thought of Western-style revelry. The moment belonged to An and Nhan.

Shortly afterwards, Jan and Peter Smark left Saigon, traveling widely before ending up back in Australia.

For journalists, the kidnapping of Wilf Arthur was further proof that South Vietnam was still well down the list of news priorities. Even in Australian newspapers, where one might have expected lively coverage, the story barely rated a mention. Their foreign pages were still focused on Soviet nuclear tests and attempts to establish bases in Finland. It wasn't until another incident, at a hamlet called Ap Bac, that interest in the civil war in South Vietnam started to grow—in Australia and the U.S. as elsewhere.

Arthur left the farm after his two-year contract was up. He declined an offer to work at the Australian mission, with Crozier still there, and opted instead to go into business with the Duck Feather King, Keith Hyland. Hyland, by now, was living like many a wayward bachelor with too much money. But business was certainly on track. A third partner joined the enterprise, a Chinese businessman named Benny Chow. From its feathery start, the Hyland empire eventually expanded into timber, freight and shipping.

Life in the palace and the circus that surrounded it was also beginning to herald change. In February, there was another assassination attempt, this time on Madame Nhu in the palace gardens, but that also failed and the perpetrators got away.

As it happened, Dr. Tuyen himself was losing his place in Madame's good books and he and his wife, Jacky, soon found themselves left off the guest lists of Saigon's more important social occasions. Dr. Tuyen complained privately in a letter to her husband. Nhu sympathized with him, but when Madame got wind of the missive, she began a concerted strategy to undermine the doctor.

Rumors of his Communist sympathies—first aroused by American suspicions of his otherwise seemingly inexplicable peasant manner—suddenly resurfaced. He didn't help his cause by appearing much better informed than Nhu at a conference on combating Communist infiltration of villages. Madame Nhu convinced her husband that Dr. Tuyen had deliberately humiliated him and urged his dismissal.

An opportunity for squaring things presented itself after two defecting South Vietnamese hijacked two fighters and bombed strategic sites in Saigon, including the palace. Until that attack, the president had remained a Tuyen loyalist. But when he summoned his spy chief after that, Diem had the files on Nguyen Van Luc, a longtime political opponent, on his desk.

Luc had been released from jail a year earlier and it transpired that his son, Nguyen Van Cu, had led the air attack. "Do you know them?" the president asked the doctor, pointing to the dossier on his desk.

"Only by name," Dr. Tuyen replied.

Luc had in fact been freed by the president himself, but his dossier was marked, "Released by Dr. Tran Kim Tuyen."

"Did you know anything about the bombing in advance?" the president then wanted to know.

"Nothing," Dr. Tuyen said.

For the first time, the president did not believe his most trusted aide and through Madame Nhu's petty jealousies, matched only by her brother-in-law's panicking distrust, Dr. Tuyen was framed but offered a way out when Diem offered him a diplomatic position in Egypt. Tuyen accepted but his diplomatic career was cut short after Cairo extended relations to North Vietnam. He then fled to Hong Kong where he was afforded protection by the British and Pham Xuan An had lost one of his most important sources.

8. AP BAC, PLACE WITH A PLANT

THE PLAIN of Reeds provided an innocuous backdrop for a train of events that would aid the rise of Hai Trung in the Communist underground. Trung got around. His ascendancy began with the capture of Viet Cong guerrillas by South Vietnamese forces during their first predawn exercise. The raid, across swampy marshland near My Tho, where An had spent much of his youth, was a mixed success. While 131 Viet Cong fighters, according to the South Vietnamese leadership, were allegedly killed*, more than 300 from the Communist army's 504th battalion escaped across the border to safety in Cambodia.

Until that strike, on July 20, 1962, there had been virtually no night attacks by South Vietnamese regulars. The idea was to destroy the entire 504th battalion. According to American senior intelligence adviser Capt. James Drummond, the battalion had massed near a hamlet bounded by two small streams that flowed through the plain. Using a technique known as "spear and net," the South Vietnamese were to deliver a lethal blow, signaling to the National Liberation Front that their Viet Cong fighters could no longer count on nighttime respite with South Vietnamese forces backed by American military superiority. Along the Plain of Reeds, U.S. helicopter transports touched down to discharge nervous soldiers of the Army of the Republic of Vietnam (ARVN). As they squished their way across the rice paddies the South Vietnamese officers leading the attack intentionally dithered until it became obvious that the 504th had already started heading for the border on the far edge of the plain. The South Vietnamese tried to make a show of making up for lost time by unleashing a firestorm

---

* U.S. internal reports put the figure at no more than 90 VC Killed in Action (KIA).

of napalm and conventional bombs and other ordnance on the vacated Communist fighting positions, but most VC troops still escaped with their organization intact. The attack had been a badly kept secret and was openly talked about at Joint General Staff (JGS) headquarters, where previously An had worked as an interpreter for Dr. Tran Kim Tuyen and the feared Office of Political and Social Studies.

The escape of so many Viet Cong guerrillas infuriated the Americans, but Dr. Tuyen's propaganda department tried their best to turn the debacle into a public relations triumph at the behest of that master of spin, the increasingly cunning President Diem. The roots of the fiasco indeed reached back to the attempted coup of 1960. Diem believed that the military leaders who had rebelled were, at least in part, aggrieved by what they viewed as needless and excessive casualties inflicted on their units due to overly aggressive anti-Communist tactics. These deaths were bad press and bad for morale—the president agreed. Accordingly, in the wake of the coup attempt, Diem verbally instructed top ARVN leaders to not look for trouble and to minimize the number of troops killed and wounded. Diem's action only reinforced a military culture manifest with a predilection to passivity and lassitude. In a practical sense, the common practice among ARVN commanders became not to get too close with Communist forces. Rather, once contact was made, standard operating procedure became to unleash a fusillade of harassing fire to essentially cover the enemy's retreat—which up to that point, the VC seemed wont to do. Given the opportunity to slink away, the VC would rarely stand and fight in the clear knowledge that out in the open they had little to counter the overwhelming firepower advantage of the U.S.-equipped ARVN and their American 'advisors'.

Although the attack, largely planned by U.S. military adviser Lt. Col. John Paul Vann, faltered, ARVN 7th division leader Col. Huynh Van Cao was trotted out as a hero. Vann saw the action as a failure, something to learn from and move on. But Cao won plaudits for what was promoted as the most successful offensive ever launched against the Viet Cong. Success was measured in enemy dead, after all, and never had so many cadres been killed.

Cao had an insatiable ego, which Vann had played up in the hope that he'd carry out military operations along more disciplined American lines. As a sense of failure deepened in Vann's mind, an overwhelming sense of accomplishment blossomed in Diem's. Radio Saigon trumpeted the victory and Cao was given a hero's parade through central Saigon. Thousands turned out for the march. The women greeted Cao and his officers with flowers, hailing them as the national heroes. Through the streets Cao rode, standing at attention atop an army jeep. The parade route included a stop at the steps of the National Assembly, housed in the 19th-century opera house opposite the Givral, where weapons seized in the operation were put on display. Then onto the palace where Cao was decorated by Diem.

This wasn't the Communists' day for winning hearts and minds. South Vietnamese regulars were being successfully billed as winners—a useful show, given recent political wavering. At Reuters, correspondents had to report on the event, a put-up job though it clearly was. As the South Vietnamese president lied his way through the charade, journalists felt duty-bound to report his tributes to Cao. The Americans, for their part, couldn't publicly contradict the president or the man they so desperately wanted to lead the South's fight against the Communists.

Though the parade was a public relations success, Lt. Col. John Paul Vann would not have to wait long for another crack at the Viet Cong. This time the target would be a hamlet called Ap Bac.

When serving as an officer in the South Vietnamese army, An had become friendly with Capt. Hoang Duc Ninh, who often turned to An for advice. The airborne intelligence officer at JGS was a regular visitor to the Reuters office in the early 1960s and would often bring with him military maps illustrating strategic positions. So there was nothing out of the ordinary when he visited An's first-floor office in November 1962.

Pham Ngoc Dinh was doing his usual job of looking after visas, and the odd Christmas card, when he noticed the captain sitting down by An's desk and pulling out a military map. Overhearing them discuss a major military operation, Dinh thought something genuinely big was afoot. Talk of a military offensive had been constant in the Reuters office. The office complement had by then grown to 15 journalists, an indication of growing news interest in Vietnam.

Ninh had in fact come to capitalize on the PR momentum created by the Plain of Reeds "victory" and offset reports that Communist forces were gaining ground in the southern provinces. Radio Catinat scuttlebutt had it that the Plain of Reeds exercise had more than a few shortcomings—indeed, that the Communists had come out of it better than expected, all things considered.

While Capt. Ninh seemed genuinely concerned about the rising strength of the National Liberation Front, he also believed the allies had finally hit on an idea that would truly turn the tide. An listened as Ninh rolled out his maps and pointed to a small hamlet.

It was called Ap Bac, about 70 kilometers southwest of Saigon. Military command got word that Viet Cong forces had recently moved into the area. According to Ninh, JGS was now in the midst of preparing an operation aimed at annihilating the guerrillas—not to mention improving troop morale in the wake of the Plain of Reeds debacle. (President Diem's public relations stunt fooled few people in the military.)

As Ninh told it, the Americans planned a ferocious attack involving air-to-surface missiles fired from an airborne armada that included bombers, helicopter gunships and troop-carriers. Again the 'spear and net' technique would be used to round up the Viet Cong as they fled. But this time, there would be no repeat of the escapes at the Plain of Reeds. The mission was scheduled for early January.

What Capt. Ninh and his U.S. advisors did not understand was that the Viet Cong had every intention of digging in and fighting on January 2, 1963.

Many of the details of this sudden strategy reversal only turned up in an official account published on the 30th anniversary of the battle. Indeed, the official story helped tie together previously published accounts. The South Vietnamese forces expected to find about 120 Viet Cong guerrillas. Instead, they were confronted by more than 350 hiding in surrounding hamlets.

The Viet Cong, of course, had long anticipated the attack, the tip-off having come from the mysterious and all-knowing Hai Trung. Besides that, separate intelligence sources in Saigon, including palace spy Pham Ngoc Thao, had reported increased supplies coming into Saigon. Meanwhile, the winter dry season was soaking up the water ways of the Mekong Delta, offering easier access for South Vietnamese troops into Viet Cong strongholds.

The Viet Cong, for their part, had some confidence-building to do, too. Locals in the delta provinces had been shaken by the ferocity of the American-sponsored attacks, embellished and made larger by Diem's spin. The National Liberation Front needed to act quickly and make it known that it was capable of dealing with an enemy backed by superior American military hardware.

The Communists believed that up to 2,000 troops from seven divisions and local militia groups would attack Ap Bac, where they had one VC company, which is to say, 100 men. Initially, they had planned to withdraw the company and leave behind women and children to receive the assault, which would have made invading allies look like bloody monsters.

Tay Ninh directors, commanding from War Zone D, had ordered the withdrawal, in fact. But 24 hours before the assault, the company was ordered to remain, while two other companies moved into the surrounding hamlets. Each company was divided into groups of 10—each equipped with rifles, Soviet made AK-47s and heavier arms—and ordered to target one helicopter per group.

The next morning this peanut-sized Viet Cong force would face two regiments comprised of 27 companies, 10 LH-125 HULA helicopters, Douglas A-1 Skyraider ground attack aircraft, two B-26 Invader light bombers, seven reconnaissance helicopters, 13 small navy tank boats capable of crossing the saturated rice dikes, six 105-mm artillery guns, 10 mortar cannons and seven C-47 transport planes.

* * * * *

DINH WAS immediately struck by the sight of An as he stepped into the Reuters office late in the afternoon on January 2. "You have come back from battle?" Dinh asked, half-jokingly, pointing at An's battle fatigues.

An was taken aback. Obviously, he had been in battle. He never wore fatigues, but this time he had donned the whole kit—military boots, khaki pants, an army green shirt (the only exception being his photojournalist's vest with its riot of pockets for notebooks, cameras, sound recorders and travel documents). And, in case Dinh needed any more proof, An's clothing was covered in stinking slime from the paddy fields, and he reeked.

"Yes," came An's answer after a stunned pause.

The exhilaration of witnessing the battle as a war correspondent mesmerized him. It was a rare occasion where everything he'd learned seemed to come together—a defining moment. "You should have seen it, Dinh," An gasped, in a rare display of exuberance. "It was a big, big battle, Dinh."

An reached for a map from his desk and described at length what he had seen—the crashing helicopters, the walls of bullets. Then he sat down to write and by 6:30 p.m., An's version of the battle for Ap Bac was on the wire to Reuters subscribers around the world.

Dinh was enthralled by the story. But then he uttered a thought, only a fleeting thought really—more of a joke than anything else. But he said it, and he said it out loud: "Bloody hell, Pham Xuan An organized the battle, not the Communists."

Dinh's words hung in the air. Reuters station boss Nick Turner, always a little doubtful of An, looked at his local staff with equal suspicion—An, Dinh, the office secretary and taxi drivers, and assorted locals who hung around the office. They were all a cause of suspicion, especially given long-lingering doubts about the so-called stay-behinds who didn't go to the Communist North as provided by the 1954 Geneva Accords. The division of Vietnam into North and South had had a widespread impact on traditional loyalties. Whose side were these staffers really on? Turner often wondered.

That night other staffers drifted in, corroborating An's report. (An, by this time, was off in his corner writing a memo, as he often did for reasons no-one could quite fathom.) The following report, based on An's account with editing by Reuter staff, appeared the next day.

FIVE 'COPTERS SHOT DOWN BY REDS

SAIGON, Jan 2 (AAP-Reuter) - Communist rebels shot down five American helicopters in South Vietnam today.

Three other US helicopters were hit by the Communist fire in Dinh Thuong province, 40 miles south-west of Saigon.

A United States Army captain was killed and three other Americans wounded.

A United States military spokesman said the captain, an adviser to Vietnamese forces, died of wounds received while aboard one of the helicopters.

The action involved 1,200 Vietnamese troops, supported by aircraft and amphibious armored personnel carriers.

Reports from military sources said the helicopters ran into heavy automatic fire from guerrillas, as they came into land Vietnamese infantry near the target area.

The guerrilla force in the area was estimated to be of battalion strength and heavy fighting was reported for several hours during the day.

Eight American helicopters were hit by Communist fire altogether, but three of them were able to return to their staging base.

* * * * *

Being a newspaper man, David Halberstam of the *The New York Times* was able to express more of an opinion, and one that proved accurate. After An's reports had been put on the wire, Halberstam filed this story within the next 24 hours.

VIET CONG DOWNS FIVE U.S. COPTERS
HITS NINE OTHERS

Defeat Worst Since Build-up Began Three Americans Are Killed In Vietnam

Communist Guerrillas armed with automatic weapons inflicted a major defeat today on United States helicopters carrying troops into an operation in the Mekong Delta. Five helicopters were shot down.

Fourteen of the 15 helicopters taking part in the operation were hit by guerrilla gunners. One was an adviser to a ground unit, one a crew chief in an armed helicopter. It is believed that six or more Americans were wounded during the long and bloody fight.

It was difficult to estimate the casualties on the ground. One source placed the South Vietnamese casualties at 50 including dead and wounded. An HU-1A pilot, who made several strikes, said he believed that up to 100 Viet Cong were killed.

This was by far the worst day for American helicopters in Vietnam since the American build-up begun here more than a year ago. Up to today there was a widespread feeling that the addition of armed helicopters had made the use of the slower transport helicopters safer.

At one point in the action, in a rice paddy 50 miles south-west of Saigon, the three Americans crews were stranded as other Americans and Vietnamese were unable to get to them...

Halberstam went on to describe how, this time, the Viet Cong did not follow their usual routine of avoiding a fight and disappearing into the bush. The South Vietnamese and American forces were again going to use the technique known as 'spear and net'. The technique required the main force of ground troops to attack the core of the opposition, sow confusion and scatter everyone, at which point helicopters moved in and flung the 'net' —essentially mowing everyone down with machine-gun fire. Halberstam closed his dispatch with:

"...a trap had been sprung after it had become known that government forces were coming into a set spot."

* * * * *

Nick Turner was also unsettled by An's odd behavior after returning from battle, and his suspicions about the Vietnamese journalist were starting to give rise to anxiety.

"He knew Ap Bac was important," Turner told the author. "The change of tactics, the Viet Cong decision to stay and fight. It was the way he told us what had happened. An came in, in a considerable state of excitement and he knew what was going on. An gave us the tip-off to stick around to 6 o'clock in the evening."

Turner didn't know if An, or for that matter Dinh, had played a role in the defeat at Ap Bac or not, but his contacts and his ability to organize interviews with the upper reaches of Vietnamese society, including known Communist sympathizers, certainly made Turner wonder which side An was rooting for. Indeed, it got to the point where he warned An: "I don't care if you work for the other side as long as you keep it out of your work here."

The morning after the Ap Bac attack, Nick Turner traveled to the battle site with Neil Sheehan, then a correspondent with United Press International (UPI), and filed his story.

SOUTH VIETNAMESE POUND REBELS IN "FIERCEST" GUERRILLA BATTLE

SAIGON, January 3 (AAP-Reuter) - An attack by the Government forces on communist guerrillas yesterday became the biggest pitched battle since South Vietnam's civil war began in 1959, military observers said today.

The remnants of an estimated battalion of guerrillas are almost surrounded but are still holding out against 2,000 Government troops in rice-fields 40 miles from Saigon.

When 600 paratroopers jumped into the area last night to reinforce government infantrymen, 20 were killed and 30 wounded. Another 120 are missing.

Government forces have lost between 50 and 100 dead or wounded in the fighting, but Communist losses were estimated to be much higher.

Among the casualties were a US Army captain and two sergeants who were killed and four Americans, who were wounded when five helicopters were shot down yesterday.

As the Government troops bombarded the rebels during the night, one officer said:

"This is the first time such a large unit has dug itself in and defended a fixed position like this.

"The guerrillas gave a good account of themselves. We pounded them with 500 rounds of artillery and 11 planes bombarded them for five hours with

bombs and machine-gun fire."

One side of the perimeter was still not sealed and officers were pessimistic about the chances of holding the guerrillas until daylight.

The operation against the guerrillas opened yesterday morning after intelligence had been received on the whereabouts of at least one battalion of guerrillas.

As airborne troops and ground troops converged from the south, the guerrillas opened fire on 10 helicopters and hit almost all of them.

Four troop-carrying helicopters were shot down and one armed turbine-powered helicopter was disabled as it tried to evacuate the crews of the troops carriers.

An American Army captain described as "one of the most brilliant officers we had" was shot through the neck by a burst of guerrilla fire while leading a Vietnamese unit into action.

He died as a doctor attended him after he had been evacuated to a tiny airstrip.

Government forces came under guerrilla fire from four locations, but the biggest concentration was a hamlet which, according to aerial observers, was heavily fortified with gun emplacements and foxholes.

The hamlet, estimated to be large enough for a population of 600, was pounded by aerial and artillery bombardments throughout the day and by evening was described as "a complete shambles".

Almost all the structures were destroyed and trees were blown down by bombs.

"The villagers probably got out beforehand but if not I'm afraid the casualties are likely to run into hundreds," one American officer said.

"There are probably 200 guerrillas there and another hundred or so in the surrounding area."

A senior Vietnamese officer estimated that the guerrilla numbers were much higher.

The battle area, one of the richest parts of South Vietnam's main rice growing region, is heavily infiltrated by guerrilla regular units equipped with mortars, machine-guns and automatic weapons.

The deaths of the US army captain and two sergeants raised to 49 the number of Americans killed in Vietnam since July 1959, when the United States began aiding the country in its war against Communist guerrillas.

Thirty of these died in actual combat with the enemy, the others in various accidents.

* * * * *

With the exception of American newspapers, most of the world's papers relegated coverage of Ap Bac to their foreign news pages. Though An could see the battle's ramifications, few others could. He was disappointed with Reuters coverage and felt the Viet Cong victory had not been appropriately trumpeted, but that wasn't in the nature of wire services. Nevertheless, Vietnam was starting to arouse international interest.

The Viet Cong won the day, giving their Communist supporters something at last to really cheer about. And cheer they did. Songs commemorating the battle were written, the heroic story was written into the school curriculum, and veteran cadres were turned into overnight heroes by the North's propaganda machine.

The Viet Cong's 261st Main Force Battalion had stayed and fought, and that was all anyone had to know. Old assumptions about how the Viet Cong responded to the South's "spear and net" tactic—essentially trying to flee and getting shot down from the air—had to be discarded. With more effective intelligence and advance notice, the Viet Cong had succeeded in turning the South's attack strategy into a counter-ambush. The Viet Cong had also become more effective in shooting down helicopters by disguising their position and firing ahead of the target. In the event, the National Liberation Front could now dispel the myth that its Viet Cong soldiers were the poor leftovers from Viet Minh days. They had emerged as an effective fighting force the Americans would have to reckon with.

* * * * *

NINETEEN-SIXTY-THREE was a bad year and it would change the mood of Saigon and South Vietnam forever. It began with the debacle at Ap Bac and ended with the assassinations of President Ngo Dinh Diem and his brother Nhu. Twenty days after their November 2 killings, John F. Kennedy was assassinated in Dallas. President Kennedy knew of the plot to rid South Vietnam of Diem. It was carried out, in fact, by South Vietnamese generals with CIA approval (and with the duplicity of Dr. Tuyen, however unintentional).*

---

* Tuyen initiated a coup plot with Do Mau that was derailed when he was 'exiled' to Egypt. Thao took over Tuyen's plan and worked inside the ARVN to gather support after Tuyen's departure. The strength of Tuyen's coup plan was that he had agents inside the palace guard and special forces as well as a network of undercover agents sewed into the structure of actual combat units, individuals who had been initially placed there as pro-Nhu informants. When Tuyen left for Egypt, he was forced to leave his family behind in Saigon to act as, essentially, hostages. Meanwhile Do Mau and

The Diem assassination left a fissured government in its wake and eventually led to an escalation of American and allied troop deployment across the country.

What gold did for San Francisco nearly a hundred years earlier, American dollars would do for Saigon, which was seized by a money rush. Its population of about 2 million would more than double within a decade, turning the city into a boozy hub of prostitutes and hustlers. The city would become crammed with people seeking refuge from the war-torn countryside. And as the South drew further into itself, billions of dollars in American aid poured in. South Vietnam was an economy almost entirely propped up by war, sex and drugs, with oddments of "normal" economic activity on the periphery—like Keith Hyland's duck down and timber businesses.

By mid-1963, Diem and his brother Nhu had grown fittingly paranoid, and with the leadership increasingly crippled, the government procrastinated. Ap Bac had been a miserable failure. The president no longer traveled outside the city, and since Dr. Tuyen's relegation to the outer circle, Diem increasingly relied on his brother and the madness of Madame Nhu for advice.

Religious repression increased. As Catholics, the brothers distrusted Buddhists and actively sought to convert them to Christianity. But as the mistrust intensified, Nhu began to exercise power ruthlessly. He had his troops ransack pagodas and arrest monks and nuns—sparking a riot at the famed seven storied Xa Loi temple complex in Saigon. Bans were imposed on displaying the Buddhist flag and a national holiday commemorating the Buddha's birth was abolished.

As part of their civic cleanup, nightclubs were also closed. Political repression intensified. Political prisoners were being routinely tortured in tiger cages, essentially pits with grilles for a roof. The government further alienated the peasantry by accelerating its strategic hamlet program, which deployed troops to identify Communist-occupied villages and force suspected Communist peasants off their land. Families were split, travel severely curtailed.

* * * * *

---

the chief of the ARVN military security assumed control of Tuyen's plot machinery and eventually enlisted Pham Ngoc Thao.

ON JUNE 11, Reuters Saigon bureau chief Nick Turner sent the office factotum, Pham Ngoc Dinh, to the Cambodian Embassy. There had been word that a 63-year-old Buddhist monk, Quang Duc, would burn himself to death in front of the mission to protest Diem's repression. A presidential motorcade was scheduled to pass by the building, which was all the more significant a location for the fact that Phnom Penh, through its wildly duplicitous monarch Prince Norodom Sihanouk, backed the Buddhist cause. Dinh himself doubted the monk would go through with the plan. But as the motorcade drew near the embassy, Quang Duc, dressed in white robes, was there as promised, sitting with his legs crossed on the bitumen road. A confederate had doused him with petrol and struck a match as the monk sat motionless.

Dinh, in fact, had arrived late and remembered spotting two AP correspondents, one of them Malcolm Browne. By then, Quang Duc was already a smoldering charred lump. "It was bad, very bad," Dinh said as he later thought back to the horror. "The body looked like a piece of burnt wood."

In pamphlets handed out to bystanders and journalists that day, Quang Duc pleaded for the government to show "charity and compassion" to Buddhists and all other religious believers. The photograph taken by Browne showed anything but that, but the picture and the accompanying story got everyone's attention on front pages around the world. While Diem seemed genuinely horrified by the suicide, Madame Nhu called the horror a "barbecue worthy of applause".

By October, rumors of another coup were circulating. This time, the plotters were top-ranking army generals intent on using the monk's suicide to rouse public discontent over Diem and his brother. Some of the plotters would later make names for themselves: Gen. Nguyen Khanh, Gen. Duong Van "Big" Minh, Col. Nguyen Van Thieu, Ton That Dinh—and Huynh Van Cao, the hero of the Plain of Reeds fiasco 18 months earlier. They were led by Big Minh with the support of An's close friend, Col. Pham Ngoc Thao, the Communist palace spy (a side of Thao that An didn't know).

Col. Thao commanded a faction made up of marines, infantry and paratroopers, as well as armored division troops, adding nearly another 3,000 men. Thao's position, both as chief of Ben Tre province and as an adviser to the strategic hamlet program, gave him automatic access to data on military and artillery stocks. Part of Thao's Communist brief was to create trouble in Saigon, and a coup would certainly help discredit the South Vietnamese and their American supporters. At the same time, the Viet Cong would be rid of a leader who had proven something of an able enemy of communism.

So it was hugely ironic that the plotters should worry that Thao might support Diem in a coup attempt. In the event, they got his agreement not to act to prevent it. Actually the senior generals were also aware that Thao had inherited Tuyen's initiative, but it is completely plausible that they viewed Thao as a regime cutout and any approach to him as a trap— as a honey trap. In the end, Thao would go a big step further and put his troops at the disposal of the rebel generals. This would be an important step in moving the coup forward because Thao actually commanded combat troops, while many of the generals had been relegated to administrative positions by the regime specifically to isolate the senior strata of military officers from the armed forces that would be required to overthrow the regime (in a practical sense). In addition, what Thao brought to the party were the inherited Tuyen tentacles that reached down into the palace guard units and special forces. This eleventh hour amalgamation of the two coup strands would prove crucial.

Thanks to his close relationship with Thao, An was in the enviable situation of being able to report incisively as plans and events unfolded. There was the added complication of a fake coup being organized by Diem's brother, Nhu, in response to the rumor. And the plan was complicated. Nhu had two units, Bravo I and Bravo II, under his command. The plan was for Bravo I to fake a revolt, whereupon Nhu and Diem would flee on cue to the seaside resort of Vung Tau. Bravo I would seize Radio Saigon and proclaim a new government committed to evicting the Americans and dealing with the Communists once and for all. The murder of prominent American officials would add credence to the project. After all the declarations, Bravo II, ostensibly off pursuing Viet Cong in the countryside, would return and retake the palace in Diem's name, allowing the president and his brother to be restored as credible leaders. That was the theory at any rate.

The plotters of the real anti-Diem coup were attracted to the project for a variety of reasons. From Hong Kong, Dr. Tuyen feared that the Communists, or Communist-sympathizing nationalists, could step in and fill the void created by the deepening paralysis and he was highly embittered by his forced exile. While it was true he had been feuding with Col. Thieu—since backing Diem against Thieu's failed coup attempt two years earlier—there was now good reason to put differences aside and show common cause. Dr. Tuyen genuinely feared Diem's increasingly shambolic administration had raised the chances of a Communist victory. And Col. Thieu needed Dr. Tuyen's cooperation. The doctor still had excellent contacts within the palace and was still a confidante of Gen. Tran Thien Khiem, the army chief of staff.

From hiding, Col. Thieu had already set his sights on leading South Vietnam. Gen. Khiem was initially a reluctant participant, until Dr. Tuyen unwittingly urged the duplicitous Thao to travel overnight from Ben Tre to Can Tho where he persuaded the general to join in. For the rest, the overriding factor seemed to be raw ambition rather than the thought of defeating the Communists or winning a better lot for the South Vietnamese. They had already profited from high standing and U.S. capital spending, a position that would only be further enhanced by a grab at outright power.

Personal ambition, in fact, proved the undoing of the fake coup. Gen. Ton That Dinh, the 37-year-old Saigon regional commander in charge of orchestrating the charade, decided to double-cross Nhu after being ordered to deploy Bravo II and carry out the counter-coup. Along with his colleagues, Gen. Dinh wanted a cabinet post and a share of power.

The Americans could have prevented the coup but decided not to act. Ambassador Henry Cabot Lodge had, by this time, concluded that the war was unwinnable with Diem at the helm. It was all rich material for An to work upon.

On November 2, troops loyal to the generals stormed the palace. After the president and his brother surrendered, the generals argued about whether to send them into exile or court-martial them. Dr. Tuyen always maintained he was opposed to having them come to any harm. In the event, the brothers were discovered the next day in very bad repair. The postmortem found that they had been sprayed with automatic fire at point-blank range before being stabbed repeatedly. Madame Nhu was touring abroad at the time; first she visited Beverly Hills and then retreated to Europe, out of harm's way. She would later claim the original intention of the trip was to expose President Kennedy and CIA scheming in her country.

The coup d'etat touched off a chain of events that would lead to the Americanization of Vietnam's civil war. The rise to power of the military in the palace resulted in an immediate purge. Dr. Tuyen, long suspected of disloyalty because of his long history with and murky connections to the *ancien regime* was jailed for three years. An was one of the few to keep in touch with him, genuinely concerned as he was for his old boss. Dr. Tuyen's confidante, Col. Thao, was assigned to Washington as a press attaché, of all things, delighting the Communists. Indeed, the banishment of Thao and jailing of Tuyen, who had voluntarily returned to Vietnam in the wake of the coup—two individuals who arguably assumed the greatest risks earliest on—was prime facia evidence of the atmosphere of distrust and conspiracy that pervaded the upper echelons of Saigon's fractured society. Tuyen, Thao and their group were allies and also co-conspirators, but also potential competitors and lingering threats, and hence needed to be neutralized.

President Diem was immediately replaced by Gen. Big Minh, who was soon ousted by supporters of Gen. Khanh. That was in January 1964. Big Minh had often toyed with the idea of a power-sharing arrangement with the Communists to avert full-scale civil war. This unnerved the Americans, who supported Khanh. But they really would have been better sticking with Diem all along. With his assassination, the political, military and religious fabric of South Vietnam unraveled.

9. SHIFTING TIDES

'America never fully realized what was happening in Vietnam,
it just inched up on them.'
- P.J. O'Rourke

ON HIS visits to Saigon, Reuters' Southeast Asia chief David Chipp had been impressed with Pham Xuan An. In 1964, Chipp was promoted to oversee the entire Asian region. He was in a position to make or break careers and An's prospects looked bright, in most respects. Chipp was aware of tension building between An and the Saigon bureau chief, Nick Turner. The New Zealander's formal nature was sometimes mistaken for snobbery—something An could never be accused of—and the fact that the two were often at odds over what made a good story was a concern. But he was prepared to tolerate their differences, so long as the reporter's politics didn't affect copy.

An's experience was unmatched in the Reuters office, but relations with Turner had permanently soured. In mid-1964, An was summoned to Turner's office. Pham Ngoc Dinh had never seen An that angry as he walked out of the boss's office. Without saying a word to his colleague, An returned to his desk, wrapped his arms around everything he could carry, marched to the nearest window, threw everything out onto the street below and left the building.

Moments later Nick Turner strode out of his office and told Dinh that An had been dismissed for writing stories that "read like Radio Hanoi".

An wouldn't have to look hard for work. He had his pick of jobs, including standing offers from *Newsweek*, the *New York Times* and *Time* maga-zine. But he decided to join American freelancer Beverly Ann Deepe, who wrote for *Newsweek*, the *New York Herald Tribune* and the *Christian Science Monitor*, among other major U.S. publications. Deepe was involved with an American marine colonel, Chuck Keever. They eventually married.

But An and Deepe were inseparable. Deepe was impressed by An's ability to generate stories and sometimes joked that he was "a good cook", pro-ducing newsworthy material on days when nothing seemed to happen. He often saved stories he knew no one else would have, leads he got through interviews with a government minister, a visiting dignitary or someone in the Viet Cong or South Vietnamese military. The steady flow guaranteed Deepe a regular income.

Freelancing didn't always provide the cache, or money, of working for Reuters and reporters, especially Vietnamese ones, wondered where his mon-ey came from. His continued friendship with Dr. Tuyen, resumed once the doctor returned from self-imposed exile in Hong Kong after Diem was as-sassinated, gave rise to suspicions that An was employed by either the South Vietnamese secret police or the CIA. Or possibly the French secret service— or just possibly, some Reuters staffers thought, An might be a Communist. He'd certainly dropped enough hints to keep the rumors flying: The spy guise would only enhance his reputation for repeatedly scooping local journalists.

This was pronounced rather loudly in August when rumors of yet anoth-er coup reunited An with old colleagues. This time the target was Prime Minister Gen. Nguyen Khanh—and the perpetrator, An's trusted friend from his JGS days, Col. Thao. Thao, of course, was a genuine Communist plant, though not even the perceptive ex-Reuters man knew about that. He had slipped back from Washington after Khanh ordered him home. The siege mentality gripping the Saigon regime had Thao convinced he would be arrested and imprisoned if he wasn't careful so on the theory that the best defense was an offence, he called a press conference.

On this freelance assignment at the Majestic Hotel down in Tu Do Street, An would be representing any number of publications and competing with his old protégé Dinh, filing for Reuters. And another JGS veteran from Dr. Tuyen's day, Nguyen Ngoc Phach, would be attending the press confer-ence. Another wearer of two hats, Phach had just returned from London for *The Daily Telegraph*, writing under his pseudonym John Draw. Phach liked the anonymity afforded by a pen-name, he also believed that Western audiences preferred a name with a familiar ring as opposed to the difficult to pronounce Vietnamese syllables.

As Phach approached the hotel, he found Thao, his old colleague, atop a South Vietnamese tank, holding forth to the assembled journalists. He was demanding the prime minister's resignation and called on America for support.

Thao's betrayal did not surprise Phach. He had long considered him untrustworthy. But he was disturbed to find An interviewing Thao about his plans in an oddly cozy manner. Even if they were old friends, An's manner seemed too familiar in the circumstances. The scene would bother Phach for years afterward.

The reporters broke up and returned to their offices to get filing. Dinh and Phach made several calls to the Joint United States Public Affairs Office (JUSPAO) to get an official reaction to Thao's demands. It transpired that Col. Thao had no U.S. support. As far as the Americans were concerned, Prime Minister Khanh's forces were free to smash the rebellion, which they did, such as it was. With time running out, Col. Thao went into hiding, but the secret police soon caught up with him and put a bullet in his head.*

* * * * *

The United States was by now heading down a slippery slope, committing itself militarily, politically and financially to South Vietnam following a series of military defeats after Ap Bac. Covering the rise of American involvement was complicated by ongoing convulsions within Saigon's corrupt government. In April 1964, after extensive time in South Vietnam, Washington appointed Gen. William Westmoreland as commander-in-chief of U.S. forces in South Vietnam. President Lyndon Johnson and Congress gave unqualified financial support to the war effort. By February the following year the United States began the systematic bombing of North Vietnam.

On March 7, 1965, America's first combat troops, 4,000 marines, landed at Danang, on the northern coast of South Vietnam. Australian, South Korea, New Zealand, Thailand and the Philippines would follow suit.

By the end of 1966, there were nearly 400,000 U.S. troops in South Viet-

---

* Thao's dual role was not known until after the end of the war, thus in an ironic turn of events, ARVN posthumously promoted Thao to general and bestowed the Liêt Si (heroic war dead) honor upon him. And while Thao was originally interned at the ARVN cemetery in Go Vap, following the fall of Saigon, his remains were disinterred and reburied amongst his Communist brethren at the Revolutionary Martyrs' Cemetery.

nam. The Americans and South Koreans were joined by smaller forces from Australia, the Philippines, and not long after that, Thailand. With Canada wanting no part of the war, large numbers of Canadians were joining the American military, some of them attracted by the fringe benefits, which included free university tuition in the United States.

As the war escalated, a staggering $40 billion a year would be spent on what was being called an international police action. Between 1961 and 1966, 637,000 tons of bombs had been dropped, more than the tonnage dropped in the Pacific area during World War II. American bombers sent Agent Orange, a chemical weapon, drizzling down, defoliating more than a million acres—including the Tay Ninh area, where the Communists had centralized their intelligence network under Gen. Tran Van Dang. On November 17, 1966, President Johnson announced that the U.S. expeditionary corps would assume control of military operations while the South Vietnamese troops would be responsible for the pacification project. Near the end of 1966, the U.S. Senate approved $17.4 billion more toward the effort. The Americans were now conducting a real, if still undeclared, war.

By late 1967, nearly 600 journalists were working in South Vietnam. The first thing arriving journalists had to do was secure Military Assistance Command Vietnam cards from JUSPAO.

Officially, they were "accredited to cover the operational, advisory and support activities of the Free World Military Assistance Forces". Bureau chiefs enjoyed the same status as a colonel, entitling them to the utmost "co-operation from the military". The open relationship between the military and the media was rare but not unprecedented, and would serve as a model for press relations following the invasions of Afghanistan and Iraq.

Journalists had broad access to transport and the battlefields throughout the South. At 8 each morning, the military would issue a three-page update giving their version of the war's progress, and every day at 5 p.m. there was a press conference, derisively known as the "five o'clock follies". As Reuters correspondent Hugh Lunn, who had arrived in February, put it: Everyone reported what was said, but "we didn't really believe it". More than 100 journalists showed up each day to hear the official story, usually delivered by a general. Tapes of each briefing were immediately sent to Washington for evaluation. What would become the longest-running front page story of the century was getting bigger, if less and less accurate.

The bulk of information was carried via the international news agencies, supported by regional media organizations, and competition was fierce. While the Vietnam War would become known as the first television war, the visual electronic media was still in its infancy and like radio relied on the wires as its chief source of information, a concept known in the trade as "rip and read", tear it off the printer and read it out on air. In fact the time it took to develop film, get it in the can and back into the studio meant much of the footage was days old when aired, and this was particularly the case in 1968. CNN changed that in the 1991 Gulf War and other networks would catch up by the time of the 2003 invasion of Iraq.

Because agencies sold their product on the strength of being first with the news, they would send two journalists to briefings so that one could leave halfway through to begin filing, while the other stayed through the question period. Very little of the information sent from the follies was fact-checked. This would not prove unique. Journalists covering military press conferences in the Balkans during the 1990s, or Afghanistan and Iraq in the following decades would experience the same problem*.

Time was the enemy here. But there were more insidious complexities at work in the dissemination process. Domestic news services in Western and Eastern bloc countries alike subscribed to the major agencies and reworked individual reports into single round-up stories before passing copy to newspapers and broadcast networks. As well intentioned as editors may have been, the practice filtered out genuine news instead of enhancing it. In effect, it created a gateway, allowing the familiar through, but rarely original stories that would qualify as scoops. Stories that could not be corroborated by other agencies were often spiked, or trashed, rather than allowed through for domestic distribution. As a result, some journalists simply regurgitated the official line to get into print. Or equally bad, stories deemed antiwar or anti-American could end up rewritten and out of context.

Occasionally reporters had the opportunity to check the veracity of a military briefing. After being told that 80 villagers near Hoi An, an ancient trading port dating from the 15th century on the northeast coast of South Vietnam, had been kidnapped by the Viet Cong, Hugh Lunn discovered they'd been merely helping evacuate Viet Cong casualties to safety. Villagers routinely blamed neighbors' absences on VC kidnappers when challenged by South Vietnamese authorities, to avoid being labeled as Communist sympathizers—and possibly becoming targets for future U.S. bombing runs.

---

* The author has covered conflicts in Afghanistan, Cambodia, Iraq, Kashmir, and Sri Lanka while spending time or writing about trouble zones from Northern Ireland and Morocco to Thailand and the Southern Philippines.

For the American military the daily meet-the-press exercise served a secondary, but important purpose; keeping reporters in Saigon and controlling the flow of information, essentially a numbers game, where casualty figures could be omitted or distorted—by a 10-to-1 ratio, Dinh later estimated. In the Ashau Valley, where Dinh was schooled by the Communists, 45 helicopters from the 1st Air Cavalry were shot down. Reuters reported 45, but JUSPAO said 15, then the next day announced a further 15 and another 15 the day after that. The two accounts converged in the end, but for two days Dinh and Lunn had to endure insinuations that their numbers were wrong.

* * * * *

AN'S STINT working with Beverly Ann Deepe lasted about a year. In 1965, she left the country to marry Chuck Keever and An was free to take up *Time*'s standing job offer. From then on, An and Dinh's friendship served to bring together staff at Reuters and *Time* and veteran journalists in Indochina. The *New Yorker*'s Bob Shaplen, freelancer Denis Warner and Don Wise were known as the Godfathers or the Three Wise Men because of their immense experience in the region dating back to World War II. Wise also bore an uncanny resemblance to actor David Niven and wrote for one of Britain's nationals, the *Daily Mirror*. Like his compatriot, Wise wasn't spare with his opinions, once characterizing *Mirror* readers, a little unfairly, as "people whose lips move when they read".

An, Nguyen Hung Vuong and Cao Giao, who had introduced An to his future bride, were dubbed the Three Musketeers. Vuong was Shaplen's confidant and on particularly good terms with Douglas Pike, who ran JUSPAO. The musketeers were the big hitters of local journalists, working for some of the most well regarded newspapers in the English speaking world. Between them they shared a wealth and experience that in Vietnam could not be matched.

And there was Neil Davis who would earn plaudits for exceptional work as a cameraman for Visnews. He was also a standing member of the group and since Visnews was half owned by Reuters, the Tasmanian could earn extra cash as a freelance writer—and thanks partly to An's contacts, Davis established himself as a highly prolific reporter specializing in South Vietnamese military operations. And finally, there were the by now widely recognized authorities—Stanley Karnow, Neil Sheehan, David Halberstam— who, together, made for a highly sophisticated network.

Frank McCulloch was *Time* Saigon bureau chief from January, 1964 till the autumn of 1966, then chief of Southeast Asia until February, 1968. He assigned An to cover South Vietnamese politics and—a longstanding ambition of An's—economics. An also became *Time*'s Mr Fix-it, organizing interviews for journalists, arranging visas and placating the palace when an irritating article was published. Unofficially, An's duties sometimes extended to getting people's favorite prostitutes out of jail, earning him the nickname "Doctor of Sexology of the Continental Hotel" where he and the foreign press pack often held court

McCulloch was impressed with An's contact book, packed as it was with CIA agents and palace numbers. By this point, An enjoyed virtually direct access to Prime Minister Nguyen Cao Ky, a French trained pilot renowned for his flamboyancy and resolve, and Nguyen Van Thieu, now president after a succession of coups. An had used his palace connections to keep Dr. Tuyen out of jail, though he remained under surveillance. But An was no friend of Ky and Thieu, who hardly trusted anyone anyway. From An's point of view, Ky and Thieu were responsible for the unspeakable treatment that befell his close friend, Col. Pham Ngoc Thao, the Communist spy.

Against all odds, Thao had survived being shot in the head after his unsuccessful attempt to oust Gen. Khanh as prime minister. The bullet had passed through his mouth, leaving him with just enough strength to get to the nearby Catholic convent at Thu Duc, where he took refuge for nearly a year.

When Ky learned Thao was still alive, he announced a reward for his capture. His whereabouts were quickly established and secret police chief Gen. Nguyen Ngoc Loan ordered his men to helicopter into the convent just 16 kilometers from Saigon. They seized Thao and took off but instead of flying back to the city, Thao's captors pinned him to the floor of the aircraft, pulled off his trousers, produced a steel nutcracker and castrated him. For An and Dinh, Thao's gruesome end at the hands of Ky, Thieu and Loan cast a sickening pall over life in the capital's bars and restaurants.

* * * * *

AFTER AN joined *Time*, people noticed he'd changed. Former colleagues remember him openly engaging in political arguments when he was at Reuters. At *Time*, where most of his fellow staffers were American, he toned it down. There seemed little point in risking a bright future for the sake of a few left-wing political essays.

An forged many friendships at *Time*, as elsewhere. One close friend was John Cantwell, a Chinese scholar from Sydney whom McCulloch used as a freelance contributor. Cantwell had a Chinese wife and two kids back in Hong Kong and shared An's infatuation with exotic birds and the zodiac. An gave him good leads and transport around Saigon in his white Renault, two more reasons Cantwell liked his company. An also proved helpful in getting McCulloch to arrange pay advances for Cantwell, who was frequently stretched supporting his wife's gambling habit.

Tim Page, an Englishman who joined *Time's* freelance stable as a photographer, was also close to An. Page and his good friend, the photographer Sean Flynn, were the life of any Saigon party, which always included a steady supply of drugs (usually via cameraman Neil Davis), booze and women. They were always good for moving the needle on Saigon's raunch meter.

For the likes of Page, Davis, Flynn and Cantwell, An was something of an uncle. He was tolerant when Page arrived at work after a three-day binge in an opium den. In return, Page rewarded *Time* with some of the best war photography he ever achieved. An's vices didn't go much beyond smoking cigarettes. Cursed with a weak bladder and with a history of TB and malaria, he didn't drink, so when others got shaky, he was always there with his clearheaded and relaxed presence. An could usually tolerate their frailties. They had at least two things going for them in An' s mind. They had an unambiguous sympathy for the Vietnamese people and they covered the war from deep in the field, not from the safety of Saigon.

* * * * *

IT IS difficult to quantify An's written contributions to *Time* because the magazine didn't byline stories in those days. But fellow staffer Oliver Todd reckoned he supplied 80 percent of copy produced by *Time's* Saigon bureau. By late 1967, all this coverage of a war going increasingly badly for America only fueled antiwar sentiment in the United States. In Hanoi, the leadership wanted to turn up the pressure and sought out Hai Trung, their well-placed operative in the South, for help.

The elusive Trung did not believe it was possible to push the Americans into the sea, as the saying went, as most Communist leaders also believed. To his mind, the Viet Cong and the North Vietnamese simply could not match American firepower and the only real possibility of a Communist victory hinged on pushing the United States into a political corner and forcing a military withdrawal. In an odd sort of way, and perhaps without knowing it, Trung was betting that American democracy would actually work—that the people would end up stampeding their political leaders into winding up U.S. participation in the war.

In late 1967, Trung received his next major assignment from the Communists. He was to do an impact analysis of a full scale surprise attack by Viet Cong and North Vietnamese forces across South Vietnam—to be launched on the stroke of midnight, Lunar New Year's Eve, January 30, 1968.

This was Tet. It would make for a thunderous and bloody start to the Year of the Monkey. About 140 cities and towns would be attacked simultaneously. The Communists would take advantage of the traditional New Year's cease fire by ignoring it. The sound of gun and rocket fire, at least at the critical opening stages of the offensive, would be lost in the riot of firecrackers welcoming in the New Year across the country. Key installations would be under-manned, as they usually were during these annual festivities, and make easy targets.

Tet was an old idea whose time had come. Trung himself suggested a massive surprise under cover of New Year's firecrackers in 1965, arguing that the Communists couldn't hope to win by conventional means.

In drawing up his impact scenarios, Trung considered each against four factors, all inter-related: The growing international resentment of allied involvement in South Vietnam; the element of surprise; the economic impact of American wealth, particularly on Saigon, and the heavy reliance of South Vietnam on international aid.

By making the war more unpalatable to the American public with this massive offensive, mounting political pressure would push the United States closer to withdrawal, leaving the South Vietnamese on their own. Tactically, American and allied forces were winning the war—but, and it was a very big but, escalating peace protests were starting to give the Communists a political edge.

For Western politicians to justify more injections of capital and military assistance, their governments not only had to be winning the war, they had to be seen to be by voters. Perceptions were critical. An American withdrawal would precipitate an exodus of foreign capital causing the almost immediate collapse of the South Vietnamese government: The Communists could then project themselves as the only alternative.

In the end, Trung's report came down to these essentials. It recommended employing ruses to divert the enemy and scatter their resources and then proceeding with the broad offensive as planned, including a lightning fast take-over of Saigon, followed by a short period of occupation. Saigon's takeover would really just be a demonstration exercise of Communist might, which, in fact, was not sustainable. So the first invasion would be followed by a retreat—to regroup for a second offensive.

The report was microfilmed and sent to Hanoi. Both Viet Cong in the South and North Vietnamese read and discussed it. The report went all the way to Ho Chi Minh's desk, and shortly before Christmas the Communists drew their conclusions. In Saigon, the Viet Cong would target the United States Embassy, the Presidential Palace, the South Vietnamese Army, Navy and Police headquarters—and Tan Son Nhut Airport.

Of all the points Trung made in his report, Gen. Tran Van Tra, who headed Communist military operations in the south, strongly agreed with one in particular: That the Americans would most likely be forced out politically, not militarily, in the end. The offensive might change the battlefield scoreboard temporarily, but what it stood most to achieve was to strengthen North Vietnam's political leverage at the Paris peace talks—and further the impression of an unwinnable war among American voters and legislators.

After Tet, North Vietnamese negotiators would call for the cessation of American bombings in North Vietnam at the 20th parallel. With the second offensive, so-called Tet II, they could demand bombing stop at the 17th—and add in an extra demand, while they were about it: Official recognition for the Viet Cong's political wing, the National Liberation Front, and for its inclusion in the Paris peace talks.

Viet Cong generals received their orders. The first attack in the sweeping offensive would be at Hue. Troops were moved south. Ammunition and stockpiles of rocket launchers, hand-grenades, AK-47s, machine guns and howitzers, originally ferried from the Soviet Union, were transported south via the Ho Chi Minh Trail through Cambodia and down the South China Sea.

The North Vietnamese and Viet Cong set out some convincing decoys. One involved building up force strength at a small U.S. military base called Khe Sanh, 24 kilometers south of the DMZ and 16 kilometers from the Laotian border. Communist troops were building up to 40,000 in the area, forcing Gen. Westmoreland to commit 45,000 American soldiers to the region, in addition to the 5,000 based inside the hilltop fort. A North Vietnamese "defector" reported the Communists were out to take control of the northern provinces to use as bargaining chips at the peace talks but only after taking Khe Sanh. It was nonsense, of course, but what was probably a staged defection was convincing.

At *Time*, An advanced the theory that Viet Cong and North Vietnamese forces would strike at Khe Sanh. Cantwell, Dinh, Shaplen—and the Radio Catinat rumor mill—dutifully spread the word. Embellished, the story was that the Communists envisioned a reprise of the Viet Minh's overwhelming strike at Dien Bien Phu, routing the French in 1954. American intelligence ate it up. The U.S. command was delighted at the prospect of traditional conflict on proper battle lines. Yet, in the weeks leading up to Tet, An was also charged by his other employer with driving Tu Cang,[*] the commander of the Communist southern intelligence service, known as the H.63 cluster headquartered near Cu Chi—and An's direct chief for most of the hot war—around Saigon in order that the two could scout targets for the upcoming attack. Tu Cang[†] posed as an old school friend of An's, a bon vivant plantation owner, in town just to visit and while away time chatting at the Givral or on the terrace of the Continental. After some primping to ensure that Tu Cang's rural origins were obscured, together they visited the Saigon port, the state treasury, chatted with a senior ARVN commander, and even frequented the *Time* office.

But suddenly, there was a new distraction. On January 23, 1968, just a week before Tet, the North Korean navy seized the USS Pueblo, claiming it had strayed into their territorial waters. The crew of the intelligence-gathering vessel was arrested and paraded with their hands in the air. Reported *Time*: "The seizure of the USS Pueblo in international waters came as an abrupt abject lesson to Americans that the world's greatest power can be roundly and resoundingly put down by the most minuscule of foes." The incident made Khe Sanh only more important in America's eyes—and fully justified more resource commitments there. So strong was the conviction that Khe Sanh was the focus of Communist attempts to defeat the South that *Time* wrote:

SHOWDOWN AT KHE SANH: Despite North Korea's obvious attempt to win prestige through belligerence, many in the top echelons of U.S. government felt that the hijacking of the Pueblo had an ominous connection with the war in

---

[*] Hoang Hai Van and Tan Tu, *Pham Xuan An: A General of the Secret Service* (Hanoi: NXB The Gioi, 2008), p88.

[†] Ibid p89.

Viet Nam. As the London Economist observed: "The North Koreans are trying to direct American attention from what could be a decisive battle in Viet Nam." That battle, shaping up around the U.S. Marine base of Khe Sanh in South Viet Nam's north-west corner, could be the biggest of the war. The Communists would not only like to distract U.S. attention and resources from the battle but also combine the humiliation of the Pueblo's seizure with a U.S. defeat or at least a major bloodletting. Such a one-two punch, they might well hope, would destroy the U.S. will to continue the war.

In January 1968, Frank McCulloch decided to tour as many of the 22 provinces in South Vietnam as he could. He had covered the region for nearly four years, the last two from his base in Singapore, and had just been reassigned to New York, where he was expected the following month. The tour lasted a week and ended in Saigon, where he met the White House representative, Robert "Blowtorch" Komer. McCulloch sensed something was wrong and told Blowtorch as much, saying the trip had been a surreal experience. "Wherever you went, no-one even looked at you."

Komer laughed at McCulloch and produced a computer read-out, which indicated the overall situation in South Vietnam was "tame".

"You're dead wrong," McCulloch said, clearly unimpressed.

Komer laughed again. They agreed to disagree and said their goodbyes.

10. TET—THE PUNJI TRAP

AT REUTERS, Dinh had more or less assumed the role An played in his early days with the agency. He'd been nicknamed "Gungadinh" because, as Hugh Lunn put it: "He was a better reporter and man than any of us." Despite the accolade, Gungadinh's English had only slightly improved since Bruce Russell had enrolled him in English classes years earlier. "Dinglish," his colleagues called it.

It was unabashed Dinglish that greeted Hugh Lunn arriving from London in February 1967. "What your grandfather do? Jail?" It was a standard joke Gungadinh reserved for Australians with their storied convict heritage. He used the same line on Bruce Pigott, when he arrived later in the year. Lunn was a laconic Queenslander. Pigott, from Victoria, came to be known as the "Quiet Australian", a man of few words outside of cynical observations about the war. He had also been posted from London, where he'd joined Reuters after passing the usual tests, which involved rewriting scrambled copy. Pigott would become close friends with David Chipp and another Brit destined for South Vietnam, Ron Laramy.

As the months passed, Pigott and Dinh became very close. Dinh appreciated his sensitivity to Vietnamese custom, a rare thing for a foreigner. All in all, Pigott was pretty understated for a foreigner. He was a nonsmoker and, unlike other correspondents, not a big drinker. He also loathed the call-girl scene that excited many of his Western colleagues. He'd fallen in love with Miss Nga, a local he wanted desperately to marry. But her parents objected —they assumed Pigott was another sex-crazed Westerner, an impression Dinh tried his best to correct.

By the end of January, 1968, former Reuters Saigon bureau chief Nick Turner was trying his life as a freelancer. Dinh, Pigott and Lunn worked under a street-smart Scotsman named Jim Pringle, who was quickly building himself a reputation as a top-flight war correspondent. Pringle had a way of endearing himself to the locals. One of his first orders ended the Reuters practice of referring to the Viet Cong as "the enemy" in copy. The change in the style manual upset U.S. officials but, as Pringle saw it, Reuters was an independent news agency with an obligation to provide balanced coverage. Given his druthers, he would have hired a Communist reporter or two in the name of balance.

Reuters was at 15 Han Thuyen Street, about 150 meters from the cathedral and the same distance from the Presidential Palace. *Time*'s offices were also on Han Thuyen Street, so Dinh and An were always trading gossip. One would always be calling the other out from his office for a chat and the routine put An at the top of Pringle's list of sources—anytime a rumor came up, he'd have Dinh run it by An.

With McCulloch back in New York, the *Time* office was in for changes, too. Bill Rademaekers arrived in Saigon for a nine-month stint as bureau chief in December 1967. His brief included orders to sort out John Cantwell, who was now routinely asking for advances to keep up with his wife's gambling debts. By the time Rademaekers touched down, they had spiraled to $12,000, equivalent to a hefty house deposit in the States then. It had to stop, and the deal was that management would forgive the advances, but would no longer use his services.

Cantwell had become a valued regular stringer—a reporter who performed well in combat zones. And just the previous month, the red-headed Australian had survived a helicopter crash near the summit of Hill 875, outside Dak To. He was a hard man to fire and Rademaekers was not looking forward to the office that morning, when Cantwell approached him having breakfast on the terrace of the Hotel Caravelle.

"I see you're having vital juices," Cantwell began.

Rademaekers stared at his cornflakes and prunes, struggling to deduce his meaning.

Cantwell broke the silence: "In China they take a dried prune and place it in the vagina of a virgin. The prune soaks up the natural juices and it's quite a delicacy."

Rademaekers managed to avoid throwing up and asked Cantwell to sit down—and then told him point blank that *Time* was letting him go. "It's the advances."

Stunned, Cantwell replayed the old tape, telling the new bureau chief a sad story about his wife's mah-jong habit and how he needed the money to pay her debts and feed his kids. Then Cantwell spliced in a counterproposal—that *Time* retain him as a regular freelancer and that management cut into his pay periodically to claw back the advance money.

Rademaekers had taken an instant liking to Cantwell, despite his lapses, and respected his work. Even more to the point, he knew Cantwell would be hard to replace, so he decided on the spot to buy his proposal.

With one big problem out of the way, Cantwell then announced he didn't want to work outside Saigon anymore. The killing was getting to him, he said, and he was becoming consumed with a sense of his own mortality. What Cantwell really wanted, without actually saying as much, was to get back to Hong Kong with his debts paid off, and work for *Time* from there.

Since Rademaekers had no wish to send a hesitant man into a battlefield, he bowed to that pitch, too. "But no more advances, John."

Happy as he was for the break, Hong Kong suddenly looked a very long way off. Cantwell had just committed himself to remain in Saigon over Christmas and the foreseeable future. Others, like Tim Page and Denis Warner, could find some release from it all. They'd both left the country for a holiday. Even Neil Davis, resident cameraman for Reuters affiliate Visnews, was away covering riots in Mauritius. Freelancer Nick Turner had gone too, but for more pressing reasons. He had been rushed to the U.S. Army 7th field hospital with acute appendicitis, and his wound turned septic after the operation. When doctors failed to contain the spreading infection with a second operation, a dangerously sick Turner was ordered home to New Zealand.

Turner's old Reuters colleagues were as concerned as anyone. On January 29, Dinh helped him pack and drove him to the airport. In the terminal, Turner said goodbye and wished his friend an enjoyable Tet cease-fire.

"No sir, no cease-fire," Dinh replied.

Turner, who'd always wondered about An with his "Radio Hanoi" copy, now wondered who Dinh really worked for. The speculation over Khe Sanh was making everybody dizzy with suspicion. The usual cease-fire, it was true, had just been implemented to take effect from midnight January 30, the first day of the lunar new year. But it was to be a much shorter period than in previous years, and this time it didn't cover the five northern provinces, where Khe Sanh remained under attack, or the southern part of North Vietnam, where American bombings continued.

* * * * *

THE FIRST whiff of something unusual came at 7 that very Monday night, the eve of the Lunar New Year. Dinh had left the office for the food vendor outside when he noticed An on the sidewalk. A routine chance meeting, they had both been working the same shift and An was leaving for home.

Dinh noticed a distinctly serious look about his friend. An greeted Dinh hurriedly, then blurted out a warning. "Be very careful. Stand by. Something very big is going to happen tonight—a Viet Cong attack." It was all a bit cryptic. An said Saigon would come under fire at 1 the next morning but he wouldn't elaborate, despite probing from Dinh.

He just walked away.

Dinh immediately returned to the office and, without divulging his source, told Pringle to keep the office open all night if necessary, because something very big was about to happen.

Hugh Lunn, "Gunsmoke" to Dinh, was sitting at his desk filing a night-lead, an overall wrap summing up recent strikes in Hue and Danang. Having noticed Lunn's girlfriend from the British Embassy waiting for him outside, Dinh walked up to Lunn.

"Gunsmoke, you tell Miss to go home."

Annoyed by the intrusion, Lunn demanded to know why.

"Tonight the VC attack Saigon. She go home," Dinh replied.

"The VC attack Saigon?!," Lunn exclaimed. "That's a bloody good story—I'll put that in the nightlead."

Dinh was stern-faced, unusually serious: "No background, no source, no report. But we must be ready. First with big story." But Pringle still seriously doubted Saigon would be attacked. It had never happened before, either with the Viet Minh during French colonial days or with the Viet Cong. Besides, a truce was in force.

But Dinh was adamant, so the bureau chief decided to keep the office open and have his reporters regroup at midnight, just in case there was anything to his crazy story.

And so the day eerily wound down. Saigon remained unusually quiet in the hours before midnight. But in a garage a short distance from the Reuters office and only about five blocks from the American Embassy on the corner of Mac Dinh Chi Street and Thong Nhut Boulevard, a score of Communist commandos from the C-10 battalion were piling into two vehicles, a Peugeot van and an old taxi. Their orders were to infiltrate and hold the American

Embassy. And across South Vietnam, 400,000 Viet Cong and North Vietnamese regulars stood poised to spring out in every direction.

Lunn, Pringle and Dinh waited till 2 a.m. when Lunn, now tired of waiting around for nothing, returned to his girlfriend from the British Embassy.

* * * * *

THE OFFENSIVE started late. Disguised by firecrackers ringing in the New Year, the first shots were fired in the old Vietnamese capital of Hue and triggered a chain of explosions across South Vietnam. At the U.S. Embassy, the Viet Cong opened fire on the military police guarding the entrance. The MPs immediately made a "Signal 300", code for the embassy coming under attack. With the grounds entrance gates shut, the guerrillas used a 15-pound explosive to blast a hole through the six-story building's safety wall, which acted as a perimeter to the main boundary fence that defended the compound.

With an M-16 by his side, Bill Rademaekers was at the *Time* office at 3 a.m., telexing New York. "Please do not call us," he typed in remarkably un-Telex-like language. "We will call you." Over at the Embassy Hotel, John Cantwell was blown from his bed by mortar fire. He raced to the roof, where he could see tracer bullets and mortar fire, and the Viet Cong battling for the Presidential Palace. From the Mekong Delta to the DMZ, the Communists were attacking on a scale no-one thought possible.

A wire service—where every minute brings a new deadline—faced more immediate pressures than a newsweekly with its next deadline still days away. Lunn was having a shower when he heard the explosions. His girlfriend rolled over in bed and said, "It's started, hasn't it?" Without answering, Lunn made a dash for the balcony and looked down to see Viet Cong guerrillas climbing out of a manhole and trading fire with American troops. Then he looked up and saw the European girl standing on the balcony across the way get hit in the crossfire (fatally, it turned out). Lunn wanted to get back to the office, but decided there was little he could do at this point except console his tearful girlfriend.

The extent of the carnage was apparent the next morning as the fighting continued. Bruce Pigott, who was based at Danang, managed to hitch a hair-raising ride on a U.S. helicopter to Hue—Reuters was one of the few news organizations to report from inside that embattled fortress—while Lunn, Dinh and Pringle concentrated on the fighting in Saigon. Pringle lived in an apartment above the Reuters office: "There were bullets flashing by the glass doors of the office as I went downstairs to file and I got the operator to douse the lights."

Even after the Communists struck Saigon, *Time* and virtually every other news organization still believed their real objective was overrunning Khe Sanh. The ruse foiled not only allied strategists, but the media, too. Rademaeker had already assigned two staffers to the hilltop garrison, and Reuters' Pigott would soon join them.

In Saigon, Dinh and Pringle set out to investigate a standoff between Viet Cong and South Vietnamese soldiers and were near the central market, when a firefight erupted. Bullets whizzed overhead, forcing both men to the ground. With their faces pinned to the pavement, Dinh felt such foreboding that he turned to Pringle and asked him to take care of his children in the event he was killed. Eventually, both crawled to safety.

Pringle and Dinh often scoured the city together, each watching the other's back, and four days later another incident tested the partnership. It was common knowledge that Viet Cong guerrillas had infiltrated Cholon, and few reporters ventured into Saigon's Chinese enclave. But Pringle had to; the Reuters transmitter was situated there and it had broken down.

This wasn't just a Reuters problem—many news organizations filed stories through the agency and the transmitter had conked out in the flood of story traffic. Pringle knew the transmitter had to be fixed so, like bootleggers, he and Dinh stocked up on American cigarettes and set off.

Dinh thought the outskirts of Cholon were eerily quiet. As they drove in, nearer the transmitter tower, the slightest noise seemed deafening. Pringle could see Viet Cong clad in black pyjamas darting between dilapidated houses. They were everywhere, Pringle and Dinh could see—in alleys and alcoves, behind piles of refuse, all armed and all watching the visitors roll towards the transmitter station.

Pringle parked the car as close as he could, but that still left them with a 500-meter walk to consider. The two briefly considered turning back but decided to press ahead. Anticipating sniper fire, they wished each other luck and set out for the tower—an uneventful journey, as luck would have it.

Once inside, Dinh got right down to business and handed over their cache of cigarettes to the resident engineer. The transmitter was quickly coaxed back to life, and Dinh and Pringle made a speedy exit. Dinh had been terrified and vowed never to return to the area, even though nothing really went amiss. Pringle went back once more to ensure he'd never have to again. When the fighting died down, he drove back and passed out 10 envelopes, each containing 10,000 piastres for each worker. The transmitter didn't skip a beat after that.

* * * * *

THE GOVERNMENT maintained a 24-hour curfew in Saigon and raised the stakes at night, dealing with offenders on a shoot-on-sight basis. Traveling in and out of the capital was impossible. In Hue, the Viet Cong were merciless. An estimated 3,000 people were shot or clubbed to death, or buried alive in the salt flats and river beds. But the carnage escaped the attention of a public preoccupied with the massacre of 100 Vietnamese civilians by American soldiers at My Lai. The gruesome spectacle would also help turn public opinion against the war, proving a propaganda fillip for the Communists whose own atrocities were grabbing much fewer headlines. America after all held a well-earned reputation for being only interested in Americans and this—as An had learned many years earlier in California—dictated what copy was sent out. In other words what mattered was newspaper sales at home.

Dinh was ringside for a horror that would make Page One around the world. Walking through downtown Saigon, he met up with the National Police chief, Col. Nguyen Ngoc Loan, in quite a state. The man who had crushed the Buddhist uprising two years earlier (and apparently masterminded the gruesome death of An's friend, Col. Thao) was on the rampage.

Dinh had earned Loan's trust but always remained wary, and he was especially wary on the morning of this chance encounter. Loan had been roaming the city in a fierce mood. The Viet Cong had killed several of his men, one in the presence of Loan's wife and children—and it was payback time. Dinh watched as Loan approached a nearby patrol with a captured Viet Cong in tow: AP photographer Eddie Adams and NBC cameraman Vo Suu had been following the unit close behind. Then, suddenly, Loan walked up to their catch, drew his pistol out with his right hand, raised his arm parallel to the deck, put the barrel to the man's head and pulled the trigger, leaving the Viet Cong to slump to the ground, blood gushing from his head like a fountain. Adams's photo of that grimacing figure at the moment of execution was front page around the world. Suu's footage for NBC made for some of the most vivid and appalling television viewing since the Vietnam conflict first flowed into the living rooms of America.

Public opinion of the war took a nosedive.

Allied fortunes had by now been declining for some time. Denis Warner captured the mood of the unraveling situation 30 years later in his book *Not Always on Horseback*:

The Viet Cong behaviour in Saigon was exemplary on the first day. The troops talked and joked with people in the streets, and apart from the attack on the embassy made no effort to single out Americans or other non-Vietnamese as targets. As resistance increased and the fighting became heavier they grew more ruthless killing marked civil servants. No-one was safe.

Nine days after the offensive began, young women in the 17-25 age bracket, dressed in grey and wearing pistols, appeared in the streets of Cholon to control the movement of the local population and to keep people from following government instructions. Locals, they didn't hesitate to shoot those who disobeyed their orders. Summary executions occurred in many places, including the grounds of Vien Hao Dao, the Institute for the Propagation of the Buddhist Faith, where six men were executed

I have seen no estimate of the numbers of civilians who lost their lives, but a figure of between two hundred and three hundred for those executed. Not that the Viet Cong were alone in this sort of conduct. Many Viet Cong agents in the city showed their hand and were killed as soon as government forces began to exercise control.

In a similar vein, Bui Tin, the high-ranking Communist and North Vietnamese journalist, was to describe what he saw from his side of the fence in Hue in his book *Following Ho Chi Minh*:

When our forces from the North, backed up by local units, first moved into Hue, they arrested hundreds of officials and sometimes whole families. The former imperial capital was regarded as a nest of feudalism, a den of enemy thugs. Special units had to be set up to detain all these prisoners as well as the many Saigon troops who were captured. Then when the Americans counter-attacked in force by sending in the marines, a confusing series of orders emanated from Hanoi. First, at the beginning of March, the General Staff instructed our troops to stand firm at all costs. This was followed shortly afterwards by an order to withdraw west into the mountains. Panic ensued and it was compounded by American bombing raids on our lines of retreat when both our troops and some of the prisoners they were taking with them were killed. Undoubtedly, however, many other detainees who could not be evacuated in the confusion of the with-drawal were massacred in an attempt to cover up the reality of what had hap-pened in Hue during our temporary occupation of the city. These efforts clearly backfired when some of the sites of the massacres were discovered and there was a tremendous outcry both in the South and internationally. Even the leadership in Hanoi had to pay attention.

In a strict military sense, the Tet Offensive had been a costly folly committed by Communist zealots with no grasp of how the general population in Saigon felt towards their cause. Their resources were overstretched and expectations that the locals would rise up in support were woefully unrealistic. Warner drew parallels with earlier events:

I had been in Hanoi in 1954 for the Viet Minh take-over there. The population was afraid and unresponsive, and the people at first watched fearfully from behind closed windows. As the battalions of troops marched into the city, however, cadres with bullhorns called the people out. The troops applauded, clapped and sang. Whether they wanted to or not, the people were cajoled and bullied into responding. By 6 o'clock in the evening, when I crossed the Doumer Bridge over the Red River for the last time, the people of Hanoi were in the grip of mass hysteria - and the Viet Minh.

The major Viet Cong units in Saigon and other cities and towns under attack tried to achieve the same effect, but this time the circumstances were entirely different. The Viet Cong had neither the numbers nor the command to convey the impression of their supremacy. Much as the people had criticized the government in the past, they had no wish to welcome the peoples court that the Viet Cong established at street intersections to administer summary justice.

An 84-year-old man, who had seen where the Viet Cong had established a local headquarters, went with the troops to point out the place. A young girl, asked by a Viet Cong soldier for a piece of pumpkin (typical Tet Food) she was eating, offered him a slice, then stabbed him.

Bui Tin didn't deny that the gains of Tet came at considerable cost:

After the military setbacks we suffered in 1968 following the Tet Offensive, it took us a long time to recover. We had lost the initiative because we were over confident and had not safeguarded our existing gains ... Indeed it was not until mid-1970 that we regained our strength in the south although we continued to manipulate public opinion in the United States to our advantage.

Who won? Certainly, it was a public relations disaster for Washington and PR wins and losses were what counted now. Bui Tin, for his part, was in no doubt as to who won:

In fact, the Tet Offensive launched on January 31, 1968, turned out to be a great victory for us, at least psychologically. Playing on the over confidence and arrogance of the American commander, General Westmoreland, we achieved total surprise with a smart and bold move to launch simultaneous attacks on more than forty cities, towns and military bases; the targets included the US embassy in Saigon. Thanks to the media, which exaggerated the damage caused by the offensive, the American public was bedazzled, and under strong pressure the US administration had to agree to negotiations in Paris with the participation of the NLFSVN (National Liberation Front of South Vietnam) which it thus implicitly recognized. At about the same time it began the process of de-escalation leading to the Vietnamization of the war.

On February 27, Robert McNamara made his last official decision as U.S. defense secretary. He rejected a renewed appeal from Gen. Westmoreland for an additional 200,000 troops on "economic, political and moral grounds", as he put it much later. The end game in Vietnam had begun. The worlds of Ho Chi Minh, Pham Xuan An and Pham Ngoc Dinh, were converging.

* * * * *

SAIGON HAD been badly hit physically and certainly emotionally. The fighting left hundreds dead and thousands wounded. An estimated 40,000 were homeless. No-one felt safe anymore, the streets always emptying as fear crept in at nightfall. Sleep came only in fits. Packed suitcases were kept ready under beds.

Dinh, caught in a routine street check, was drafted into the army. Hugh Lunn finished his posting, grateful to be returning to Brisbane. He was replaced by Ron Laramy, from Devon in the south of England. Pigott had left for a well-earned holiday in Manila. Cantwell, still stuck in his rut, wanted desperately to go home to Hong Kong to his wife and children.

Denis Warner, on the other hand, had returned to take up the search for the kidnapped Australian businessman Keith Hyland. (The Duck Feather King had been captured after venturing into Cholon looking for his missing sister who disappeared during the offensive.)

Time executives wanted a meeting in Saigon to find out what on earth was going on with this war. An helped co-ordinate. Company brass knew of Nguyen Ngoc Phach through his (London) *Daily Telegraph* byline John Draw and invited him to the meeting, along with Dr. Tran Kim Tuyen, despite Tuyen's ambiguous status within the upper echelons of South Vietnamese life. Shaken by the events of January and February, management kept pressing Phach, An and others on where things were heading. They got nothing firm—critical for a magazine that liked encapsulated, easy-to-understand answers. But that in itself was revealing and Phach, as he later told the author, soon detected *Time* toning down its support of the war; indeed, he began to feel the magazine was on the verge of opposing America's military presence in South Vietnam.

If Tet had left *Time* changed, An could see Cantwell had changed, too. The attacks, and the almost permanent cloud of death hanging over everything, affected everyone, but Cantwell especially. He couldn't concentrate and rarely laughed any more. The bravado was gone. Hyland's kidnapping unnerved him, too; it proved that when the Viet Cong needed money, they didn't discriminate between military or civilians—or worry much about nationality. The Viet Cong had taken the war to the diplomatic and political edge. Nobody was safe. Cantwell had already survived a chopper crash after covering combat across the south—and survived a mortar explosion in his hotel room during Tet. To An, he look liked a man who knew he'd pressed his luck and had resigned himself to some horrible fate.

An's interest in fortune-telling widened from Chinese horoscopes to tarot cards and handwriting analysis. He would size up friends' handwriting at random in after-hour moments, often for a laugh. (A common finding, revealed by loops in Ys and Gs, betrayed sexual frustration—it was good barroom material.)

But he took horoscope reading seriously enough to check Cantwell's. An began to worry the Australian's premonitions of death might become a self-fulfilling prophecy and he found nothing in his favor. "Big fish-eyes," as An sometimes called him, "... is going to die," he said to himself.

At Reuters, Pham Ngoc Dinh, for very different reasons, coincidentally reached the same conclusion about Bruce Pigott, his friend who wanted to marry Miss Nga. In his book *A Reporter's War*, Lunn records what Dinh had confided to him 30 years earlier. "Bruce not long live man," he told Lunn.

* * * * *

LOCAL SUPPORT for the Communist offensive proved very weak, and American and local troops soon fended off the Communist challenge and restored order a fortnight after Tet had begun. As the fighting subsided, Neil Davis, Tim Page and Denis Warner each returned to Saigon to discover that few of their colleagues had been untouched by the battle. Warner was in Australia when he heard about the offensive and immediately booked a flight. But he wasn't cleared to reenter the country for a week, by which time Tet was winding down. By mid-February most of the fighting around Saigon was over, though fighting continued in provincial cities, including Hue, where Pigott had won accolades for his reporting.

Warner had a shock settling in. It was only after his return that he learned his close friend, Keith Hyland, had been kidnapped by the Viet Cong. The memory of the Australian Embassy's mishandling of Wilf Arthur's abduction still rankled.

Page found his return unsettling, too. He was met by a driver using the same Mini-Moke which had earned a reputation for trouble. (The jeep-like vehicles were originally developed by Morris Motors as cheap transport for the British Army in the 1950s and they didn't like them much either, opting to fleet up with Citroen 2CV light trucks instead.) Page had heard the vehicle had been in a firefight and since been patched up, repainted and sold to *Time*—and Page had wanted it ditched, convinced it was jinxed.

This seemed to be a time for confronting old doubts and suspicions. Throughout the offensive, Hai Trung sat alone at his desk at home. Occasionally, he broke curfew, leaving his apartment to stroll through the streets to see first hand the city broken and bloodied.

Just a few days earlier he sat in the same seat staring aimlessly towards the kitchen door, wondering about how the unfolding war matched his predictions, when his wife walked in. She stood and stared. Trung knew exactly what was on her mind. "Okay," he calmly answered her unspoken challenge. "I work for the other side." Nothing more was said.

11. TET TWO, ENCORE

FROM A military standpoint the Tet offensive was a dismal failure for the North, but plans were well advanced for a second offensive. Although Hai Trung had recommended a second strike as part of the overall strategy, he was unaware of the date strategists had settled on.

Intelligence at the outset of the Tet offensive confirmed the best course would be to stage an attack on Saigon, then occupy the capital for a short period, withdraw and attack again later. The second attack would demonstrate the North's sustainable military might and strengthen its negotiating hand at the Paris peace talks. On a political level, the Communists calculated that the perception of an increasingly uncertain military situation for the allies would further weaken support at home for the U.S. war effort and ultimately force the Americans to pull out, leaving the war to Vietnamese.

But Hai Trung was beginning to wonder if a second attack should go ahead. Appalled by the slaughter of the Tet offensive, Trung decided to oppose the idea, even if it meant losing his position within the Viet Cong. He first sounded out his VC connection, the shadowy Maj. Nam. Trung argued that all the civilian deaths, added to Viet Cong military losses during Tet, had raised doubts about the viability of a military victory. And the fact that Operation Phoenix, launched by the Americans in retaliation for the Tet offensive, had annihilated thousands more Viet Cong agents only lent further weight to his argument. Phoenix had also taken out key contacts needed for guiding troops through unfamiliar territory for a second attack. Indeed, logistics and supply lines were in disarray as a result of the American counteroffensive.

Maj. Nam relayed his concerns but they went largely ignored, so Trung decided to approach his superiors directly. Gen. Tran Van Tra agreed that the attack should at least be postponed. He had no interest in wasting any more troops in fruitless battle. And privately, other senior Viet Cong officers agreed with Trung.

But Communist Party officials, in particular the overzealous Tran Bach Dang, couldn't be budged. They held steadfast in their belief that popular support for the Communists was strong among the peasants, and they overruled objections to launching another major offensive.

Like Trung, Tran Bach Dang began his life with the Communists in the youth associations, but any similarities ended there. Dang was ruthless and decades within the movement had delivered him enormous clout within Communist Party circles. In Saigon he had lived under several aliases, which enabled him to evade the authorities and travel intermittently. Although his freedom to move had been hindered by a well-publicized $100,000 reward on his head, Dang's knowledge of Saigon won him the right to lead the second offensive inside the capital. And lead it, he would—the political commissar could not be swayed. Furthermore, Dang said, Saigon would be taken in the name of Ho Chi Minh, who was nearing the end in Hanoi. But to launch an offensive just so Ho could catch it before he died made no sense, Trung thought.*

In April, Viet Cong Lt. Col. Tam Ha, who was opposed to the second attack, defected. An, along with several others, learned from him that "Tet II" would begin early the following Sunday morning, May 5. More importantly An had learned that Ha had revealed the Viet Cong's strategy to the South Vietnamese military and An obtained transcripts of his interrogation. This was crucial and enabled Communist forces to change tactics and avoid any potential ambush.

Soon after An arranged to meet Cantwell early on Sunday morning, to go shopping. Cantwell was keen to buy a green nightingale imported from Hong Kong, and An decided this was an ideal excuse to visit the markets and steer clear of the fighting.

On Saturday, another freelance journalist, Frank Palmos, who had known Pigott and Cantwell from previous exploits, returned from Danang. The three joined scores of journalists at a follies briefing for the usual run-down on the day's events and American wins and losses. It was after that

---

* Tu Cang, who had holed up with An during the fighting, initially reached the same conclusion as An after driving around Saigon with him in the aftermath of the Tet offensive. He changed his mind and decided to proceed with a second offensive after talks with senior cadres and a realization of the psychological impact the first offensive had had on American public opinion.

that Cantwell and Palmos planned to reacquaint themselves over a meal and a beer at the Pagoda restaurant on Tu Do Street, northwest of the Givral, which was normally a popular breakfast haunt among correspondents for its coffee blends and dainty Chinese waitresses.

Later that evening, Cantwell returned to the *Time* office to begin his shift and not a few hours had passed before he heard a loud explosion. The night ripped apart from that point. Altogether, 122 targets across South Vietnam were shelled and bombed. Forty cities and towns were hit in a matter of hours. Seven airbases and dozens of allied installations were struck. The attack did not carry the same ferocity as Tet but caused extensive damage. Scattered mortar shells fell on central Saigon and heavier fighting was reported in the south, in Cholon, District 5, where the city's Chinese were concentrated. *Time* later reported that a Viet Cong battalion had positioned itself in a military cemetery by the entrance to the airport and described a battle being fought "[from] headstone-to-headstone and house-to-house." At the aptly named Y Bridge leading from southern District 8 over the Saigon River and Kinh Doi Canal to central Saigon, Communist saboteurs tried to demolish its main section where it forked into two sections feeding into the city while fending off attacks from helicopter gunships. Elsewhere, 80,000 refugees choked the streets seeking safer parts of town. When the smoke had cleared, authorities counted 2,000 shacks and houses destroyed.

Under Political Commissar Tran Bach Dang and Gen. Tran Van Tra the Communists had massed their troops just inside the safety of Cambodia* and now ordered them to move in overnight. In groups of five and six they slipped through allied troops ringing the city. A group of Viet Cong women brazenly marched across the Saigon River and into town. But again the Communists ended up foundering. Many soldiers were kids, some as young as 13. One unit tried to enter the city from the west only to be greeted by U.S. troops who forced them into swampland where they were cut down by fighter-bombers and helicopters. Again, hopes of sparking a popular uprising were proving fruitless, as Hai Trung had predicted.

On the morning after the initial attacks, Sunday, Cantwell telephoned Rademaekers, forgetting his appointment with An. Cantwell wanted to investigate the fighting around the Y Bridge, but Rademaekers rejected the idea. There was no point taking any risks. Deadlines had passed anyway,

---

* Communist forces, Viet Cong and North Vietnamese soldiers, had long been given permission to use Cambodian territory by its head of state, Prince Norodom Sihanouk, a disastrous decision which would lead to his ousting and the rise of the Khmer Rouge.

so reports from the field now would be outdated by the following week. Besides that, Cantwell's deteriorating mental state made Rademaekers nervous; Frank McCulloch in New York had been told that Cantwell "had a real sense of foreboding". Cantwell had by now started carrying a handgun in the small of his back, defying everyone's advice.

Dinh, now in uniform after being drafted, also heard the explosions. He had been given weekend leave and, ignoring military protocol, returned at dawn to the Reuters office instead of his army post—to write a story on the attacks. Shortly after he began filing, Bruce Pigott walked in. Pigott had just returned from R&R in Manila, a reward for his efforts at Tet, and was pleased to see Dinh. He had brought him a traditional Filipino shirt as a present and had planned to talk about Miss Nga. Bruce was a typical man in love, easily given to boring others by talking about it. Just a week earlier he had decided to marry Miss Nga, assuming her parents would finally bless the union, and he wanted to return to Melbourne with his bride.

Dinh was eager to catch up, but that would have to wait for dinner later. There was no time now. Dinh and incoming Reuters bureau chief Tony Baker had agreed to check on fighting in the north end of the city.

Pigott himself was to check out Cholon. Palmos met him outside the Reuters office, and the two of them strolled over to the Continental Palace Hotel where *Time-Life* was. Cantwell was waiting outside by the office Moke, its windshield emblazoned with the familiar red *TIME* logo. Presently, two others came by—Mike Birch from AAP and Ron Laramy, who had replaced Lunn at Reuters. Cantwell had no intention of going anywhere, but they pressed him to ferry them around in the jeep. He gave in, despite his misgivings about the expedition—and being a lousy driver.

They drove south towards Cholon in District 5. Nothing seemed to be happening so the five decided to return to Saigon. His stops and starts were jerky, but Cantwell drove serviceably when the vehicle was in motion. Birch sat in the front passenger seat. Laramy sat behind Birch. Next to him was Pigott, and Palmos sat on a half seat in the back with his left leg dangling over the side.

As they entered Cholon, Saigon's Chinatown, helicopter gunships loomed almost directly above them. They were firing rockets at targets 800 meters to the north, where smoke was pluming up. The group decided to investigate. As they neared Keith Hyland's deserted duck feather factory, Cantwell turned down a side street, moving against the throngs of refugees trying to escape the carnage.

"It's always the people who suffer," Pigott groaned.

As they drove people yelled, "Viet Cong!—Vee Cee, Vee Cee, you're going the wrong way!"

As the swollen lines of refugees began to thin, Palmos, who had a higher seat and a better view into the distance, suddenly yelled: "The VC are up ahead—Stop!"

Three times he told Cantwell to stop. Repeatedly ignored, Pigott stepped in and said: "Oh, go ahead anyway."

Seconds after Pigott told Cantwell to press ahead, Palmos noticed a sharp change in Pigott. His face had gone pale. Now Palmos called for Cantwell to stop, then Birch, or possibly it was Pigott again. In the event, they were headed for a deserted intersection near the Minh Phung Market. As they drew nearer, Cantwell spotted a roadblock erected from used oil drums. He swerved to the left and began to reverse as the bullets began ringing out across the intersection.

Palmos recognized the types of bullets by their sounds. They were fired from an AK-47 and a burp gun. For 10 seconds two Viet Cong guerrillas pumped bullets into the Moke. With his left leg hanging off the side, Palmos jumped off and pretended to be hit before falling to the ground. There the pretense ended. Cantwell had been struck at least six times and was now lying at the side of the Moke. In the eerie silence of briefly suspended gunfire, Palmos could now hear Mike Birch pleading; "bao chi, bao chi." Bao chi was Vietnamese for newsmen but it didn't impress the Viet Cong. Palmos heard two more bullets.

"I don't know whether he fired at Birch or anyone," Palmos later wrote. "I hoped they weren't dead, but from his face I could tell he thought they were dead."

Cantwell was still alive. Semiconscious, he dragged himself to his knees. Resting on his hands he began to crawl towards the side of the road. A Viet Cong walked up behind Cantwell and at close range shot him in the back of the head.

With his left leg tucked under his body, Palmos pushed himself forward and fled as fast as he could. "I weaved and ducked and twisted and dodged, left and right, the last 30 meters before the corner," he later told Pat Burgess for a piece in the *Sydney Morning Herald*.

Palmos didn't realize it at the time, but the two Viet Cong who unleashed the terror had emptied their clips, giving him a life-saving head start. The attackers reloaded and opened fire, one giving chase. Palmos, capable of running 100 yards in under 10 seconds in his youth, managed to sprint clear.

Dinh had just returned from a tour of the city's north end when he got a call from Gen. Nguyen Ngoc Loan, the South Vietnamese chief of National Police. Loan wanted to know if any Reuters correspondents had driven to Cholon earlier that day because he had a report that at least two Westerners had just been killed.

Dinh feared the worst and told the chief he would go out and see if he could identify the bodies. Gen. Loan protested, calling him crazy for even thinking of going. Certainly, Dinh was scared—the reports placed the shootings in the same part of Cholon where he and Jim Pringle had once been pinned getting the Reuters transmitter repaired. Dinh knew the journalists had strayed into extremely dangerous territory. It was a place to which he himself swore he'd never return.

Despite air bombardments and sporadic gunfire, Dinh proceeded towards the market in Cholon. From 50 meters he saw two men dressed in the Viet Cong's trademark black pyjamas, armed with AK-47s. They pointed their weapons at him. Palmos would later report the guerrillas wore khaki uniforms and Ho Chi Minh sandals, standard Viet Cong foot ware cobbled together from old tyre rubber. While Palmos's and Dinh's apparel stories conflict, it is possible that replacements were brought in after Palmos had fled.

"Where are you going, boy?" a guerrilla demanded of Dinh. In a local peasant dialect Dinh explained that he lived in the area and was trying to escape the fighting. Dinh was not the enemy to them anyway, so they told him it was all right to leave. Instead, Dinh moved closer to Bruce Pigott. On the verge of crying, he asked if the body was that of an American GI.

"No, that is CIA, we must kill them," a Viet Cong said.

Dinh was obliged to agree, and in an attempt to win their confidence, he told the VC they had done the right thing. But he had to get closer. He had to touch the body of Bruce Pigott, which under Vietnamese custom would enable Pigott's spirit to join Dinh.

"CIA do a dirty job in Vietnam... let me see the body of CIA?" he asked.

They acceded to his request.

The head of Bruce Pigott was slumped on the ground. His legs were still lodged inside the Moke. Dinh put his hand on Bruce's heart and confirmed he was dead. Dinh spent a few seconds, as long as he could, before moving to the remaining corpses. Laramy's body was rigidly fixed in the back seat. Birch was dead in the front seat. Cantwell's body was lying by the roadside.

Dinh returned to the police station and reported that four journalists had been killed by Viet Cong guerrillas.

Palmos managed to find his way back to Saigon and to the *Time* office. There, in the company of Tim Page and Bill Rademaekers, he slowly summoned the will to speak. Rademaekers sensed the immense fear in Palmos and handed him a bottle of scotch. As the grim tale unfolded, Rademaekers began cursing himself as he thought of Cantwell and all the what-ifs. "If only I had sacked him. If only his wife didn't gamble. If only he had learned to drive." The last thought allowed Rademaekers a slight laugh, even if he was on the verge of tears.

Palmos emptied the bottle within a half-hour, numbing himself as the others grieved. Mike Birch was 24, Bruce Pigott 23, Ron Laramy 31 and John Cantwell 30.*

Later that afternoon, after the Viet Cong had retreated from the intersection and withdrawn from the city, the bodies of Cantwell and his colleagues were retrieved by combat police and taken to the morgue. An was silent as the bloodied corpse of Cantwell was wheeled past on a trolley. Later, he took on the task of washing the blood off the car.

The Viet Cong had failed to recognize that the journalists were civilians, grimly ironic given how media reports were proving more effective than VC bullets at wearing America down. Their deaths were among hundreds of civilian casualties that day. The first secretary of the West German Embassy was discovered in the back of his white Volkswagen at the Phu Tho race track with a hole in the back of his head. The following day UPI photographer Charles Eggleston was killed. The American was all of 23.

After the occupation of the U.S. Embassy grounds, Johnson partially halted bombing raids of North Vietnam and then stunned the world by announcing he would not seek a second term as president. Vietnam had become symbolic of all America's ills. The daily television diet of violence from Indochina was sickening the American public, and the assassinations of Bobby Kennedy, after his recent makeover as an antiwar presidential contender, and Martin Luther King, only raised the pressure to get out. In early 1969, newly elected President Richard Nixon began withdrawing American troops.

The process of "Vietnamization" had begun. Unfolding military events

---

* In 1994 the author was employed by Australian Associated Press. A request for access to the files of Mike Birch was submitted but the author was told those files were lost during a shift of offices.

were still proving true to Hai Trung's original prognosis. Now Viet Cong chiefs were coming round to his way of thinking. His thesis that South Vietnam, and Saigon in particular, would have to sink to its knees economically before the Communists could win popular urban support was finally gaining credibility with top strategists. In recognition of his efforts, the Communists promoted Trung to the rank of colonel.

Possible outcomes were few. As the Australian journalist Wilfred Burchett, celebrated and derided for his Communist connections and sympathies, noted: "A neutral and truly independent South Vietnam is the best solution Washington can hope for, a Vietnam in which North and South live on terms of friendship." This even he fully anticipated, adding: "It will be the eventual solution".[*]

---

[*] Burchett, Wilfred. *Passport*, Thomas Nelson, Melbourne, 1969, p275-276

Top (24): Pham Ngoc Dinh and his wife Vy in the backyard of their Sydney suburban home; *Above (25):* The political commissar Tran Bach Dang who insisted on pushing ahead with a second offensive in the wake of Tet 1968 believing this would spark a popular uprising in South Vietnam. It never materialized.

Top (26): Photographer Yana Sisi who worked with many foreign correspondents; *Below (27):* An early portrait of Ho Chi Minh hangs in government offices of the city that now bears his name.

Top (28): The bridge that divided North and South Vietnam at the 17th parallel.

Right (29): The Vietnam War Memorial in Washington DC.

Left (30): Photographer Tim Page in the grounds of the Royal Palace in Phnom Penh.

Right (31): Photographer Al Rockoff (left) chats during an Old Hacks reunion at the Majestic Hotel in HCMC. The Hollywood actor and friend of Sean Flynn, George Hamilton, is in the background.

Bottom Left (32): Dutch photographer Hu van Es with long time partner Annie during a charity ball hosted by the Foreign Correspondents Club in Hong Kong.

33

Above (33): Vietnamese troops on hand during commemorations marking the 40th anniversary of the "liberation" of Saigon.

ÉT LIỆT CHÀO MỪNG KỶ N[...]I LẦN THỨ 35
NGÀY GIẢI [...]NG HOÀN TOÀN MIỀN NA[...] THỐNG NHẤT ĐẤT NƯỚC
(30/4/1975 - 30/4[...]0)

Top (34): Ho Chi Minh drapes the Independence Palace in what was once South Vietnam.

Left (35): Supporters of the old South Vietnam are prosecuted in a HCMC court after attempting to raise an insurgency.

36

Top (36): Catholic Churches dot the North Vietnamese landscape. Catholics fled North Vietnam in 1954 following the division with South Vietnam. They then fled South Vietnam following the Communist annexation in 1975; *Above (37):* Vietnamese flags drape the buildings of Ho Chi Minh City.

Top (38): Correspondents Jim
Pringle, Peter Arnett and Perry
Deane Young during an Old Hacks
reunion at the Majestic Hotel in
HCMC.

Left (39): Tran Hung Dao, a famous
admiral points the way. When
South Vietnamese were looking
to leave the country after the
Communist takeover, they would
often say "go see the admiral".

Below Left (40): North Vietnamese
tank 843, which crashed though the
gates of Independence Palace and
sealed the fate of South Vietnam on
April 30, 1975.

PART THREE:
1970-2006

12. SUN SETS OVER SAIGON

HOPES OF an outright allied victory evaporated after Tet. America continued to withdraw its troops and leave the running of the war to the Vietnamese. The United States still participated on the edges, with strategic bombing runs into neighboring Cambodia where the murderous Khmer Rouge were on the rise, and securing supply lines for their Communist brothers across the border, but the end of U.S. involvement was fast approaching.

The Americans and their allies withdrew in 1973. They left behind an arsenal filled mostly with despair, an apt legacy for a remnant of a country about to be steamrollered into history by the events of April 1975 and the final routing of Saigon.

Mayhem within the ranks already suggested the allies had suffered a collective nervous breakdown in the run up to the withdrawal. Stories, many going out on agency wires, of widespread drug use and the fragging of officers by freaked-out noncoms were legion. At home, returning soldiers were embraced by relieved family and friends, at least briefly, but their reception otherwise ran the gamut from unspoken respect to vicious name-calling. Society had long ago split into hawks and doves, the latter rallying around the amp-fired lyrics of Jimi Hendrix, the Grateful Dead, the Rolling Stones, the Beatles, Buffalo Springfield and others. It had been a time of sex, drugs and rock 'n' roll, all part of the general rage against war and its establishment sponsors. The soldiers had lost and the doves had won, and the righteous didn't mind flapping their wings about it.

In Vietnam, green plastic body bags continued to pile up. In the villages soaked by the defoliant Agent Orange, birthing women got their first look at their grotesque newborns and suckled them on mother's milk laced with toxins. With men in such short supply, polygamy, outlawed and against every Vietnamese tradition, was rampant. In field hospitals on both sides of the DMZ, the hopelessly injured waited to die.

Families from all political sides were torn. Reporting their plight was the job of the South Vietnamese press corps, which was divided into international and domestic camps. Pham Xuan An sat comfortably in the first, working for foreigners, but he kept in contact with his compatriots working for Vietnamese newspapers, radio and television.

Local reporters, unless they worked for international news organizations, did not hang around the Givral cafe or the Continental with the foreigners. Instead, they congregated in the back-street bars where an affordable beer (and more agreeable company) could be found. An naturally considered local reporters a good source of information and they, for the most part, considered him the most senior journalist in Saigon. His reputation stirred both admiration and jealousy, of course. An's uncanny ability to predict what the Communists would do next tended to raise suspicions among friends and detractors alike. There were always whispers about him being a Communist or CIA agent.

An simply knew too many things he shouldn't have known in advance, the rumor-mongers said. There was his prescience concerning the North Vietnamese Army advance over the DMZ in March, 1972 and the American decision to begin covert bombing runs over Cambodia, albeit Kissinger and Nixon have claimed with the permission of Prince Norodom Sihanouk who had done his best to play one side off against another throughout the conflict*. Considering the pattern, going back to his mysteriously acquired Ap Bac scoops and his interviews with highly placed Communists, it all looked very suspicious. But for all that, or perhaps because of it, many local reporters were in awe of Pham Xuan An, the man who proudly wore the badge of "*Time* magazine correspondent".

Saigon News reporter Nguyen Thu was a friend of An's and occasionally ventured into the international camp—with the help of Bob Shaplen, he even did some moonlighting as fixer for *The New Yorker*. Thu had his suspicions, too. An had unnerved him by canceling a dinner date around the time of the Tet Offensive, claiming the restaurant in District 5 where they

---

* Prince Norodom Sihanouk's official biographer Julio Jeldres told the author that in 1968 the head of state said he would 'close his eyes' if the American military were to pursue hot Vietnamese targets across the border and into Cambodia territory. This could be interpreted as permission for the U.S. to invade Cambodia but Sihanouk did not sanction any bombings. Jeldres quoted Sihanouk as saying if 'one Cambodian water buffalo is killed I will raise hell in the United Nations'. He never did.

were to meet—across the Y Bridge on the far side of the Saigon River—had been singled out for attention by the Viet Cong. "I don't want to become a target for the NLF," Thu remembered An telling him.

Thu was astonished, because the restaurant was considered safe, but the information later proved correct and the establishment was blown to smithereens.

An's position at *Time* and his contacts in the palace, and his good working relationship with President Thieu, afforded him what security he needed. An could usually avoid being seriously implicated by innuendo—at least long enough for gossips to tire of the topic and focus on someone else.

An was a smooth operator with a humanitarian side. He used his Communist contacts to help secure the release of *Time-Life* staffer Robert Anson, who had been captured by the Khmer Rouge in Cambodia. But he was only sorry he could not do the same for freelance photographer Sean Flynn, the rollicking friend of Tim Page and son of Hollywood star Errol, nor Dana Stone, a photojournalist dubbed by the marines as "mini grunt". Both perished in the hands of Pol Pot's rebels—or so it was thought after renting Honda motorbikes in Phnom Penh and heading up to the frontlines towards the Vietnam border in April 1970. Nor could he help the kidnapped industrialist Keith Hyland, held captive for nine months by the Viet Cong. Hyland won his freedom in the end, thanks in part to a deal engineered by Bob Shaplen working with his CIA contacts—who cooked up a package which included ransom cash and a U.S. visa long denied to Australian journalist and Communist Wilfred Burchett.

* * * * *

FOR MEMBERS of the Fourth Estate, the press, life grew more miserable as the war progressed. Tim Page was arguably luckier than some. On April 17, 1969, the Englishman drove the same jinxed Moke that had taken his four colleagues to their deaths to Cu Chi, where he boarded a D-model Huey helicopter for a mission across the 25th Division's tactical area of operations, which included Tay Ninh on its northern edge. After briefly detaining two guerrilla suspects, the next stop on the tour was to rescue a soldier caught in a booby trap. Page jumped into the chaos and took several frames with the Nikon strapped around his neck. Then, suddenly, he felt groggy with his legs about to buckle. Somehow he struggled back to the Huey, and the next thing he knew he was in a medical ward. He'd been hit by an exploding mine, shrapnel blasting into his skull. Technically, he died three times on the operating table when his heart stopped, but he was revived each time. Eventually he gained full health, despite losing a large chunk of his brain.

Ho Chi Minh died in September 1969. By then North Vietnam was being run by a Communist elite under the stewardship of Le Duan, South Vietnam's NLF leader who escaped capture in the south more than 10 years earlier. The war was becoming protracted, despite efforts by President Nixon to extricate America from Indochina. His national security advisor, Henry Kissinger, had found Hanoi's Le Duc Tho a tough negotiator at the Paris peace talks.

Cambodia was proving an obstacle. By March, 1970 Prince Norodom Sihanouk had been ousted by his trusted prime minister and long serving defense minister, Lon Nol. Unlike Sihanouk, who feigned neutralism while playing the myriad of sides off against each other and tolerating the U.S. bombings of VC hideouts in his country, Lon Nol backed American efforts in Indochina wholeheartedly, support which should have been of some comfort to Washington. Exactly a year before Sihanouk's ouster by a vote in parliament, in March, 1969, Nixon had ordered the cross-border bombing runs into Cambodia. Sihanouk had a habit of saying "yes" and "no" to all sides when it suited him, a policy that would cost his country dearly in the decades to come.

The rise of Pol Pot's Khmer Rouge had been rapid and by 1970, with more and more of the Cambodian countryside under their command, they threatened to overrun the entire country. To counter this, the Americans devised an ambitious plan to invade Cambodia with 20,000 U.S. and South Vietnamese ground forces using air support. Besides pushing back Pol Pot and routing the Viet Cong from their sanctuaries, the Americans were especially keen on destroying what was known as the Central Office of South Vietnam, the COSVN under Gen. Nguyen Chi Thanh, the North's top official in the South. This was the Viet Cong headquarters, which had been reestablished inside Cambodia after its original base at Tay Ninh across the border was destroyed.

The decision to invade was taken on April 26, 1970, and the offensive was launched four days later. Freelance correspondent Denis Warner was preparing to leave Saigon for an R&R break when he was advised by U.S. sources to hang around for something big. Others, too, got the hint—reportedly Bob Shaplen, his offsider Nguyen Hung Vuong and An were fully briefed. An was key because the U.S. military considered *Time* ideal for dropping leaks. *Time*'s contacts within the palace and foreign embassies were formidable.

Jim Pringle returned for another stint as Reuters' Saigon bureau chief, exactly one day before the U.S.-led invasion, and Dinh was pleased to see him. The pair hadn't met since 1968, when Pringle returned to investigate the killings of Cantwell, Pigott, Laramy and Birch.

Pringle and Dinh were again in the thick of a major offensive only a day after the bureau chief's return. The 20,000 troops should have provided enough strength for an easy allied victory but they achieved little. With ample warning, the Communists had no trouble evading capture. Pringle, Warner, Dinh and the rest of the Saigon press corps followed the troops into Cambodia but found little to write about. Most Viet Cong and their sympathizers had been evacuated, leaving the South Vietnamese to carry out search-and-destroy missions on abandoned huts. Their reports were an anticlimax and both Dinh and Pringle arrived at the same conclusion: Someone had tipped off the Viet Cong weeks in advance.

Months after the invasion, An dug up a report he'd written nearly a year earlier and left at the office, addressed to *Time's* Robert Anson, the correspondent he would later get freed from the Communists. The note essentially predicted what would happen—that the Americans would expand the war by invading Cambodia, that is if the process of de-escalation was prolonged. An wanted to impress upon Anson the extent of America's problems in Vietnam by highlighting the paradox. At the bottom, An appended a note: "You damned Americans. You read, but you never learn."

The invasion's failure left South Vietnam on a steeper section of the slippery slope. Viet Cong leaders remained on the loose and their network was left unscathed virtually till Saigon's capitulation. In the United States, the antiwar movement gathered more momentum. To capitalize on the enemy's organizational deterioration, the North Vietnamese began planning a large scale invasion of their own to further buttress their negotiating strength in Paris. The Nixon administration, meanwhile, was fulfilling its pledge to withdraw American troops. By early 1972, more than 400,000 soldiers had gone home, leaving 70,000 Americans on the ground, but only 6,000 of them actual combat troops. Of course by honoring its withdrawal commitments, the United States only weakened its bargaining position in Paris.

On cue, the North Vietnamese Army (NVA) went on the offensive with attacks on three different fronts beginning on March 30. While 30,000 troops and 100 tanks rolled across the DMZ and rapidly captured Dong Ha and northern Quang Tri province including a necklace of key fire bases that included Khe Sanh, far to the southwest 35,000 attackers emerged out of Cambodian sanctuaries to pounce on 7,500 ARVN defenders at An Loc, just 90 kilometers north of Saigon. The siege of An Loc would later be compared to Stalingrad and Verdun. Then, in early May, with South Vietnamese forces reeling, 50,000 NVA fighters supported by armor rolled out of the Truong Son mountain range of southern Laos with the objective of overrunning the two already isolated and strategically important central highland towns of Pleiku and Kontum. Politically, the offensive was designed to sway the American voter against Nixon, who would be facing off against the just-nominated Democratic Party contender and antiwar candidate Sen. George McGovern in November's presidential election.

Nixon was under increasing pressure to end the war and "win the peace." Vietnam was as hot an issue as it had been in the LBJ-Barry Goldwater race in 1964. And 1968, when, days before the election, Nixon sought to derail the peace talks, win the presidency and keep the war going.

Nixon feared that Vietnam peace efforts by President Johnson in the run-up to the November, 1968 U.S. presidential election could wreck his bid to defeat Hubert Humphrey, the Democratic candidate, and capture the White House. Nixon's response to Johnson's efforts was to use a go-between, Anna Chennault, to urge South Vietnamese President, Nguyen Van Thieu, to resist efforts to force them to the peace table. Nixon's efforts paid off spectacularly. On October 31, Johnson ordered a total halt to the bombing of North Vietnam, the precondition for getting the North and their Viet Cong allies to join the talks. Two days later, under intense secret urgings from Nixon and his lieutenants, Thieu announced his government would not take part. Nixon was elected president less than a week later, a victory measured by less than a one-point margin in the popular vote over Humphrey.

As planned, more than 120,000 NVA troops moved in sync through the northern provinces of South Vietnam, along with thousands of Viet Cong guerrillas. Armed with Soviet-made tanks, artillery and rockets, the Communists formed a three-pronged attack, moving simultaneously north from Cambodia through the Ashau Valley, and then directly south from North Vietnam and across the DMZ. Militarily, the Communists had hoped to improve their negotiating position at the ongoing Paris peace talks: They understood that territory not held on the battlefield would likely not be won at the conference table. They also intended to fracture South Vietnamese civilian and military morale by pushing home the point that even a well-funded client army, like ARVN, ultimately lacked the initiative, spirit, as well as logistical capacity to defend everywhere all the time. The population of South Vietnam was fatigued and psychologically spent after decades of war, and the Communists recognized the value in cultivating the South Vietnamese self-doubt spawned by the imminent U.S. withdrawal. And in the end, despite horrendous losses, the Communists achieved their basic objective of showcasing ARVN's shortcomings as only the massive application of U.S. airpower—wave after wave of B-52 strikes and tactical air-support sorties—was capable of buttressing the thinly spread, beleaguered South Vietnamese ground forces against the NVA onslaught.

The provincial capital, Quang Tri, fell on May 1. Hundreds of government posts in the area were overrun. In Hanoi, intelligence chief Bui Tin received information from Hai Trung, one of several Communist plants in Saigon, saying President Thieu's best troops would be sent to blunt the main force attacks, making it easy for the Communists to seize large tracts of fertile land—and undermine the South Vietnamese government's pacification program aimed at redistributing better farm land to peasants.

The attack had been anticipated in Washington. At that, the Communists resisted the urge to continue the push. Had they overwhelmed the South, there was the danger that the peace talks might stall, or worse, prompt a re-escalation of U.S troop deployment, as Hai Trung once warned.

Quang Tri was eventually vacated by the Communists in September. The following month, October, just ahead of November's presidential contest, a draft peace proposal was concluded between Kissinger and Le Duc Tho, though both conceded, it was "only 99 per cent completed". The problem was, however, that South Vietnamese President Nguyen Van Thieu remained unaware of the contents of the agreement until a series of meetings with Kissinger in Saigon in mid-October. When Thieu discovered that Kissinger had acceded to the North Vietnamese demand that NVA troops already in South Vietnam could demobilize in place—that is, not be required to withdraw north—after the conclusion of the agreement, the president exploded. Moreover, by signing the Kissinger-Tho draft, Thieu rightly concluded that he would be tacitly recognizing the NLF as a second legal South Vietnamese regime—with its own territory and its own capital. Thieu was livid, arguing that for him to sign the agreement was akin to committing suicide. Kissinger returned to Washington on the 23rd, his 'October surprise' gift to Nixon slowly disintegrating as he flew east across the Pacific. Three days later, Kissinger, after learning that Hanoi was about to leak the text of the draft, decided to pre-empt the North by claiming that "peace was at hand" and despite apparently insoluble North-South disagreements, a final settlement was within reach. But it wasn't. Thieu claimed the draft text amounted to a betrayal by Washington of a loyal ally, while Tho refused to accede to Saigon's demand that all NVA troops be required to leave South Vietnam. Indeed, Nixon, now reelected, fell briefly back on his old conviction that the Vietnamese Communists could be bombed into submission, while recognizing that the brutal air campaign he planned would have the ancillary benefit of reassuring Thieu that U.S. airpower would be ready and available to come to his rescue—even after the U.S. withdrawal—in the event of a serious North Vietnamese violation of the agreement. Fed up with the never-ending peace talks, and impatient to break the impasse—and to once and for all shed the millstone of Vietnam—Nixon initiated Operation Linebacker Two a week before Christmas. Over an 11-day period, beginning on December 18, B52s flew an estimated 1,000 sorties over North Vietnam, breaking only for Christmas Day. It was the most intensive air bombardment of the war. Over 40,000 tons were dropped, but the damage to Hanoi and Haiphong, the North's most important centers, was minimal. Most civilians had been evacuated to rural areas but key installations—ports, radar, ammunition supply depots, power plants and rail yards—were destroyed.

In a tactical sense—and apart from any moral, ethical or legal context— the bombing worked; the pummelling of North Vietnam's urban centers coaxed the Vietnamese back to the negotiating table. On a strategic and domestic political level, however, the bombing would turn out to be a trap that would later ensnare Nixon himself when the very intemperance of his action would boomerang on the president by igniting the ire of the congressional doves. Despite the ostensible goal of the bombing campaign—concluding a peace agreement—several months later, with the Watergate crisis closing in around him and his political capital wasting, Nixon would find himself defenseless to fight back against a determined campaign among lawmakers to circumscribe his presidential war-making powers; they wanted Nixon defanged. The unrestrained brutality of the Christmas bombing, combined with the ongoing 'secret' bombing of neighboring Cambodia, essentially ensured that Nixon, by the end of the summer, would never bomb again. On January 27, 1973, an agreement for the American withdrawal was signed in Paris.*

---

* Film maker Rory Kennedy noted in his *Last Days in Vietnam* that in the U.S. Embassy the agreement was toasted with Bloody Marys. The film also noted that the total U.S. commitment, including contractors, advisors and support staff, was reduced to between 5,000 and 7,000 people

It differed little from the draft agreement signed three months earlier. While the accords provided for a council of national reconciliation between the North and South to be established, there was no mechanism or timetable to ensure that it happened. Nixon promised Hanoi, confidentially, that he would deliver on $3.25 billion in war reconstruction aid to "heal the wounds of war" while the Communists were expected to release all U.S. servicemen who were being held as prisoners of war. But Nixon also made a secret commitment to Saigon in personal letters to Thieu; that Washington would stand ready, in the event of a clear violation, to rescue South Vietnam by sending the bombers back. Unaware of Nixon's whispering, Congress would unwittingly obviate these promises when politicians tabled their bombing halt legislation the following August.

The Communists were allowed to keep the areas over which they had gained control during the previous year's three-pronged attack, along the South's western border, up through the Ashau Valley and along the DMZ right to the South China Sea—the city of Dong Ha would never revert to Saigon's control. Indeed, the territory of this new, third Vietnam administered by the Provisional Revolutionary Government of the Republic of South Vietnam, resembled an inverted 'L'. As America disengaged, more than 150,000 NVA troops remained emplaced in this southern zone. It was estimated that South Vietnamese President Thieu controlled 75 percent of South Vietnamese territory and 85 percent of the population. Overall, the North was in a stronger military position, despite the significant numerical superiority of the ARVN—or at least as it appeared on paper.

Through Hai Trung, Bui Tin learned that President Thieu had quietly developed a strategy aimed at recapturing ground lost during the NVA offensive 12 months earlier—and increasing support for his regime in the bargain. Yet morale was crashing; as the ebullience many felt in the immediate wake of Paris faded, trepidation over the continued fighting grew. The already wobbly South Vietnamese economy began to totter with the withdrawal of direct and indirect American largesse. With the mountains of dollars that the massive U.S. military presence spun off now gone, and gone for good most believed, black marketeering and corruption, long entrenched, exploded.

To counter the economic decay, Thieu in 1973 began touting an eight-year program of development mega-projects that included massive highway

over the next two years.

and pipeline building as well exploiting newly discovered offshore oil finds off South Vietnam's southeast coast.* At their one and only post-Paris meeting held at Nixon's 'Western White House' in San Clemente, the South Vietnamese president presented his development and reconstruction plan to Nixon and asked for $1.5 billion in economic aid. Nixon demurred, but agreed to the sum as a "target". Though planning continued, the simmering post-war war ensured that major private investors steered clear of South Vietnam, and the U.S. Congress—Saigon's primary benefactor—began trimming aid allotments in the belief that feeding Thieu's coffers only fueled the ongoing military conflict. Thieu also committed to hold national elections in mid-1975 as scheduled, but showed little willingness to open the political process to NLF participation as laid out in the Paris agreements. For all of their acuity when it came to the military facets of their struggle, the Communist leaders in Hanoi never really gained a clear sense of the depth and breadth of Thieu's legitimacy. Like an oft-discussed phantom, their trope of a popular uprising of the South Vietnamese against the government in Saigon never really materialized. In the end, they were cautiously optimistic that Thieu's support was wide but not deep, yet nobody—including Gen. Tran Van Tra, Gen. Vo Nguyen Giap and Bui Tin—believed a Communist victory was possible before late 1976 despite Hai Trung insisting an earlier victory was indeed possible. And it was a fair appraisal—for all of the much reported brittleness that afflicted the socioeconomic reality in South Vietnam, Thieu stood atop a well-equipped and increasing confident million man army.

Bui Tin could live with Trung's sometimes contrary, and in this case, cautious positions. He had become a steady source of reliable information and, with Tet, had earned his place as Hanoi's number-one spy.

* * * * *

THE END came quickly after the Americans pulled out in late March, 1973. When consulted by his superiors in Hanoi how an invasion and occupation of South Vietnam might unfold, Hai Trung suggested that, as during the Tet Offensive, North Vietnamese regulars should follow the coastal route south, then enter Saigon from the south through Cholon. A

---

* The future of this program would have proved doubtful in any case. Oil and gas reserves developed by Australia, British and French interests off the southern coast in the early 1990s proved disastrously low.

second front should then be launched in the central highlands in order to overrun the ARVN force concentrations guarding the western approaches from Laos and Cambodia at Ban Me Thuot, Pleiku, and Kontum. If the South Vietnamese were to lose control of this string of towns spaced like pickets along Route 14, it would be a short march for the Communists to the coast—a manoeuvre that would essentially slice South Vietnam in two and isolate Hue and Danang from Saigon and the southern rice basket. As far as the Communists were concerned, there was never any serious intention to honor the terms of the Paris agreement nor respect the already compromised sovereignty of South Vietnam. Within days of signing the accords, though specifically prohibited in the text of the treaty, the Communists launched a massive infiltration campaign that siphoned tens of thousands fresh troops along with their equipment down the Ho Chi Minh Trail to staging areas along the western border of South Vietnam.

It was well understood that the almost impenetrable mountains of the Annamite Range, by planners in Hanoi—and by Trung—would need to be the first objective, if the final objective was to carve up Thieu's territory and forces and ultimately trigger a total collapse. Balancing the importance of the central highlands as a military objective was the possibility that the South Vietnamese would probably get increased U.S. military aid if the Communists launched a full scale attack—and in an emergency, even actual U.S. ground troops top-covered by dreaded B-52s. So while among Northern leaders the fear that the United States might re-enter the war remained palpable, as time passed and as Trung witnessed how the constant stream of revelations poured from the Watergate investigations progressively hobbled Nixon, Hai Trung became more and more convinced that Washington would never again send its troops to defend South Vietnam as they had in the 1960s. Importantly however, it was a thesis that needed to be tested.

Gen. Tran Van Tra, commander of liberation forces in the south, had himself reached many of the same conclusions as Trung, and was directly involved in the military planning that would shape what was intended to be a coordinated dry-season offensive aimed at capturing and permanently occupying large slices of the Central Highlands that ran along the western spine of South Vietnam and opening invasion routes that would touch the coast. But, as Trung had pointed out, weakening the ring of defences around Saigon and the belly of the beast was, for Tra, equally important though many in Hanoi—including Giap—disagreed. The senior generals remained concerned that a broadside attack on Saigon was foolhardy if undertaken too early in the game; it could, once again, mean a profligate waste of men and materiel. These disagreements festered among the senior leadership. And hence, much of the Communist military planning remained contingent well into early 1975. There was no masterplan; just a stack of alternatives. But first the test.

In mid-December 1974 the NVA 4th Army Corps attacked Phuoc Long province, hitherto a strategically marginal area for the South Vietnamese located at the southern end of the Annamite chain as it tapered down into the lowland plains around Saigon. But for the Communists, the battle would serve two main purposes: Capturing Phuoc Long (as they expected to do) would help link up Tra's rear area in Cambodia with the Central Highlands and, as importantly, it would test the U.S. reaction to a major Communist offensive and a significant ARVN defeat. After a month of brutal fighting, it was done. The province was completely in Communist hands. And despite calls for increased military aid to Saigon from the new U.S. president, Gerald Ford, U.S. lawmakers refused any additional aid appropriations with a large number of members claiming they saw no 'national interest' in expending new resources propping up Thieu and his army.

With their answer to the American question in hand, the Communists turned north against Ban Me Thuot—a key strategic location linked by road to Nha Trang on the southern coast and Pleiku to the north. Besides straddling a crucial crossroad, Ban Me Thuot was the location of the ARVN's largest ammunition stores in the entire highland region. The Communists launched the attack early on March 10, 1975, after intense fighting that lasted two days, the NVA won control as South Vietnamese units staged a disorganized withdrawal toward the coast. Hanoi began hearing reports of officers deserting, of troops exchanging cash for gold and of soldiers evacuating their families south. The panic fueled a mass exodus of civilians that added to the confusion. The events in Ban Me Thuot prompted the North Vietnamese to re-evaluate the incremental moves they had made to date and settle on a new plan to launch an all-out offensive designed to capture Saigon along the route Trung recommended. They would still punch east first—to sever South Vietnam on an east-west axis between Ban Me Thuot and Cam Ranh Bay—while they continued north against Pleiku and Kontum. Once their rear area was safe, they would then swing south to Saigon; the coastal enclaves north of line would be left to whither and mopped up later. The Communist generals, by early March, saw all the signs that the ARVN was nearing the point of collapse and their strategy involved essentially drawing and quartering South Vietnam to eliminate any hope of its military regrouping in a coordinated way.

When this second wave of attacks began—not even the Russians or Chinese knew Hanoi had actually decided on a full-scale invasion of South Vietnam. And while southern military leaders like Tran Van Tra and Pham Hung who were stitched into the NVA high command understood that Saigon had become the final objective of the Ho Chi Minh campaign, it is not clear that the rank-and-file Viet Cong and its political organization, the National Liberation Front, were aware of the monumental decisions being taken in Hanoi.

But once again events overtook Hanoi's planning. In the aftermath of Ban Me Thuot, Thieu panicked. Now finally fully convinced that he had been abandoned by Washington, forsaken, Thieu unshelved a plan—"light at the top; heavy at the bottom"—first proposed by an Australian advisor, Ted Serong. The retired brigadier had suggested to Thieu that his armed forces were over-stretched and that the thinly spread ARVN should all but abandon the northern provinces of South Vietnam save for cordoned areas around Danang and Hue. These freed up forces, should then be concentrated and realigned for the stalwart defence of the southern Cochin-Chinese heartland—an area bordered on the north by a chord running from Nha Trang west to Cambodia and then extending down into the Mekong Delta. Concerned that such a radical move could irreparably shatter the already brittle South Vietnamese psyche, Thieu had previously rejected Serong's proposal. But now, with the threat to his country clearly existential, Thieu re-evaluated—and ordered the plan into action. Had such an evacuation been attempted in peacetime, it would have been traumatic. Managing it under fire, in the midst of a siege, proved impossible. The action entailed 'quietly' redeploying tens of thousands of troops, with their equipment, from the highlands to the coast moving, not by highways, but along third-class roads while delaying a civilian exodus until after the military withdrawal was complete. Almost predictably, the manoever, intended to be a strategic retrenchment, developed into a fiasco, a rout, and a tragedy of staggering proportions. The civilian population—many of them family and friends of the soldiers—immediately realized what was happening and jammed the roads out of town slowing the military columns to a grind and making them easy targets for NVA forces that were moving from Ban Me Thuot who, not surprisingly, pounced on the entangled rabble of soldiers and civilians. In the end, the human cost was compounded by the fact that the tattered remains for the ARVN units that eventually emerged at the coast, arrived piecemeal, in scattered groups without equipment, and in no condition to fight. Moreover, the rout in the highlands triggered panic in Hue and Danang, further fed by the decision of an increasingly fraught President Thieu—now overcome by fears of a coup at home—to order several elite units back to Saigon. Orders got crossed, contradicted, and countermanded, and the situation in these two major political and military centers quickly unravelled. Military units simply melted away as officers dithered or abandoned their posts. And again townspeople fleeing the Communist advance, choked ocean ports and roads heading south. Hue fell to the Communists on March 26th, and Danang only four days later. By April 2, only three weeks after Thieu's fateful decision to withdraw from the highlands, South Vietnam had been shorn of all of its northern provinces, and two of four army corps. A rump South Vietnam persisted, but the remnants that survived in the wake of the debacle, societally and militarily, were irreparably fractured. No longer, it was increasingly clear for the South Vietnamese, would Washington be there to backstop the failures of their own leaders. For the Communists, by the first week of April, the road to Saigon was open.

Both Trung and Bui Tin still both believed victory was another 12 months away, but the swiftness of the North Vietnamese Army's advance under Gen. Giap was making them, and others in the South, wonder. As suspense intensified, An sought his colleagues' opinions. Denis Warner had returned to Saigon after traveling with the stream of refugees fleeing south, just a short distance ahead of the advancing Communists.

An managed to corner Warner in the lobby of the Continental Hotel.

"What do you think will happen?" he asked Warner.

"It's all over," Warner replied.

"But who will win?" An countered.

Warner assumed the answer would be obvious to An, given the latter's reputedly impeccable Communist contacts.

"The North," Warner answered, a little impatiently.

Until Warner had said it, the end hadn't been at all obvious to An. Now it suddenly was, if only because a man of Warner's stature had said it. An hastily arranged the evacuation of his wife and children.

* * * * *

DAYS LATER, *Time* correspondent Oliver Todd joined a table outside the Givral. An, Bob Shaplen's factotum Nguyen Hung Vuong and the man who brought An and Nhan together, Cao Giao were all talking about the North's current position. It was rumored the Communists were preparing to attack Tay Ninh, where the North's Central Office of South Vietnam (COSVN) used to be before allied attacks forced it to relocate in Cambodia. An was telling Giao and Vuong he'd already advised several people to get out.

Then talk turned to Saigon and the potential for a mass slaughter if the city fell. An became defensive and sought to allay their fears. "The Communists don't bother with sentimental considerations. It's in their interests to set up a provisional government, so that's what they're working towards," he said, dismissing the possibility of a rash of payback killings.

By mid-April, thousands of people were planning their evacuation. The climax to Vietnam's long, sad story was about to unfold. Neil Davis wanted to cover the end of the war for U.S. broadcaster NBC, but was trapped in Phnom Penh, then bracing itself for the arrival of the Khmer Rouge. Unlike the Communist Pathet Lao of Laos, or the Viet Cong of South Vietnam, Davis genuinely feared Khmer Rouge and didn't at all mind missing that story, although Cambodia was his favorite spot in Southeast Asia. And luck was on his side. Davis had a chance meeting with an old and useful friend—Andrew Peacock, the high-profile Australian politician who used his CIA contacts to organize a chopper flight for Davis and himself back to Saigon. (Peacock was later to become Australia's ambassador to Washington).

On April 21, President Thieu resigned in favor of Tran Van Huong, who was shortly replaced by Gen. Big Minh, the suspected Communist sympathizer who had briefly occupied the hot seat before. Minh had held the distinction of being the first South Vietnamese Chief of State following Diem's overthrow—and would be the last. When the Saigon legislature went around the constitution to replace Huong, they hoped that Minh's neutralist tendencies, and his de facto position as the leader of South Vietnam's nebulous 'Third Force' movement would have Minh appear to leaders in Hanoi as a reliable negotiating partner, such that the surviving shard of South Vietnam still under Saigon's control might survive something short of complete capitulation. The Communist appetite for total victory well whetted after three decades of war, their hopes, it would turn out, would prove forlorn.

A few days before Minh's investiture, on April 25, Denis Warner and

Keith Hyland left Saigon, together. Much as he had reasons to hang on, Warner* was emotionally exhausted. This doyen of Indochina journalism did not want to wait to see the capital fall—there were too many friends he could do nothing for.

Hyland left behind assets he himself put at $8 million.

Gen. Minh's appointment had surprised Bui Tin. He knew through Hai Trung in Saigon that there might be a coup, possibly splitting military units into competing camps—and confusing advancing Communists in the process. Tin had anticipated one last bloody stand costing several thousand civilian lives, but fortunately his intelligence from Hai Trung was wrong this time. North Vietnamese forces quickly overran the hapless South Vietnamese. Their grounded air force, the fourth largest in the world, had literally run out of gas, following the U.S. Congress decision to restrict additional funding to cover only the cost of the evacuation—not a cent would be appropriated to continue the war. Last-minute pleas for American military aid from Saigon were ignored.

On the morning of April 29, final evacuation preparations were being made across the city. People tuned to American Forces Radio, awaiting confirmation of Vietnam's worst kept secret. Nguyen Ngoc Phach, or John Draw to his *Daily Telegraph* readers, knew it was time to leave when he heard the order to evacuate. It was delivered in code on Armed Forces Radio, an announcement that said "the temperature is 105 degrees and rising" then followed by eight bars of Bing Crosby's White Christmas.

Phach had planned his escape carefully. His family had already evacuated to Rach Gia, a fishing port in the Mekong Delta where his brother owned and operated a fleet. On the last morning of the war, Phach drove to Than Son Nat Airport where he bribed his way onto a helicopter heading for Can Tho. From there he paid a taxi driver to take him the remaining distance —through infested Viet Cong territory.

Pham Ngoc Dinh didn't get as far. Realizing the fight was all but over, he headed for the U.S. compound at JUSPAO. There, six buses had been allocated to transfer designated American and Vietnamese citizens to the airport. Reuters had already paid for Dinh's passage out of Vietnam, but he found hundreds of people desperately clawing their way to seats. He ignored the first bus, seeing the queue of women and children. But realizing there were

---

* The British journalist Clare Hollingworth would often complain to the author, across the bar of the Foreign Correspondents Club in Hong Kong, that Australia had failed to fully recognize the achievements Denis Warner had made throughout his career.

hundreds more people than seats, Dinh began squeezing his way to a seat on the second bus. No sooner had he sat down than an American MP kicked Dinh off the bus, not caring whether he had a ticket or not. Clutching his ticket, he began queuing at the next bus.

An was happy to stay put. *Time*'s senior staff had repeatedly asked him if he wanted to be evacuated and join his family in America, now staying with his former colleague, Beverly Ann Deepe. Each time, he politely declined, explaining that professionalism required him to stay on. Besides, he had a comfortable situation. *Time* had moved An and his elderly mother to the second floor of the Continental Palace Hotel, just where the office was. She was too old to make the trip to America in any case.

* * * * *

AN'S OLD JGS boss, perennial contact and longtime friend, Dr. Tran Kim Tuyen, faced a very uncertain future. As former head of South Vietnamese CIA operations, Dr. Tuyen's prospects under Communism were bleak indeed. He had been incarcerated by the Communists after the First Indochinese War and now faced that possibility again, only this time he'd be lucky to get away with only jail time. The Communists weren't likely to look kindly on the little man reputed to have put to death thousands of Viet Cong and suspected Communists.

Dr. Tuyen had refused to make his getaway earlier, convinced that President Thieu's troops would stave off the latest attack; worst case, a deal brokering a North-South coalition government would be made, buying him time, and perhaps a way out of his predicament. Attempts by Bob Shaplen to get Dr. Tuyen out with the foreign press corps had failed. There was nothing else he could do but give Dr. Tuyen 50,000 piastres and the key to his room at the Continental.

An and Dr. Tuyen were together in the Continental on the last day of South Vietnam's short political history. On this day of uncertainties, there was one certainty in the air—Dr. Tuyen was convinced beyond a doubt that An was a CIA agent and could get him out.

"If you can't leave today you can go with me to my house and I will try later to find a house for you to live in," An told him.

It was all he could say. But it was as much as Dr. Tuyen needed to hear. He was convinced, as indeed *Time*'s management was convinced, that An would get himself out to the United States—and that he would be going with him.

* * * * *

ON BOARD a small fishing vessel, Nguyen Ngoc Phach decided to re-tire his pen name John Draw and leave the *Daily Telegraph* as he and his family headed for the open waters of the South China Sea, where the U.S. Seventh Fleet was stationed. The tiny vessel was not designed for the open seas and lacked basic navigational equipment. The boat and its passengers were tossed about, the man at the wheel unsure which direction to take. On the horizon Phach saw another boat, similar to their own. The captain decided to follow. Hours later they sighted scores of other boats following each other. After 10 hours or so, the U.S. flag, loomed on the horizon.

Dinh, meanwhile, was greatly relieved to find a spot on one of the four remaining buses. South Vietnam was finished. He needed a new country, perhaps America where his estranged wife and children lived, or maybe Australia, he thought to himself as the bus left the U.S. compound. Right now, his destination was unknown, but at least Dinh had a ticket out. As the planes swooped overhead he heard sporadic gunfire and the massive cracking explosions of North Vietnamese shells raining down on targets around the city. After two hours of meandering, the bus arrived at Tan Son Nhut Airport. It was closed—and suddenly it dawned on him: The driver, obviously a Viet Cong, had deliberately gone as slow as he could because waiting planes made easy targets for the North Vietnamese who'd been pounding the airport relentlessly. The now crater-scarred tarmac was strewn with scrap metal.

In the end, the driver turned the bus around and headed back into central Saigon where Dinh got out and wandered back to the office, crestfallen.

The city was in even more mayhem than he'd left it. Tens of thousands, locals and foreigners, diplomats, military and civilians, were hurriedly packing their bags. The panicky ones tried to call in favors or resorted to threats, bribery or blackmail, whatever worked, to escape the encroaching Communists. Earlier that day, Dr. Tuyen was shocked by the sight as An steered his Renault through the chaos of Saigon's main thoroughfares, to-ward his apartment all the while puzzling through escape options. They drove past the palace and embassies where Dr. Tuyen once held court, but not much farther. The roads had become impassable and An decided to give up for the moment and return to the hotel.

An was prepared to risk his own security with the Communists to save Dr. Tuyen. If necessary, he could hand Dr. Tuyen over to the Communists, claim a reward and seek leniency on the doctor's behalf—though this wasn't an option he wanted to pursue. Back in the *Time* office, at about 4 in the afternoon, An got a call just as Dr. Tuyen was about to make his own way to An's place. It was Dan Southerland of the *Christian Science Monitor*. Southerland knew both men and spoke briefly with An before telling Dr. Tuyen he would talk to the American ambassador. Southerland called again 30 minutes later. The doctor's escape had been organized.

* * * * *

FOR FOUR hours Dinh moped around his modest apartment before deciding to phone the office. "Reuters. Neil Davis speaking." Dinh was relieved to hear that voice. The freelance cameraman had gone to the office to get a camera. "It's Dinh here, I'm stuck, I can't go," Dinh rattled down the line.

Davis was surprised. He thought Dinh would have easily escaped with the help of Reuters. Sensing panic in Dinh's voice, Davis told him to remain calm and to stay at home until the clamor subsided. Tomorrow they would report to the Communists together.

Feeling slightly better, Dinh spent the rest of that night on edge, though the thought of Davis hanging on after so many journalists had left gave him courage. Dinh admired Davis immensely, for being a good and wild man at one and the same time. Davis couldn't stay away, and he was one of perhaps 60 journalists who had decided to remain that day, a small number compared to the many hundreds in Saigon weeks earlier.

At the Continental, An bundled Dr. Tuyen into a car and drove him to the American Embassy. The gates were locked but, with An helping, Dr. Tuyen could squeeze his tiny body through along the ground. Tuyen's thumb-size stature had for once worked to his advantage. On the other side Dr. Tuyen turned and squeaked a thank-you before heading for the embassy's rooftop helipad.

From the balcony of the UPI office in down town Saigon, looking north, a young Dutch photographer named Hu van Es, could see the cathedral and a housing block called the Pittman apartments. The elevator shaft on the roof of the building, which housed CIA officers, had been reinforced, and was capable of holding the weight of a helicopter. Amid the last gasps of South Vietnamese history Van Es heard a bellow from his bureau chief Bert Okuley, who had remained behind with fellow UPI staffer Ken Englade.

"Van Es, get your fucking ass out here, there's a chopper on the roof."
Van Es was never slow off the mark.

"I dashed out, grabbed my camera put on the longest lens, and left the office. It was only 300 mm but it had to do. There were around 20 or 30 people on the roof, climbing up the ladder to an Air America Huey helicopter. At the top of the ladder stood an American, pulling people up and shoving them inside."

The Dutchman took aim and shot 10 frames, and in the race to transmit he clearly wrote in the caption that it was a helicopter taking off from the roof of a Saigon building. Van Es had captured what would become the signature photo for the finality of the Vietnam War, although for decades to come photo editors would ignore the caption and imply the shot was a portrayal of the last chopper fleeing from the roof top of the U.S. Embassy.

As that helicopter lifted off, Neil Davis was standing by the U.S. Embassy gates, wedged into a mass of thousands pressed up against the compound. America's last undignified hurrah was to be an ungainly chopper wobbling up and out to sea. The United States had given up, leaving no rescue plan for the many thousands left stranded—only tear gas for people struggling to climb aboard the departing aircraft. Nearby, Bob Shaplen, James Fenton from the *New Statesman*, Jim Laurie and Peter Arnett watched. Davis got his camera and began filming as the marines lobbed tear-gas canisters at these left-behinds. As the awful reality of their situation sunk in, the crowd was swept up by a strange but oddly bracing esprit de corps. Soon Davis stopped filming and joined in with the Vietnamese shouting at departing Marines. "Do ma, do ma!" they cried. "Go fuck your mother."

* * * * *

THE DANGER for the cameraman is getting so wrapped up in the image in the frame that he doesn't see dangers bearing down on him from outside the viewfinder. Davis had known this strangely blinkered existence for years and always knew where he would shoot his final scene of the war. Early on the morning of April 30, he met Dinh and Bernard Edinger at the office. Edinger had been sent by Reuters in London for a short stint, purely to cover the Communists' arrival.

Saigon was unusually quiet, the looting and chaos of the preceding days having coming to an end. The city was staying in today. Reuters was quiet and lonely, too, as the trio waited for the end to come. At 11:30, Davis got a call from the palace. He was told that Bui Tin would soon be arriving there: Would Davis like to take pictures? Tin was coming at the head of advancing tank units. Today, he was playing a dual role. As deputy editor of the North Vietnamese Army newspaper, *Quan Doi Nhan Dan*, he wanted to cover the "liberation" of the South. As a high-ranking Communist official, he planned to accept the formal surrender.

Davis lit a cigarette, picked up his cameras and walked towards the palace under the shade of tamarind trees. While Gen. Big Minh was inside, sitting out his final moments in charge, Davis picked out a site for shooting, not far from where Tom Aspell, also of Visnews stood, waiting for something to happen.

Back up the road, Dinh wandered outside the Reuters office for a smoke and watched the first North Vietnamese tank roll in—No. 843, a Russian-built T-54. Davis saw the tank, too, and got filming just outside the palace. Fearing his camera would be mistaken for a rocket launcher, Tom Aspell put his camera down as the palace gates cracked and buckled beneath the weight of tank 843. Davis kept his camera rolling, capturing the tank smashing through as a soldier, carrying a massive Viet Cong flag, leapt off and raced towards the palace. As Davis paced the flag-bearer, he caught in the corner of his eye a soldier pointing a rifle in his direction. He kept filming, but only for seconds more—the soldier finally caught up with him and punched the barrel of his rifle in Davis's stomach. "You're American," he shouted. Davis raised his hands. "No. I'm Australian," he countered. "Welcome to Saigon, comrade."

At just that moment, South Vietnamese troops flooded out of the palace to surrender. The confusion was enough to distract Davis's captor and he nipped back to the Reuters office with his film. Davis knew he alone had captured something very special.

Bui Tin arrived at the front of the main tank group. He marched up the palace steps and across its marble interior, where he found Gen. Big Minh and his cabinet waiting. Jean-Louis Arnaud and Francoise Demulder from Agence France-Presse watched on.

Minh said he had been waiting since early that morning to transfer power. Bui Tin then delivered his famous reply: "There is no question of your transferring power. Your power has crumbled. You can not give up what you do not have."

Outside the Reuters office, several hundred meters away, Dinh and Davis stood staring down the street, puffing away on cigarettes. Davis pointed to the new flag flying above the palace and turned to Dinh. "Now the war is really over."

13. A PEOPLE'S LIBERATION

FEARS THAT the annexation of South Vietnam would unleash a fresh wave of payback killings appeared groundless at first. Compared with the Thieu regime's long descent into chaos, the Communists brought stability, in fact. The North Vietnamese military acted largely with restraint, at least long enough for Communist politicians to consolidate their position and exert their clout.

It was almost a week after his botched airport trip when Dinh next saw An. They bumped into each other at the Givral, which had survived the onslaught intact. It was that encounter, Dinh later remembered, when his suspicions about An began to jell. "Don't worry," An told him, "everything will be okay."

The pat reassurance was to be expected, but why did An then warn him not to try to escape? An's behavior struck Dinh as odd in other ways. He spoke as if he was in control of an uncontrollable situation, which spooked Dinh. An asked him why he hadn't fled before the Communists entered Saigon. Dinh told him about his airport misadventure. As the conversation continued, Dinh regained confidence and guessed that An's position at *Time* gave him some leverage with the Communists.

Dinh asked after Nhan and the kids and their evacuation to the United States. He was surprised to learn they were still with Beverly Ann Keever, his former freelance boss and enduring friend, and wondered if the link might compromise An's relations with the regime. An jumped on Dinh when he asked if his kids would settle permanently in the United States. "I want my children to be Yankees?!" he snapped incredulously. Usually, An had kept his thoughts to himself. But he had been weighing up the benefits of uniting his family abroad and was waiting to see how events in Vietnam would unravel.

Dinh was unable to file anything at Reuters. But An capitalized on the confusion over new rules governing the media and ran *Time*'s Saigon bureau for about another 12 months on his own, providing fodder for the rewrite desk. Shortly after the South's capitulation, *Time* reported:

With incredible suddenness it was over, not only Viet Nam's agonizing Thirty Years' War but also a century of Western domination. This massive, 20-year American struggle to build a stable non-Communist government in South Viet Nam was finally and definitively ended, an all but total failure. When Communist soldiers in Saigon fired salvos into the air and shouted, "Victory! Victory!" the stubborn inextinguishable dreams of Ho Chi Minh and his heirs in Hanoi were fully realized.*

Repression came subtly at first, but as the months after passed, curfews were imposed and eventually, a daily schedule of public executions. Re-education camps were opened and filled with thousands who were denounced as American collaborators. Libraries were raided and books and official documents were destroyed. Independence Palace was renamed Reunification Hall and the train linking Hanoi with Saigon was rebranded as the Reunification Express. An was aghast at hearing historical documents were being used as toilet paper. He himself had to obtain and carry a license entitling him to keep his personal library. In an ensuing dispatch, *Time* also noted:

The Communists began to target the Western influences in South Vietnam. Men with long hair were ordered to have it cut. Nail polish, miniskirts, blue jeans and lipstick were frowned upon and the newspapers closed. Some signs of change were becoming more notable.

An, it turned out, was ill-prepared for life under a Communist government. He never anticipated that peasants would actually end up running the country—peasants from villages in closed areas that had been cut off from the world since 1954. It had been An's spark and savvy that prompted the Viet Minh to make him a platoon leader at the end of World War II— now the brightest and best were an anathema.

Tran Bach Dang, the zealot and political commissar, certainly had little

---

* *Time*, May 12, 1975.

time for them.* He was one of the people who said Tet would stir a popular uprising and end the war seven years earlier. Dang was put in charge of media oversight in South Vietnam and immediately sounded An out on his politics. An told Dang that he preferred cockfights to the political arena, not the kind of reply his interrogator might have expected since the Communists had banned the blood sport.

The new regime in the South viewed An with increasing suspicion. Even old friends grew suspicious of him. He started turning up in the khaki uniform of the newly reorganized Vietnamese army, its red lapels and gold insignia announcing him as a colonel. Since An had a knack for ingratiating his way into different camps, Dinh assumed the designation was honorary-proof that his instincts for currying favor worked as well with the new order as the old. To Dinh, this really was a sign An would be useful.

The truth was An was embarrassed at the attention the uniform was causing. He wasn't wearing it out of choice. He didn't mind friends seeing him as someone who sympathized with nationalist ideals—besides, he was just networking with the latest set of power brokers, something An had done time and again. But he didn't want friends thinking he had any part in bringing down South Vietnam.

It was a hard sell. Journalists became deeply unsettled by An's close ties with the Communists and even suspected him of spying on them. He did seem to be keeping a close eye on Nguyen Thu, the *Saigon News* reporter with links to *The New Yorker*. They were still friends but Thu had really suspected something since the day An canceled their dinner date, advising Thu the restaurant was a Viet Cong listening post and potential target. Unlike other locals, Thu used his real byline and tended to be scathing where the Communists were concerned before "liberation". He was a natural target for interrogation and both An and Dinh were under immense pressure to denounce journalists the Communists suspected of being CIA agents (essentially, anyone who wasn't a Communist).

They resisted, but at their peril. An and Thu met several times after liberation and in their encounter one evening in May, 1975, An knew his friend was in grave danger. Shortly after that meeting, Thu was accused of working for the Americans and sent to a re-education camp, where he

---

* Tran Bach Dang was indeed harsh. This was evident during interviews conducted when the Khmer Rouge were still active in neighboring Cambodia and proving troublesome along the Vietnamese border. Asked if another war was possible he said: "... when they attack Vietnam we will retaliate". *Asian Business Review*, May, 1993. p19.

was beaten daily with the butt of an AK-47 and left to languish in solitary confinement on a diet of 50 grams of rice a day. Released in 1988, he fled to Hong Kong, where he was placed in a repatriation camp before winning asylum in America. But before leaving for Hong Kong, An and Thu met, the first time in 13 years. Thu later remembered how An, almost apologetic in manner, offered him assistance. Thu only wanted An to answer to two nagging questions. Had he been working for the Communists all along? And had he denounced him?

An, as always, gave nothing away.

* * * * *

BILL RADEMAEKERS was in *Time*'s Paris bureau when An's wife, Nhan, walked in with her daughter and three sons. who had flown in from New York. *Time* had asked the Paris office to organize their tickets onward to Hanoi via Moscow.

Rademaekers was naturally curious to know what was going on because he, too, had heard the report about An being a colonel in the people's army—and all the conjecture along with it. American journalism had indeed come to an amazing pass, when a *Time* correspondent could double as a senior officer in an invading army, but *Time-Life* management really didn't want to know about An's connection with the regime. New York preferred to accept a simple home truth, so to speak, and leave things there—that Vietnam was his home and home was where An and his family wanted to be.

As far as anyone outside Vietnam really knew, the whole Communist connection could have been cooked up by him to placate authorities. There were too many theories and counter-theories for anything to make sense, even to Rademaekers and Bob Shaplen. In any event, tickets for the onward journey were secured and Nhan and the kids left Paris bound for Moscow after a minor shopping spree that included a new fur coat.

In Saigon, Dinh and An maintained daily contact. Occasionally, An would anxiously read the latest telegram, giving Dinh a blow-by-blow account of the family journey home. Reaching into his shirt pocket, he would retrieve the slip of paper and say: "My children are in Moscow." The next message would be about arriving in Peking; then Hanoi. Then finally: "Tomorrow they come home, to Saigon."

They arrived as An's career seemed to be going from bad to worse. He had refused to join in the liberation celebrations and had shunned officialdom when he could. He did attend obligatory events such as Gen. Tran Van Tra's media lunch marking Ho Chi Minh's birthday. Dinh, still struggling to maintain the Reuters operations, was also ordered to attend.

It was the first time An had met Gen. Tra, the man charged with military operations in the south, and a month later, he found himself appointed head of the foreign press corps in Saigon, a sensitive role as he would quickly find out. For starters, the difficult and suspicious Tran Bach Dang asked him to deliver a speech to local journalists spelling out the regime's expectations on reporting news.

Instead of arguing for media control and the case for journalists joining in the national effort to build Vietnam's Socialist paradise, An gave a face-saving talk about a journalist's life of honest toil reporting the truth and supporting the family. He spoke of a journalist's duty to report fairly and accurately but he also, in a pointed aside to the new regime, said it was wrong to persecute the messenger for delivering bad news.

No surprise, his performance fell far short of expectations and Dang lit into him, denouncing An on the spot, leaving some startled faces in the audience. An managed to keep his job and continued to monitor the few foreign journalists who ventured into Indochina. But he kept his distance from the reporters themselves to avoid having to justify his actions to former colleagues. Neil Davis, who returned often to the country, was the exception.

* * * * *

PHAM NGOC Dinh missed his estranged family and his old journalist friends. He also missed the ambiance of a city which always seemed to thrive on the edge of destruction. Now he strolled down Dong Khoi Street, only remembering it as Tu Do Street. Nothing seemed alive anymore. The familiar hustle and bustle, the gossipy crackle of Radio Catinat, were all gone now. Each day he would be greeted by the Reuters plaque, now sharply indented by gunfire, and begin another day of playing reporter: Right now, his main job was maintaining a Reuters presence, not running the bureau in the normal sense—because the censors shredded anything of value. Getting copy out of the country was virtually impossible now. But his problems were slight compared to those of his contacts. If they were found with any offending notes or copy, they would be reported to the authorities.

In a perverse kind of way, the new regime gave the party faithful a say in the day-to-day running of government. Power, in theory, was evenly spread from Hanoi, down through the provincial and urban central committees, to the Local Peoples' Committees (LPC). The LPCs were the vanguard of street -level communism, but often the power wound up in the lap of party lackeys with scores to settle. This made reporting difficult, if not hazardous. The organization of everyone into small street-block committees gave everyone ample opportunities to report on each other. The block committees reported once a week to a central committee and the overlay of reporting structures proved highly efficient in organizing and controlling people's daily lives.

The LPCs also provided an important information network and supported secret police efforts to keep tabs on dissidents. Like millions of others, Dinh forced himself to become a creature of habit to avoid creating suspicion or standing out from the crowd. Habits became formulas to prevent being singled out as an enemy of the common good.

On February 16, 1976, An wrote for *Time*:

Like countless other communities in Asia, Ho Chi Minh City—also known as Saigon—last week celebrated Tet, the Vietnamese lunar new year. Eight years after the devastating, decisive 1968 offensive, flowers bedecked the streets although perhaps not so many as in years gone by. The City's florists did not believe that South Viet Nam's new Provisional Revolutionary Government (PRG), would allow such a luxury. As one of them put it, "we were not prepared to grow flowers on time."

Communist policies and media control continued to compromise An's management of the *Time* bureau. Initially Hanoi liked the idea of An being *Time*'s man in Saigon. But then it realized it had no control over editors in New York, ignorant as they were of news operations. *Time* was scrutinized each week by party officials, who held An responsible for North and South Vietnamese content.

They were often enraged by the most prosaic of headlines, including this one appearing a short time later.

VIET NAM: Early Smiles Are Beginning To Fade

In this story, *Time* quoted Western journalists saying North Vietnamese troops were unable to cope with widespread corruption. The magazine also reported:

Saigon has been plagued by a near epidemic of theft and lawlessness. At first the Communists were quite casual about patrolling the streets; soon they began making rounds heavily armed and only in groups of at least five. Lawbreakers have been dealt with harshly.

"Harshly" came down to summary execution in certain circumstances. To Hanoi, the word also implied the accusation of acting unfairly. An's role as *Time* bureau chief became more untenable by the week and his telex machine was eventually seized, cutting off communication with the outside world, and on May 10, 1976, the *Time* bureau was closed,

The final curtain was also falling on South Vietnam. On the morning of July 2, Dinh went for his habitual walk around town. His route took him past the Roman Catholic cathedral, now missing its three-meter statue of Mary, and then down Dong Khoi Street, the former Tu Do Street, towards the boarded-up Givral. Across the street a huge map of Vietnam had just been erected on the facade of the Opera House, which had been used as the South Vietnamese National Assembly. The map showed three cities and there was no north-south border markings. Instead, there were three dots marking Saigon, Hue and Hanoi. Hanoi had an extra circle around it.

Later that day Hanoi announced South Vietnam had been unified with the North and Hanoi was now the capital of Vietnam. Saigon was renamed in honor of the father of the revolution. As Ho Chi Minh City, the former southern capital became known by the messy acronym HCMC—though to locals, at least in private, the place was still Saigon.

The future for Dinh looked pretty bleak, as it did for the media scene generally. Diplomatic entreaties to lighten press controls got nowhere with the new regime. On top of these problems, Reuters had to defend Dinh against charges that he was a Communist spy. The company refuted the claim leveled by an Australian journalist. But it only made the burden a little lighter. Dinh's bureau activities had been severely curtailed, as Reuters' own house organ reported.

All those people who ever worked in Saigon will be interested to hear that the indomitable and invaluable Mr Dinh, who acted so bravely during the tragic killings, is still working for Reuters at 15 Han Thuyen, although almost all our activities have ceased since the Viet Cong took over the country in 1975. He was made Manager/Correspondent after all non-Vietnamese staffers left. Unhappily at the moment the government, based in Hanoi, will not allow Reuters to file from Ho Chi Minh City (Saigon) nor allow us to open a bureau in the capital, and has also so far rejected Reuters efforts to post Mr Dinh to Singapore.

Life had certainly changed. During his early morning strolls he'd now see hundreds of homeless children rise from makeshift beds in the city's parks, their parents mingling with former bar girls, Buddhists and Catholics. Old distinctions were fading and everyone seemed to be converging into one communal people's blob.

The dilapidated colonial facades on the city's tree-lined boulevards were getting their third makeover, spiritually if not physically, since World War II. After the orderly flourishes of the French regime and the unruly and garish motifs of the American era, a thick cloud of Soviet and Bulgarian gray had descended.

Life was hardly better outside the city center. Thu Duc, a village on HCMC eastern outskirts, was strangely at odds with the picture put out by the party. As Dinh approached it by a bridge spanning the Saigon River, he wanted only to retch. The stench was awful, effluent oozing everywhere. Electricity ran only intermittently. Families were jammed into filthy spaces.

Along the Kinh Te, the Ben Nghe and Thi Nghe canals, HCMC's poorest lived in shanties made of scrap materials and propped over the stinking black silt on bamboo stilts. Here huddled thousands of war veterans: Former South Vietnamese regulars, Viet Cong freedom fighters, and soon there would be more—returning from Cambodia where Vietnam would be dealing once and for all with the murderous Pol Pot. Incapacitated and unable to provide for their families, these veterans from hell relied on handouts from food vendors. Supplies were generously given while political leanings in the past were ignored.

Most spent their days idle, hunched against doorways in front of their hovels. The limbless, the brain dead and the horribly scarred were cared for by nurses and doctors in ill-equipped veterans' hospitals. Survivors of napalm attacks, having survived the repair of melted or fused skin, now faced a different hell; skin grafts removed all elasticity, leaving the victim encapsulated in a rigid cocoon.

Five years of the new order left Dinh near exhaustion. Perhaps he should have escaped on the boats to Hong Kong or Australia like the thousands before him. "If you don't like Vietnam," the saying went, "go and see the Admiral." The Admiral was the 13th century warrior, Tran Hung Dao, who had defended Vietnam from the invading Mongols and Chinese. He stood cast in bronze overlooking the Saigon River with one outstretched arm pointing towards the sea. To go and see the Admiral meant to go and find a boat destined for Australia, Indonesia or Hong Kong. It meant risking everything. The owners of often barely seaworthy scows would take your wealth and what they didn't manage to grab often went to the murderous pirates combing the South China Sea—for these bobbing refugees made easy targets for plunder and often murder.

Dinh wanted to see the Admiral badly but he had started a relationship and wanted to marry. He didn't want to put his new girlfriend through the hazards of that kind of journey. Dinh had met Vy at the bank which handled the Reuters accounts. Any vestiges of his first marriage were over.

Apart from catching the teller's pretty smile, there was no real need for Dinh to visit the bank. There was no money to deposit or withdraw. But there was the matter of keeping up routines, to avoid arousing suspicion and being reported to the nearest LPC. Some routines, it turned out, had their compensations.

To keep the suspicious in check, Dinh kept his distance from visiting correspondents. As it was, he was taking chances with Vy as that relationship developed outside banking hours. Her three brothers had fought in the South Vietnamese Army and been sentenced to 10 years' imprisonment. But steady nerves kept the relationship on the rails and they eventually married and produced a son.

Suddenly, the Admiral called, or so it at first appeared. In September, 1979, Australian Immigration Minister Michael Mackellar had written to Dinh (and Reuters and partner AAP) to say that Dinh had been granted a visa to Australia. But the visa hadn't come via the usual channels—the minister wrote that Dinh was getting it for "extraordinary services to Australian journalists during the 1968 Tet offensive".

Reuters immediately applied to Hanoi for Dinh's exit visa, but that turned out to be the beginning of more trouble for Dinh. Here he'd spent the past five years trying (with An's help) to convince the Communists he had never worked for the Americans. And now the Australians came up with what looked to Hanoi like a payoff for working as an agent for Australia which, by definition, meant the United States.

A day after Dinh got Mackellar's letter, there was a knock at the door. The secret police had come to take him in for questioning, three months of questioning, it turned out. Over and over the same questions came: "Why did you work for the Australian Embassy, boy? Why the special visa? What did you do to earn it? What specifically did you do to help these journalists? What were their politics?" The conclusion his interrogators drew was that Dinh had spied for the Australians.

"I spied for no-one," he said a hundred times. "They gave me a visa for humanitarian reasons. I have no job, no food, no clothes, my children are hungry."

Dinh was on his own, there was nothing Reuters could do apart from lodging the usual diplomatic protests and Dinh was sinking fast with the possibility of exiting this hell looking more and more remote. He told his interrogators he didn't care whether he lived or died. (Later, he said he couldn't remember whether he was being brave or stupid in saying that, but exhausted he certainly was.)

In standing up to his interrogators, Dinh began to notice a shift in their attitudes. The harder he stuck to his arguments, the more his attackers seemed impressed. "If I have done something wrong, then put me in jail," he told them. "If not, then let me be free. I don't care if I stay or leave—just tell me what the fuck you want from me."

Dinh discovered his interrogators were Viet Cong veterans, fellow southerners who could put two and two together after a fashion. They grew to respect his pluck and came round to the notion that he was no more than another displaced compatriot—albeit one with an option he desperately wanted to exercise. But did that make him a spy?

14. MISSING LINKS

'Minimize Harm.'
– Second ethic of the Society of Professional Journalists

PHAM XUAN An's dissatisfaction with the north was also growing, as Bui Tin knew from An's letters. Hanoi and the Viet Cong were supposed to liberate and unify Vietnam, not subjugate part of it like a colonial power. But that was what was happening. In April 1980, An, concerned about the fate of his old colleague and friend Dinh, contacted the police and began the process of trying to convince the authorities over many visits that his friend had never been a spy. Eventually, he offered to act as Dinh's guarantor.

Later that month, interrogators asked Dinh to write down his opinions of the new government—a request he only complied with after repeated pleading from his wife. After relenting, he asked Vy to take down a letter and address it to Hai Linh, the chief security officer for foreigners and immigration in the south.

Dear Hai Linh,

Please forgive me for how I address you because I want the following opinions to be expressed between two brothers, not between a citizen and an official.

Dinh went on to say that Hanoi had lost sight of the fundamentals laid down by Ho Chi Minh and his prescribed stages for union—namely, liberation of the South, then financial and physical reconstruction, and only then reunification. Hanoi, he said, had loused up everything by being totally preoccupied with reunification at the cost of southern goodwill.

In a subsequent letter, Dinh cautioned: "The diamond you can buy. Position in government you can buy. A beautiful wife you can buy, but you can't buy love for your country."

Dinh had moved a good deal closer to getting exit visas for himself, Vy and little Vou, but it wasn't entirely on the strength of clever homilies. An had been essential in securing them. Before leaving the country, Dinh and Vy visited An in District 3, Saigon's old Embassy Row district. As usual, they were greeted by a barking dog. Although northerners dispatched by Hanoi viewed An with great suspicion, he still enjoyed status. His two-storey stucco house had been a British diplomatic residence, confiscated property An was given for services rendered.

After the usual pleasantries, An told his visitors how he had agreed to be their guarantor. Then, with the story of the exit visas behind him, An dropped the bombshell.

"I made a mistake," he began. "I realized we fought for the independence of South Vietnam, but the reality was not what I wished for. Many people said I was Viet Cong. I never denied this but I never confirmed it. But now, before you go, I would like to show you a magazine and you'll know what I mean."

An then went to the wooden cabinet in his library where he kept a safe. Dinh remembered the piece—it was the cabinet An had fussed over when Dinh had helped him shift house more than 10 years earlier. An had become furious when Dinh approached it and had ordered him not to touch it. Now, An seemed driven to expose its secrets. He opened it and pulled out an old issue of an in-house organ, a magazine designed for internal Communist Party consumption. He handed it to Dinh, who was stunned by what he saw. It was a picture of An standing proud as a peacock with Ho Chi Minh. It had been taken in late 1968, when An had secretly visited Hanoi to be decorated for his services during the Tet Offensive. Col. An, it turned out, was a national hero with links to the highest echelons of the Communist Party. In the photo, An, in civvies, and the patriarch in his army uniform, stood side by side. "Comrade Pham Xuan An with Uncle Ho," the caption read.

Standing in the small library, Dinh and Vy took it all in and as they did, An began turning white with rage, as if the act of divulging his double life made his "mistake" all the more vivid. Shaking and sweating feverishly, he began swaying precariously, then, just as suddenly, he collapsed.

* * * * *

IT WOULD take years before Dinh could fully piece together An's life as Hai Trung but he certainly smelled a story that last night in Saigon. It went back to 1945, when An left home to fight the French alongside his fellow Viet Minh. Though he'd never formally left the organization, malaria and tuberculosis forced An into seclusion. That hiatus stretched beyond his recovery, until after his return from California, 20 years earlier. The next phase of Communist activity didn't begin until he took the job with Dr. Tran Kim Tuyen's secret police within Joint General Staff (JGS) headquarters. Although An's status was more akin to sympathizer than serious operative, he was well placed to leak information to Hanoi after the separation of North and South Vietnam in 1954. Nguyen Ngoc Phach, who also worked within JGS as public relations chief for the South Vietnamese military (also known as John Draw, to his unwitting *Daily Telegraph* readers in the United Kingdom), is convinced it was An who tipped off NLF leader Le Duan in time for him to escape arrest—a view Dr. Tuyen himself eventually came around to.

But his career as a Communist was more a product of unforeseen circumstance than anything planned. An's rise within the Viet Minh got an unexpected lift through a process of attrition. He was studying journalism in America when Duan convinced the North Vietnamese to reactivate hostilities in the South. In response, South Vietnamese President Ngo Dinh Diem and Dr. Tuyen instigated a crackdown on Viet Minh sympathizers resulting in the deaths of thousands. One estimate suggested that up to 90 per cent of all cadres were eliminated.

Whatever the actual number, the losses were severe enough to create openings for people like An, who by late 1959 had just returned from the United States and secured his job at Reuters. By this time, Duan was coordinating attacks and delivering supplies via the Ho Chi Minh Trail that linked North and South via Laos and Cambodia entering South Vietnam near Tay Ninh. Other routes were also used, land, sea and air. A central structure for coordinating operations was needed in the South.

To remedy that, high-level Viet Minh agents, including hard-liner Tran Bach Dang, organized a meeting—sanctioned by Duan (who by this time had been named Communist Party secretary general)—at Tay Ninh in December 1960. Out of those discussions, the National Liberation Front (NLF) was created largely from the remnants of the Viet Minh. Essentially, the front was the collection of Communists in the South committed to raising peasant support for reunification with North Vietnam and independence, goals laid down by Ho Chi Minh nearly 20 years earlier. It was South Vietnamese President Diem who dubbed this reinvented front the "Viet Cong".

An had returned from two years' study in the United States with near-perfect English and a good grounding in American customs. And he had a good record so far as supporting the cause went. He had been a regular financial contributor and fought against the French. More important, he now had an understanding of the South Vietnamese economic and power structure and top contacts within it, including Dr. Tuyen. As a Reuters journalist, he was well placed to use those contacts in the service of the NLF, which was developing an intricate intelligence network permeating all levels of South Vietnamese society, based on a very effective cell structure—where Communist agents were deployed into hostile areas and lived quietly as locals until needed.

The Army of the Republic of Vietnam (ARVN), even the army's own intelligence department—even, indeed, the American military advisors under Col. Daniel Boone Porter—were oblivious to its existence, until July 1962. That was when captured Viet Cong guerrillas told American interrogators that the VC had gained access to .50 caliber American-made antiaircraft guns and had established a school for training Communist fighters in the art of blasting helicopters out of the air.

As An was re-establishing himself following his return from the U.S., he was seconded to this intelligence network at a meeting at Tay Ninh, headquarters of the NLF's Central Office of South Vietnam (COSVN). Tay Ninh's area of operations would later be known as War Zone D. Located 100 kilometers northwest of Saigon near the safety of the Cambodian border, Zone D was pivotal to supply-line organization. Here Viet Cong political commissar and intelligence supremo Gen. Tran Van Dang established six levels of military intelligence as one branch of the NLF. An was part of a rare breed of trained and educated spies who reported to him after becoming ensconced within the power structure of the South.

An's decision to resume Communist activity wasn't hard. He had made the commitment 15 years earlier on the grounds of the Viet Minh training camp in Can Tho, when he was told membership was for life. His three Confucian priorities—family first, then country and humanity—also sat well with his decision. And back from America, An still viewed communism as the most realistic vehicle for uniting North and South Vietnam.

Spies usually had one contact person, nearly always female. The NLF chose women because men always faced the risk of being drafted into the South Vietnamese army, wrecking established lines of communication. An's contact was Nguyen Tse Van, known to him as Maj. Nam. For the Communists An worked under the name Hai Trung—Commander Hai Trung. He worked in conjunction with an extended organization of informers within the general population, plus ARVN infiltrators monitoring troop movements, plus others gathering information abroad.

Within the Tay Ninh hierarchy, Commander Trung had like An, climbed up from platoon leader, the rank he held in 1945. His immediate contacts were Maj. Nam and Gu Van, who headed guerrilla activities and espionage across the south usually from the Cu Chi tunnels near Saigon. And ultimately, there was Gen. Dang at Tay Ninh. Very occasionally, Trung would drive out to Cu Chi, where the Viet Cong had dug an underground base around a network of tunnels, to be briefed by Gu Van. Information would then be passed from there to Hanoi via different conduits, usually diplomatic missions in Phnom Penh and Hong Kong. But Chu Chi meetings were rare for security reasons.

Rank within the Communist system was often informal, sometimes honorary and not always comparable with Western military hierarchies. Maj. Nam, with 10 years' operational experience, outranked Commander Trung. Officially, Trung had been assigned to Research and Systems Analysis, a name borrowed from a similar department in the Pentagon.

He was to contact headquarters only by courier and pass information only orally or in notes written in invisible ink. Invisible ink could be bought at the local chemist or made from boiled rice. Once dry, the ink left hardly a mark. (Splashing iodine on the paper revealed messages.) The only other medium to be used was microfilm, which had to be passed along undeveloped. Trung carried a small camera to film documents and passed his undeveloped rolls to Maj. Nam. If either was caught, the rule was to immediately expose all film. At first, Trung turned in pictures that were out of focus, a problem addressed by attaching a length of chain to his camera to measure off the correct distance between the lens and the document being photographed. With that innovation, crisp shots were virtually guaranteed.

At Tay Ninh, Gen. Dang would compare Trung's information with intelligence from others like Pham Ngoc Thao in the field. Dang would then liaise with headquarters officers such as Gen. Tran Van Tra. From there, the information was passed to Hanoi, ending up with intelligence chief Bui Tin—who could arrange for it to be published in Hanoi newspapers when warranted.

Once intelligence was received and evaluated, orders would be given by radio and later by wire after a telegraph line was strung along the Ho Chi Minh Trail linking Tay Ninh and Hanoi. As the years passed, An, a.k.a. Trung, became quite brazen. As a *Time* writer, he had developed sufficient contacts within the ranks of the South Vietnamese military to phone officers in the middle of battlefield action from his office at the Continental Hotel.

Together, Maj. Nam and An belonged to one Communist cell; in Tay Ninh they were known as B1 and B2 and signed off reports using those designations. In the early days, the demands placed on Trung were relatively light. He dabbled in negotiating the release of kidnap victims and Viet Cong prisoners with mixed success. When he could, he tried to protect those he liked, regardless of political affiliation. In those days An had no trouble juggling the two sides of his life. But for An as for everybody else, the Second Indochina War crept up at a pace few contemplated.

Trung took it upon himself to organize the release of kidnapped farm manager Wilf Arthur. Even though Arthur's Ben Cat guerrillas operated with some autonomy from Tay Ninh and virtually had a free hand in deciding the Australian's fate, An managed to convince them they'd be better off trading him for desperately needed supplies.

Trung's knowledge of the region and his contacts in the hamlets and villages from Cu Chi to Tay Ninh and across the Mekong Delta were formidable, but Gen. Dang wasn't always swayed by his agent's charms. He ordered Trung to end his affair with the daughter of the Cao Dai anti-Communist doctor—and he ended it as ordered.

In the early 1960s, An spent most of his time at Reuters, where he began to put his inside knowledge to use, both for the National Liberation Front and as a career journalist. Whatever the obvious conflicts, he brought to his journalism unmatched inside knowledge of how the Communists operated, writing dispatches no-one but an insider could possibly have written:

SAIGON, January 4 [1962] Reuters - The top ranking members of the Communist guerrilla movement in South Vietnam are meeting near the Cambodian border to reshuffle their high command, authoritative intelligence sources said here today.

According to intelligence information the guerrillas were reshaping the high command to improve co-ordination between the military and political arms of the Communist movement. The meeting was also believed to be aimed at bringing the guerrillas more solidly behind the front for the liberation of South Vietnam—the popular front movement being used by the Communists.

An, of course, could quote himself (Trung) as a source. That unusual convention aside, An later maintained he always observed one self-imposed rule: Never write a false story or mislead a colleague on questions regarding his stories. Not quite. He did bend truths, tell outright lies about his sources and break his own rules, notably when Khe Sanh was turning nasty.

This limp claim aside, there was every reason not to get caught playing tricks on colleagues. Getting caught would have meant summary dismissal and that would have disabled a key intelligence gathering post.

His rise within Communist ranks was slow, in some ways pacing the tempo of the war itself. When that picked up, so too did the opportunities for advancement, a case in point being the Ap Bac debacle in early 1963. An was the first on the scene, which was a coup for Reuters and a coup for Gen. Tran Van Dang's intelligence network, which helped ensure a decisive victory for the Communists. In modern day parlance, it was a win-win outcome for the two sides that made up the An-Trung split personality.

That story, of course, had been handed to Trung on a Christmas platter, for it was in December, 1962 that Capt. Hoang Duc Ninh, the airborne intelligence chief at JGS headquarters, walked into the Reuters office, unveiled a map and gave all the army's secrets away. He pointed to a small hamlet called Ap Bac, 70 kilometers southwest of Saigon, and virtually gave the where-and-when details of the army's plan to rout Viet Cong forces—a scheme the U.S. military took pains to keep secret after leaks undermined their Plain of Reeds offensive a few months earlier.

Trung had sent word to Tay Ninh through Maj. Nam, who passed it along. Dinh first met her that fateful night before New Year's Eve—when she came to the Reuters office looking for An. The thought she might be a Communist agent never occurred to Dinh, of course. But years later, Dinh found it staggering that An had helped the Viet Cong achieve their first military victory of the war while sitting at his desk at Reuters. Dr. Tran Kim Tuyen similarly concluded years later, as more pieces of the puzzle fell into place, that An had been working on two fronts: Not only had he warned the Communists of an impending attack, he also misled the South

Vietnamese as to how many VC companies were placed in the Ap Bac area—suggesting there was one, instead of three, the real number. Tuyen suspected An's dimwitted conduit was Capt. Ninh.

When An and Reuters were first with the story, Dinh was impressed—but also a little suspicious, as was bureau chief Nick Turner, who was always doubtful about An and eventually fired him. But such suspicions were not unusual in this game of scoops, as Dinh himself would find out when he was accused of being a Communist agent.

The fact was the structure of the Communist espionage network didn't really accommodate people like Dinh. True, he had received three formative years of schooling with the Viet Minh, but that only left him with a permanent distaste for their methods. (The Communists' treatment of prisoners violated every moral principle his father taught him and he could never forget the anguish of tormented French prisoners.) Besides, he wasn't very good at taking orders he disagreed with.

An and Dinh did share a mutual desire for independence, but that was about as much common ground as they had. By the time they met in the Reuters office, An had 14 years of service with the Communists ranks and Dinh had long since said goodbye to them.

He wouldn't have got his foot in the door at Reuters had he been a Communist anyway. An made sure of it. He would not abide anybody connected with the Viet Cong working with him for fear of being detected—and ran a check on Dinh before recommending him for a job. Being detected would have wrecked everything.

15. ENTRENCHED

'Act independently.'
– Third ethic of the Society of Professional Journalists

AS HAI Trung, An had begun to distinguish himself with the victory at Ap Bac. And just as Western media coverage of Vietnam rose with America's growing involvement in the war, An's twin careers as Viet Cong officer and international war correspondent ascended in parallel.

He became his own best source of information. Through Col. Pham Ngoc Thao, An cultivated sources inside the palace, although An didn't know Thao was a Communist spy, too, and had been working from within for years. Working for Reuters gave An what few local journalists had—credibility, and with that, a reputation for objective, independent reporting. The job allowed An to spend his working day entirely on the war, developing contacts within government, the CIA and the intelligence organizations of Britain and France.

An also cultivated contacts within the foreign embassies of the United States, Taiwan, South Korea and Australia. He considered the Australian diplomats among the best informed because of their trusted links with their counterparts in the U.S. Embassy. Though they never knew it, An routinely targeted these diplomats for debriefings at parties, lunches or over coffee at the Givral or breakfast in the Pagoda. Initially, he used his Australian journalist colleagues to open doors at their embassy, then dubbed "Little Brother" (Big Brother, of course, being the American Embassy). And with his fluency in French, the French Embassy was clear sailing from the start. His Communist credentials, or rather Hai Trung's credentials, opened doors at an array of different embassies and missions.

In many ways, An's work for the Communists was not unlike that of a Wall Street analyst researching and writing company reports, critiquing economic or military strategies and assumptions underlying plans of different entities.

Analysis became his preoccupation when the South Vietnamese and American governments began putting together a joint military and economic plan aimed at shoring up support for President Diem. Announced on January 5, 1962, the multifaceted program aimed to expand health and education services and promote agriculture and industrial development. The United States wanted Diem to get out the message loud and clear: Only the South Vietnamese regime, not the Communists, could offer security, substantial material benefits and improved living standards. In tandem with the announcement, President Diem said that the government would increase borrowing as a portion of annual revenue from 25 to 40 percent, translating into an extra $400 million a year.

An, wearing his Trung hat, sifted out the implications of the policy shift and relayed his analysis to Gen. Tran Van Dang in Tay Ninh. In this instance, the announcement suggested the South's deepening dependence on the United States—a sure sign of decline—but, equally, how any rise in living standards would make locals even harder to win over to communism. With the growing disparity of living standards between North and South uppermost in his mind, An, or Trung, urged his superiors to give economic considerations higher priority. Pragmatists like Gen. Tran Van Tra understood the agent's concern. The problem was ideologues like Tran Bach Dang, the VC political commissar who plotted the 'second Tet offensive' in 1968 who wouldn't abide such capitalist running-dog thinking.

An equated America's economic clout with military clout and concluded that North Vietnam could not win, not for years anyway, despite its decisive victory at Ap Bac. Tran Bach Dang continued to believe all Vietnamese would rise as one, if not to support communism, then to expel the American foreigners—just as the French had been expelled after Dien Bien Phu in 1954.

An was convinced the Americans could only be defeated on their home ground, that is politically, by continually fueling antiwar sentiment in the United States. That meant ensuring a continuous flow of news feeds showing the war's futility. In battle terms, An argued that the Communists—as the weaker and underequipped belligerent—could only survive by their wits. This explains his early enthusiasm for Tet, the brainchild of Gen.

Nguyen Chi Thanh (according to North Vietnam's intelligence chief, Col. Bui Tin). Thanh was the North's top man in the South, of course, and as such, headed the COSVN, the Central Office of South Vietnam. Both he and An saw the potential of hitting the Americans fast and hard when their guard was likely to be down.

An was pivotal to both Ap Bac and Tet operations but he played smaller roles, too. Working on both sides of the fence, he had helped secure farm manager Wilf Arthur's release from Communist captors and he also tried, in vain it turned out, to get a fellow Communist out of a bad jam with the South Vietnamese. Nguyen Van Troi was an electrician and part-time Viet Cong guerrilla who had tried to assassinate U.S. Defense Secretary Robert McNamara. Like many nationalists, the inexperienced Troi made this his own mission, without even telling his higher-up in the Communist Party about it. Not far from Saigon's Tan Son Nhut Airport, Troi had placed enough dynamite under a bridge to blow up both bridge and McNamara as his limousine passed over on its way into town. He ran the detonating wire from the bridge to his house nearby but didn't anticipate military police making a security sweep of the area. They discovered the wire and followed it to the house, where they found Troi fast asleep—and promptly took him into custody.

The Viet Cong immediately asked An to organize negotiations for a prisoner exchange but inquiries at the palace and with the Americans, initially through Bob Shaplen, proved fruitless. The problem was An could argue the case for a would-be assassin's release only so far without raising suspicions. The rescue mission had to be aborted and Troi was executed just after An left Reuters. An's understudy, Pham Ngoc Dinh, went to the execution and spoke to Troi before the end, when his cries of "Long live Ho Chi Minh", rang out across the yard of Chi Hoa prison.

Troi's flaky heroics resonated beyond the prison walls, with nationalists in the south and Communists like Tran Bach Dang, who saw Troi as an icon that could be used to motivate peasants across South Vietnam. But Dang, as usual, overestimated the impact of Troi's example on people at large, just as he overestimated their enthusiasm for the cause in general.

An's negotiating skills were kept fully engaged in and around the Reuters office. With his talent for navigating through Saigon's steamy denizens of pimps and prostitutes—and bailing them out of jail after vice sweeps—colleagues called him "Dr. of Sexology". But laugh derisively as some might, these grateful night workers were often useful sources of information. And servicing customers on both sides of the political fence as they did, An could keep up to date with South Vietnamese and Communist operators alike. Between these sources and highly placed contacts, An honed his already uncanny ability to accurately forecast a palace revolt or some other event that would surprise everyone else. With this growing wealth of information, An could endure digs from colleagues who called him "Dr. Revolution" or "Master of the coup d'etat".

On two occasions, the Viet Cong put out contracts on Nick Turner, An's boss at Reuters before he fired him for his "Radio Hanoi" copy. Why the VC wanted Turner dead had to do with an alleged CIA connection, an allegation An successfully disabused them of. On another occasion, there was talk of Turner's illicit tryst with a local girl whose husband had Viet Cong connections. Like so many others, Turner had been a victim of the Radio Catinat rumor mill but it was a trap he managed to climb out of with some quiet help from An.

Hateful though Radio Catinat could be in some ways, it was exactly that gossipy atmosphere that enabled An to cover his work for the Communists. Sipping tea in the Givral on Tu Do Street just around the corner from the office, he was free to chat with the numerous unknowns—Maj. Nam, and the "spooks and spivs", Peter Smark used to call them—who floated in and out. An could be an effective Communist agent right in the open. There were so many rumors for him to fathom, when he wasn't fueling them himself. For all anyone would know, An might be a CIA operative or perhaps a harmless government flunky. Or maybe a Communist, or just an unadulterated, unaffiliated nationalist. Or maybe just a guy sipping tea between sales calls. As Dinh later observed: "No-one could ever tell with An—he was just too aloof."

An knew how to play the game on any level and wasn't above turning a toilet—and his tormented bladder—into a prop. Often he would disappear into the washroom for 30 minutes or an hour and his colleagues at *Time*/Reuters accepted the unusual pattern as a matter of course. If An was not at his desk, he was on the toilet—which was isolated and free of distractions. It became a satellite office, where he made notes in invisible ink, sorted rolls of film, or just stole time to think. In this case, he was genuinely cursed (or blessed, Hanoi might say) with a bladder problem, but An could come up with infinite ruses to explain his behavior. He justified long absences from the city telling people like Nguyen Ngoc Phac, the ARVN public relations man and correspondent, that he had a holiday house in the countryside.

Excursions to this bogus retreat could run to four days, giving An plenty of time to meet with Communist chiefs Gu Van or Maj. Nam in the Viet Cong tunnel network at Cu Chi.

An wrote on politics and economics for *Time*, custom-fit beats for collecting on and off-the-record information for both his daytime and nighttime jobs. In confidential briefings, military spokesmen—as in most conflicts before and since—would often tell journalists of impending strikes on condition information not be printed or broadcast. The military could at least be confident An would respect publishing embargoes, though they would never have guessed the reason: One cheap scoop could see him barred from future briefings and his listening post closed down.

With access to helicopter transport across the South, An would also take hundreds of photographs for *Time* detailing the terrain, military installations and troop deployments below. After handing over his *Time* films to the photo department, he would organize and date rolls destined for North Vietnamese intelligence, attaching notes written in invisible ink and signed B2.

The unprocessed film would be passed to Maj. Nam, or B1 in Tay Ninh's code. Once rolls were received in Tay Ninh from Maj. Nam, the likes of Gu Van would direct them on to Hanoi via diplomatic missions in Phnom Penh and Hong Kong. In Hanoi, cartographers would assess local conditions while strategists figured out appropriate North Vietnamese army troop deployments and logistics for fighting alongside the Viet Cong.

On rushed jobs An would bundle his notes together and head for the bathroom where he could work without suspicion. Occasionally his espionage work was done at home, although he was reluctant to carry out these activities with his wife and children there.

It was against this background in early 1967 that An began preparing the report making his case for Tet. It was also at this point that he started misleading his fellow journalists. Knowing the Communists would carry out simultaneous strikes all across South Vietnam, An encouraged colleagues to focus on Khe Sanh, deluding them just as Hanoi sought to delude U.S. strategists into thinking the base was the sole focus of the anticipated Communist offensive. *Time* bought An's story and promptly published the report based on his nonsense.

Tet, or the idea behind it, was an old story in fact, discussed as far back as 1965. The plan had been proposed and shelved three times, each time the Communists concluding they hadn't resources for an offensive on that scale. Ironically, Ho Chi Minh only came round to the idea after Gen.

Nguyen Chi Thanh, its original architect, died of heart failure. In the event, Tet finally happened and the Viet Cong rampaged through Saigon, but An's role in talking up Khe Sanh qualified as mere deception compared to what was to come.

It was only after Tet—or really after Operation Phoenix, the allies' lethal counteroffensive—that An committed the first of what *Time* bureau chief Bill Rademaekers called his "two great lies". After Phoenix, which involved jailing and/or executing every possible suspected Communist in South Vietnam, the Viet Cong were severely depleted—by 90 percent, An himself believed. Yet the perception that the Viet Cong had come out on top of the Tet-Phoenix match and rematch inexplicably prevailed.

In the office and in the pages of *Time*, An promoted that lie, maintaining the Viet Cong had survived the offensive in good repair. Arranging backdoor interviews with fake high ranking Viet Cong agents, he duped his colleagues into believing they were talking to Communists of substance and power. With his disinformation program in full swing, An spoke and wrote of meetings in shadowy locales around Saigon to leave the impression the South was still thick with Communists. The absolute priority was convincing the Americans that the Viet Cong were a very real and present danger, to give the North maximum leverage at the Paris peace talks.

An's second "great lie" was using *Time* to convey an ever more sickening picture of American and South Vietnamese barbarism. While the allies certainly generated some genuine raw material (the My Lai massacre rating near the top), An took things a good deal further and repeatedly concocted stories of stomach-turning horror. One of his most imaginative concerned Viet Cong prisoners being decapitated and having their brains extracted while other prisoners looked on. Rademaekers didn't doubt their veracity and saw that they were reported, accepting An's argument that all sides of the war must be reported objectively.

The irony was that peace activists saw the U.S. government and America's military-industrial complex as the biggest liars of all—and their involvement in Vietnam, the great lie. Now this unseemly alliance was in danger of being sunk by more convincing lies fashioned by Communists like An. The fact was more and more American voters were being deceived into thinking the United States truly faced an unbeatable enemy, when it wasn't the case at all.

An used other vehicles besides *Time* in his disinformation campaign. He wasn't shy about using friends at Reuters, for instance, to spread tales of American woe, "tipping off" Dinh and others at Reuters about "news" about to break, strengthening Viet Cong units or new cruelties visited on VC prisoners. These tip-offs were all bogus, of course, but news organizations had to investigate them and since no-one knew who was telling the truth anymore, denials were taken as lies anyway. Each of An's lies had a way of affirming what more and more people assumed—that the Americans were liars and always had been.

And An knew how the hunter-gatherers of news worked and fed off each other. As *Time*'s Rademaekers was to observe much later: "An understood the dependency between news organizations on each other and played this wonderfully well—like a Stradivarius."

As Hai Trung, An had correctly judged a military defeat for the Viet Cong during Tet but had successfully turned defeat into a public relations win—not unlike the Plain of Reeds exercise six years earlier. But Tran Bach Dang, the political commissar in Tay Ninh kept pushing, foolishly in An's opinion, for a second offensive. An protested to his chiefs at Cu Chi, arguing more Tet and Phoenix-scale killing of innocent people could not be justified—especially given the real state of Communist preparedness. Gen. Tran Van Tra and Gen. Dang sided with An, even accepting his argument that the Viet Cong risked alienating the local population with further bloodshed. But Tran Bach Dang refused to back down, he won out.

Reluctantly, An returned from Tay Ninh to Saigon to wait for what would be known as the Battle for Saigon-Tet II, or Mini Tet. Wearing his two hats of reporter and spy, he also wanted to keep a close eye on the luckless John Cantwell, and protect him as best he could.

U.S. Ambassador Ellsworth Bunker, along with everyone else in the American camp, was stunned by the second attack on the Saturday night of May 4, 1968. The next morning, An was in the *Time* office growing fidgety after Cantwell failed to meet him, then he disappeared. He wandered the streets in the vague hope of finding Cantwell while listening to the thunder of air strikes, rounds of AK47s and grenade explosions in the distance. "If I should die," An wondered in that dark moment, "who would know what I did?"

Several hours later, An returned to his office. Freelancer Frank Palmos was there having just finished a bottle of scotch, and told him and anyone within earshot how Cantwell, Pigott, Birch and Laramy were gunned down by the Viet Cong in Cholon.

An sat quietly as the news shot around the office in whispers. As he cried for his friend, he privately cursed his Communist superiors at Cu Chi—

and himself, for he knew he had a role in this tragedy.

* * * * *

AFTER TET, An's work as Trung became increasingly important to the Communists. He met briefly with Ho Chi Minh afterwards and was pronounced "safe and effective", a minimal rating one might think but a rarely bestowed honor in Communist ranks where paranoia reigned supreme. From that point on, he was Col. Hai Trung.

In Saigon, he monitored allied troop strength and determined which commanders could be bought by digging up dirt on them—finding out who was sleeping with a colleague's wife or girlfriend and so on. There were myriad vignettes An collected and passed around. Sometimes he would divulge snippets to the South Vietnamese government or the CIA to keep their trust. Using just this trick, he got South Vietnamese President Nguyen Van Thieu to cancel death threats against certain foreign journalists, including Denis Warner.

When President Nixon began formally withdrawing troops, Gu Van was working from the tunnel network at Cu Chi. He ordered An to draw up a report on political and economic scenarios assuming a complete U.S. withdrawal. With five months to prepare the document, An provided a military snapshot that included troop positions and ammunition stores, and political analysis covering the palace and mood of the population in the capital and the countryside. He also provided economic data covering food production, the South's trade position, GDP status, the state of its national accounts and demographic analysis.

The report was passed to Hanoi and surprised An's superiors with a prediction that the Communists would win the war by the end of 1973. An was wrong, of course, having underestimated the extent of U.S. military aid and having overestimated the strength of the North Vietnamese Army. But almost immediately after completing and dispatching his report, he had to send some late-breaking news: The Americans planned to extend operations into Cambodia.

Col. Bui Tin, the North Vietnamese journalist, was in Hanoi when An's news flash arrived. Bui Tin had been a trusted ally of Le Duan and Ho Chi Minh and only vaguely knew of Hai Trung in the earlier years of the war—and he did not think much of his prediction that the war would be over by the end of 1973. But now, with the Cambodia bulletin, everybody within Hanoi's intelligence network was stunned.

"We knew the Americans were going to bomb Cambodia because An told us," Bui Tin said later. "And the operation was another failure for Washington." Tin praised An's report, noting it also provided an outline of the targets and projected the likely intensity of response. Although An had years earlier predicted the United States would expand the war into Cambodia, the strikes surprised many because they contradicted Nixon's determination to extricate America from the war.

As 1974 began, it had become obvious that South Vietnamese forces were capable of holding their end of the country for some time to come. In a later report An prepared, in fact, he suggested victory was unlikely until 1976. In his 15 years as an analyst, An developed an unparalleled talent for getting useful intelligence and passing it on. He was less skilled at joining all the dots together and predicting the what, where and when of events. So while he could envision the United States invading Cambodia years before it happened, he couldn't pin a date on it until he secured specific information on the strikes. In the same miscalculating vein, An predicted a last bloody stand costing perhaps several thousand civilian lives. It never happened. North Vietnamese forces overran the tired and hapless South Vietnamese in surprisingly short order, they were abandoned after their pleas for America to supply even fuel for the air force having gone unanswered.

As An awaited Liberation he assumed his work for the North would make life easier for him under a Communist regime—although he still harbored misgivings.

* * * * *

THE ANTICIPATED bloodbath never came, but uncertainty dominated most peoples lives. No sooner had An been berated by the hard line political commissar Tran Bach Dang for failing to toe the party line than he and his liaison officer, Maj. Nam, were called to Independence Palace where the pair were commended for services to the Communists during the war with America.

Bui Tin, the journalist and northern propagandist who accepted the South's surrender, met An again at the 1976 military party congress in Saigon. An liked Tin for his commonsense, unfettered manner. They were like-minded people, both journalists (at least in a loose sense) and both senior officers in the Communist army. Through Bui Tin, An was introduced to Gen. Vo Nguyen Giap, who had led the Viet Minh in battle at Dien Bien Phu in 1954 before spearheading later North Vietnamese offensives.

An had arrived at the congress with Maj. Nam, and Bui Tin was fascinated to see how the pair moved about the hall. He was surprised to learn their respective ranks. Nam outranked An, but this was not how the two behaved. An was not so much Maj. Nam's subordinate as her big brother. Tin was touched and he felt the pair offered an insight into the way the Viet Cong had fought and survived the war. The two were declared "Heroes of the People". Hai Trung's citation read: "Each year he has procured many secret documents from the military operations of the American forces."

Col. An and Maj. Nam had led extraordinary lives. They had evaded the authorities almost completely. Only once had Maj. Nam failed to arrive as scheduled—but other than that both their records for evading detection remained unblemished through years of highly productive undercover work.

Bui Tin met with An again in 1977 and later in 1980. They forged a close friendship, more as pen pals than anything else. An's letters grew steadily more scathing of the Communist regime, and raged after Hanoi's decision to invade Cambodia to defeat Pol Pot. He understood the brutalities of the Khmer Rouge and that an invasion of Cambodia threatened another bloody war which, An believed, his country was ill-equipped to cope with.

An's life under the Communists had been further complicated in 1978 when he was ordered to Hanoi, where officials had grown increasingly suspicious of him. There had been signs of trouble, one of the first coming when they rejected his request to leave Vietnam and live in America where he mistakenly thought he could resume work as a journalist—and also spy for the Communist East. Given that An was still very much a part of the media and intelligence network as head of the regime's Saigon press office, the rejection was shortsighted, from their standpoint at least. He still had many active and trusting contacts within the CIA. But the Communists in Hanoi feared An had been living in deep cover too long. Coming out from the shadows didn't translate into an easy-going existence, though. Obeying orders, An reported to Hanoi and spent a year under indoctrination. Despite his best efforts to win his superiors' confidence, Hanoi continued to have reservations about An's commitment to the party.

The fact was deep fissures had split even blue-blood Communists and they cut along North-South lines. An was a southerner and essentially a part of the Viet Cong military, mere militia material rather than solid army material. Making matters worse, animosity and distrust increased markedly as more northerners migrated south after unification. Many of those shifting northerners assumed senior positions in the regime, to the chagrin of southerners who were already soured by the conviction they had borne the greatest losses during the war. On top of North-South rivalries, disputes bubbled up between the army, which tended to be less ideological and more pragmatic, and the party—which, like Communist parties elsewhere, thrived on dogma.

An had his allies, like Bui Tin, who sought to protect him. He was even promoted to brigadier general, a rank that afforded some protection, particularly among petty bureaucrats and the meddlesome local people's committees with their street corner courts. But An's rank was a hollow title. "I am a general with no-one to command," he joked bitterly.

Eventually An was allowed to return home, but he was forbidden from making contact with foreigners and lived under virtual house arrest. Occasionally, party officials consulted him on international matters, Vietnam's invasion of Cambodia, ironically, being a case in point. He continued to argue against Vietnam's involvement. But these were really pro forma consultations—few in authority heeded his counsel any more.

16. TWO LIVES—ONE LEGACY

'Be accountable.'
– Final ethic of the Society of Professional Journalists

AFTER AN slumped to the floor at his house, Vy and Dinh dragged him off the tiles back onto the nearby couch. His wife—who always kept a healthy distance from her husband's work—was nowhere in sight. Even semi-conscious, An was shaking a white-knuckled fist in a full-throttle tantrum. Dinh tried to calm him down, but for the first time in years, for the first time that anyone could tell, An had lost control.

An's rage was aimed at the Communists. He was fed up with Hanoi's hardline attitude to all things foreign and equally enraged at his country's isolation and descent into further poverty. He was convinced Vietnam's failure to move ahead economically was directly linked to Hanoi's prohibitions on everything—on teaching and speaking English and other foreign languages, on travel, on meeting foreigners—and its almost complete reliance on aid from the Soviet Union, which only embedded a regime of total dependency.

He gradually composed himself and after a bewildering 10 minutes or so of silence, began to speak. He wanted Dinh to help him escape and asked him to contact Bob Shaplen. An thought *The New Yorker* writer was now based back in Hong Kong. Anyway, he wanted Dinh to tell him that he, An, wanted to defect—not as An the foreign correspondent but as Hai Trung the Viet Cong spy (full of secrets to pass on to the other side). If Shaplen could pass this message to the CIA, An was sure the agency could organize a helicopter getaway. Assuming the CIA had reestablished a strong presence in Vietnam by now, An thought this would be an easy job to do.

But he was wrong on at least one count. Shaplen was seriously ill and in no position to help. But more than that, An's scheme seemed ready-made to put Dinh's new family in jeopardy.

Five years after the "liberation of Saigon" and his ill-fated bus trip, Dinh, Vy and Vou boarded an Air France flight for Bangkok. It was on May 8, 1980, and goodwill messages had poured into Bangkok from Reuters offices around the world. He'd been inundated with requests for lunch and straight cash offers to help him start a new life in Australia.

At a brief meeting with a Reuters contact in Bangkok, the family was given cash and travel gear. At that point Dinh had only what he was wearing. Then it was on to Sydney, where a rented house on Bondi Beach and a job at AAP were waiting.

Ex-Reuters hand in Saigon and later senior writer at *The Australian* Hugh Lunn devoted a number of full-page articles to extolling Dinh's deeds and the bravery he displayed during the Tet offensive and ensuing battles. Lunn still felt the weight of it on him. He had spent years writing his manuscript, *A Reporter's War*, but was unable to finish it. What bothered him most was how Dinh knew of the Tet offensive in advance. Pham Xuan An had tipped him off, Dinh told Lunn only then. The Australian was amazed at the revelation and immediately declared it one of the war's truly outstanding stories, a story he wanted to write, in fact. Dinh, fearing for An's safety, urged him not to pursue it. Everything, he insisted, was off the record and deep background.

Later, after Dinh's anxiety eased, Lunn squeezed a piece of the story into a memoir and referred to An as the spy who worked for "one of America's biggest weekly magazines". One passage of Lunn's account showed Dinh enraged at everyone's blundering over An's role:

With his eyes blazing, Dinh said: "How can America win war? How can ARVN win war? What CIA doing? Something corruption, black market? He very important in the war for VC. Any story he have all information he can give to VC, but, more important, he can give American journalist anti-Vietnam war information. Dinh said that no doubt [An] gave the U.S. Embassy information, and not good information.*

* * * * *

---

* A small portrait of Pham Ngoc Dinh and his wife Vy hangs in the Foreign Correspondents Club in Hong Kong, alongside the Reuters shingle that once hung at the entrance to the Saigon bureau. Dinh took the shingle with him upon leaving Vietnam.

ENGLAND WAS not Dr. Tran Kim Tuyen's first choice for retirement, but he had few options. Western countries had shunned Saigon's former intelligence chief. Had it not been for An and a bit of luck, Dr. Tuyen might have been confined in a re-education camp indefinitely, or shot. London was a reluctant host but finally agreed to the doctor's pleas for asylum on the grounds that his oldest son was studying architecture at Cambridge University. There was one proviso attached to his coming, though: He was never again to speak publicly about his involvement in the Vietnam War.

He and his wife, Jacky, dutifully fell into a quiet life, running a bed-and-breakfast on Chesterton Road in Cambridge. Life was pleasant, but old scores had a way of catching up. Seven years after arriving in Cambridge, Dr. Tuyen received a disturbing call from Nguyen Nhu Cuong, an economics professor from the Law School of Saigon and a mutual friend of Dr. Tuyen and An. An had lost hope in Shaplen and Dinh. He was looking for alternative escape plans and was prepared to call in all favors in his bid to defect. Cuong reminded Dr. Tuyen how An had saved his life in April 1975 and told him that An wanted the doctor to use his CIA contacts to organize his escape. Dr. Tuyen ignored the request. He had been granted asylum in good faith by the British government. Besides, he didn't see there was much he could do.

An bided his time until a second opportunity came. A former South Vietnamese justice minister, Tran Minh Tiet, contacted Jacky, when both of them were in Paris. Tiet told her that An was under the impression that Dr. Tuyen still worked for the CIA and was therefore in a position to have An and his family smuggled out of Ho Chi Minh City.

An put out a third call for help a year later, in 1985, through a Communist doctor, whom Dr. Tuyen declined to name during a series of interviews with the author. She regularly traveled from Vietnam to Paris and repeatedly called Cambridge from Paris relaying An's request, but to no avail. An had become a pariah—although, unlike others who refused to help him, Dr. Tuyen still could not bring himself to believe rumors that An had been a Communist spy.

In 1987, former BBC and London *Daily Telegraph* reporter John Draw, a.k.a. Nguyen Ngoc Phach, traveled to Cambridge to meet Dr. Tuyen. The doctor was eager to see the good-natured Phach, who never apologized for his up-front anti-Communist ideals. Though a product of French boarding schools, Phach's English was impeccable, as was his taste for the bourgeois life. On that cold day at the tail end of an English winter, Phach and Tuyen strolled across college grounds as Phach told how he'd been evacuated to Australia in 1975. In bouts of homesickness, Phach would dial Radio Hanoi on his shortwave and one day, he heard the strangest thing. A presenter started into an item about how Pham Ngoc Thao's remains had been retrieved for re-burial at the Cemetery of Heroes outside of Saigon. Dr. Tuyen's own trusted staffer and former senior South Vietnamese government official (and presidential aspirant, no less), it turned out, was a much respected Communist spy.

(Though An would never have suspected him as a neophyte NLF operative in the early 1960s—around the time of Ap Bac debacle—any intelligence he gathered was run by Thao before being passed along the chain. Though Thao was his downstream gatekeeper, it was only after 1975 that An himself learned that Thao was a spy. Whether Thao ever knew that An was a Communist and the one passing on all this information has never been known.)

At one point Phach looked at Dr. Tuyen and told him that he knew beyond all doubt that An was a spy—and at least a colonel in the Viet Cong. Dr. Tuyen seemed stunned at his assertion but immediately knew the implication: He had given both men their start in South Vietnamese intelligence. "It was because of people like An and Pham Ngoc Thao that people like Le Duan got away," Phach said, laying it on with a trowel.

Dr. Tuyen simply shook his head from side to side. "No," he protested. But he wouldn't or couldn't elaborate.

* * * * *

IN HO Chi Minh City, An's despondency was nearing its peak when he heard Neil Davis had been killed during an attempted military coup in Bangkok. Davis was one of the few Western journalists to make regular forays back to Vietnam, although his assignments with NBC had also taken him to Africa and the Middle East. Davis had earned the trust of the Communists and had been asked to organize a television link-up between the Indochinese capitals for celebrations marking the 10th anniversary of "Liberation".

An abandoned all hope of defecting after Dr. Tuyen repeatedly blew him off. But visitors still arrived eager to see him. CBS's 60 Minutes reporter Morley Safer, or "Stone Face" as he was known, came by twice, landing An in trouble the second time. Parts of their conversation that winter evening in 1989 ended up in Safer's memoirs published the next year—even though An considered the entire conversation off the record. Benign as his comments seemed at first, they angered Communist hardliners in the early years of the 1990s, An and his family were put under 24-hour surveillance.

An often headed the must-see lists of returning journalists, especially as rumors about his double life spread. Most often, visitors came and went in secret, satisfied they had learned the truth. Stanley Karnow was barred from seeing An on his return in 1981 to research *Vietnam: A History*, but his efforts nearly a decade later proved fruitful. An and Karnow, the spy and the chronicler, hugged in that 1990 visit. "If An and Thao had fooled correspondents like myself," Karnow would recount in *Vietnam: A History*, "they also duped the U.S. Central Intelligence Agency, which had counted them among its contacts."

As the years passed, the Communist authorities eased up. "Anyway, they are not under any illusions about what I think," An told the author in a 1992 interview, the first of many. Indeed, when asked by one visitor about his decision to bring his children back from the United States in 1975, An was nothing if not blunt: "It was the stupidest thing I ever did."

He made no effort anymore to hide his dissatisfaction with Hanoi. "I admired the Communists as nationalists," An told me. "But their ignorance and arrogance have only given us misery."

Some time after Safer's visit, the former head of JUSPAO, Douglas Pike, came by, bringing a copy of Safer's book *Flashbacks*, where An figured as The Spy in Winter. An wasn't so much shocked at what it revealed as he was by Safer making him look like he'd thumbed his nose at the authorities. The deal was he wasn't to speak to visitors on the record without permission.

Safer contended An knew what was and wasn't intended for publication, dismissing journalists who said otherwise (only off the record, of course) as jealous strivers. "I suspect they wanted to do it themselves." Certainly, naming An publicly as the spy who worked for *Time* magazine was a scoop. Safer also revealed how An had organized the escape of Vietnamese CIA chief, Dr. Tran Kim Tuyen—the man responsible for the execution and torture of hundreds of political prisoners—and backed Dinh, his former protege at Reuters, in his efforts to get out. For An, there was enough in *Flashbacks* to annoy party higher-ups and make enemies of VC friends and contacts in the bargain.

Time correspondent Robert Sam Anson also went back for a visit and discovered only then that An had been the secret agent who had vouched for his release when he was held captive by the Viet Cong and Khmer Rouge in Cambodia. Just as An could break the rules of journalism when party duties called for it, he could also break with the conventions of spying and help friends in the enemy camp. Anson asked him why and later wrote of the exchange.

"We were on different sides, you and I." An looked at me thoughtfully, as if disappointed that after all his teaching I had failed to grasp his most basic lesson. "No," he said. "We were friends." Anson later asked An if he still wanted to come back in his next life as a songbird. An replied: *"In Vietnam there are truths that never change."*

* * * * *

BY THE 1990s there was still little official evidence from the Communist side of An's covert life. Indeed, there are no known copies of the photo taken of An with Ho Chi Minh—the picture he showed to Dinh and Vy before being seized by rage. In his book *Following Ho Chi Minh*, Bui Tin did pay tribute to An in a brief passage, later explaining he was disinclined to discuss his former colleague in any detail, given An's deteriorating relationship with the Communists. But Tin did allow that, "An was the West's highest rated journalist and our highest rated spy". In his memoirs, he wrote:

Pham Xuan An, known to us as Hai Trung, had studied journalism at an American University and worked for Time-Life group for many years. He was a confident [sic] of Tran Van Don and Tran Kim Tuyen and worked hand in glove for the CIA. He was also close friends with American, British, French and Japanese journalists based in Saigon. He accompanied them into battle on American helicopters and then spread all sorts of stories on Radio Catinat, in other words the rumor mill which stretched the length of the bars and cafes of Saigon's main boulevard. At the same time, he dispatched numerous valuable documents and photographs to Cu Chi for transmission to Hanoi. This intelligence network consisted of only two people. Pham Xuan An and a woman who acted as courier. Amazingly, both of them were able to carry out this task for twenty years without once being exposed, and they were both honored as heroes in 1976.

This was perhaps the first known commentary on An from the Communist side, albeit from a defector. But many people could never be sure exactly what An was really up to. Douglas Pike, who often ran the five o'clock follies and later became an Indochina scholar at UC Berkeley, believed both An and his Vietnamese colleagues were selling information to the CIA, leading him to conclude An was a double agent. "An was confusing in nature," remembered Pike, who met An for the first time in 1960. "Politics did not seem to be in An's nature—he would prefer to talk about sports and personalities."

Frank McCulloch, his first boss at *Time*, remembered An never talked about himself but he always knew what to do with information he got from others. "When I look at it in hindsight, the information he would have come across at *Time*, just through talk in the office and over coffee, would have been absolutely invaluable," McCulloch said.

Jan Smark was shocked to learn much later that An had been a spy—but impressed that An could cling so tenaciously to his ideals. Husband Peter, on the other hand, felt duped and said so in a January, 1993 column in the *Sydney Morning Herald*:

All reporters who have misspent much of their lives covering wars and revolutions have their own warm memories of favorite press pubs. Mine are of the Continental Palace in Saigon, the Hotel Constellation in Vientiane, and a hotel whose name I have forgotten on the island of Labuan, off Borneo. The Continental Palace, on Tu Do Street (Rue Catinat), wasn't Saigon's smartest hotel 30 years ago, when I was the bureau chief for the British newsagency Reuters. But the gossip on its pavement terrace was fabulous. I used to sit there in the early evening with other reporters, including my Vietnamese offsider, Pham Xuan An, who seemed to know half the passing populace, from Ngo Dinh Diem's chief torturer to assorted spivs and CIA men. I didn't know An was a one-star general. I especially didn't know his army was the Viet Cong. That became clear years later when the Americans fled. An, by then a staff correspondent of Time *magazine, refused evacuation and declared his affiliation openly. The news is said to have induced several heart attacks at* Time's *New York headquarters. I didn't feel too good about being conned, either; I still don't.*

The details of An's secret life leaked out slowly after 1975, and in the postwar days his deeds were subject to just as much conjecture as during the war.

His legend was recast again and again by writers who romanced the Vietnam War. Among the first was David Butler, whose gripping account; *The Fall of Saigon*, thrilled readers with An's efforts to help in Dr. Tuyen's escape at the climax of 30 years of war. Others include Denis Warner's *Not Always on Horseback* in which he wrote:

> *I found it hard to understand how An had managed for so many years not to betray himself, to make the sort of deep friendships he had made with Americans like Shaplen (and, the way he talked, his affection for Bob was deep and genuine) and at no time to let slip where his real loyalties lay. But this, I suppose, must be the characteristic of all great spies.*

On the eve of the new century An remained holed up in his villa with his wife Nhan and children, a semi-recluse with his over-sized German Shepherd, and a songbird that stood watch in a cage suspended from the ceiling of his library—for which An still carried the necessary authorization papers.

This was where Vietnam's native-born great war correspondent watched the days go by. On shelves near the front entrance, squeezed neatly between some French and English literary works, sat two volumes containing an anthology by Lord Byron in English and Russian, the gift of a colleague returning from Moscow.

Byron's words should bring him solace if the jury comes out and declares An something less than a great journalist, and perhaps he should keep this couplet ready:

> *A man must serve his time to every trade*
> *Save censure—critics all are ready-made.*

He was a man who concocted stories, misled his colleagues and had his publication printing the most foolish things. Indeed, he conducted himself as if he were the enemy—which was what he was. If the jury comes out and condemns his bad journalism, they should be sent back to the jury room to weigh the evidence on the right charge.

Pham Xuan An was not just an average sort of enemy but a spy and in many ways a pretty good one. Amazingly, he wedged his way into the places where virtually all the allied secrets were cooked up and stored—and went undetected the whole time. But he also broke the rules of spying by helping friends in the enemy camp, and he paid for the lapse by spending years on a leash. And though superb at obtaining information, he proved less skilled sometimes at putting different pieces together. His prediction of a Communist victory was out by a few years.

But he paid till his dying day for his worst piece of guesswork. He assumed a Communist regime would bring prosperity and progress to his fellow people rather than tyranny and prohibitions on any activity that diverted from the color of gray.

That An realized his terrible error was evident in his three embarrassingly hopeless attempts to defect. An landed in his own kind of punji trap. And after numerous attempts to escape, he finally realized what he would have realized long before were his analytical skills less flawed—that Vietnamese traps rarely give up their catch.

Pham Xuan An, of course, might turn to Byron in the face of this judgment, too.

'Tis pleasant, sure, to see one's name in print;
A book's a book, although there's nothing in't.*

---

*   *Both cits: English Bards and Scotch Reviewers*

AFTERWORD

IN 2002, I made my eleventh visit to Vietnam in almost as many years with the intention of conducting a third series of interviews with Pham Xuan An. He looked much healthier than on our earlier encounters and had officially retired in March the previous year. He had since conducted a series of interviews for Vietnam's state-controlled press and this had culminated in a biography entitled *Pham Xuan An, a General of the Secret Service.*

An had looked at me sternly from behind the iron gates of his house, he smiled and waved me in. I followed him into his living room where we talked and he handed me a signed copy of his book. He said many of the answers I had sought were inside these pages and urged me to read it.[*] Indeed there was much, importantly it contained confirmation of his highly secret exploits for which I had independently obtained through interviews. As a cross-reference it was marvellous and removed the doubts I had encountered over the years, doubts that were pushed by Vietnam era journalists, spies, politicians and businessmen who had their own take on events.

I looked at An with one question in mind.

"All I need to know," I began with, "is what was your code name? I have heard of many aliases but I would like to know what was your name?"

An stared at me for only a second, smiled again, and simply said: "Hai Trung."

His mood had changed for the better over the years, as skerricks of information about his double life became public. More relaxed about the secrets he had once vowed to take to his grave, An seemed content to throw his

---

[*] On the inside page, Pham Xuan An wrote: "This small book resumes the old stories [from] 27 years ago."

past up to the winds of history.

The biography, part of *The Many Faces of Vietnam* series, was written with all the color and flavor the Communist Party of Vietnam could muster. As a piece of propaganda it was a grand testament to writings of the Cold War era, full of compromises that often sidestep the heart of what actually happened.

Still, it spares no effort in lionizing An as the man who made an enormous contribution to the Communist victory in the Vietnam War and happily touts him as one of the great spies of the 20th century. It details his military decorations, he was awarded the highest in the land as he rose through the ranks—An was awarded four Liberation Exploit Medals and earned the absolute accolade; People's Army Hero and that title enabled him to become a general. Following the battle at Ap Bac in early 1963 just two Liberation Exploit medals were handed out by the Communists, one went to the battlefield commander, the other to An. This according to the biography was An's "first accomplishment". During 1962 he had sent 24 rolls of film which according to his then handler Muoi Nho contained; "all plans related to the U.S. Special War strategy. They included the master plan of the war, the materials concerning the buildup of armed forces, the support of American troops, the Strategic Hamlet plan, the plan of re-occupying liberated zones and the plan of consolidating the puppet army with American military equipment."

As for the three remaining Liberation Exploit Medals, a second was received for judging and leaking information of American plans to deploy its first Marine division, landing in March 1965, a third was awarded for his role during Tet in 1968. No reason was given for the fourth although it was also made in 1968 and was possibly linked to the offensives that followed Tet, which had unnerved An so much.

The Hero title was also officially bestowed in 1968, and quite possibly by Ho Chi Minh in Hanoi later the same year or early the next, for his exploits leading up to and after the Tet Offensive where An—as well as being minutely involved in the strategic planning—convinced the world that Washington was losing militarily in Vietnam when in fact they were not, and this proved pivotal in turning the tide of opinion against U.S. involvement in South Vietnam, resulting in their eventual withdrawal and a Communist victory in 1975.

However, the evidence that An actually met Ho Chi Minh is derived solely from the last encounter between An, Pham Ngoc Dinh and Dinh's wife Vy. There has been no further corroboration and it's a subject that An and his official biographers, Hoang Hai Van and Tran Tu, declined to discuss. An did not deny the meeting. According to the official account, An's grand title was only announced in 1976 when it was considered safe to declare, albeit without detail, An's true affiliations.

In An's own official words: "I was informed of the general offensive plan three months before and was entrusted to study the situation, provide information, analyze concerned factors in the military, political, social and economic fronts, developments in enemy forces and their defense capability." He went slightly further, and acted as chauffeur and personal advisor to Tu Cang, head of intelligence at the time. The pair scouted Saigon in late 1967 and early 1968 picking out targets, mapping and formulating a battle strategy for the Tet offensive.

Certainly Ho was well aware of An's work, as noted by his old handler Nho: All those documents were submitted to Uncle Ho and were then kept in strict secret. "Hai Trung's contributions were indispensable."

Further citations were received for the final invasion of South Vietnam in 1975. Alongside his usual strategic work, An allayed Hanoi's greatest fear that the U.S. would not intervene again in South Vietnam, victory was in sight.

An did not want his wife's full name used in publications. This was more for personal reasons and as an author I was happy to oblige. His wife, Nhan, had always been a house wife and had nothing to do with her husband's journalism or his covert activities for the Communists. This became clear in An's state-sponsored biography where the interviewers displayed a genuine curiosity in Nhan to the point of revealing that she was simply an unknown quantity for Hanoi. Certainly, in the later part of An's career, she was aware her husband was spying after An was forced to confirm her suspicions, but that was where the matter ended. An was also quite possibly annoyed by Communist interference in his personal life. It would appear that at least twice his handlers had objected to his choice in women. The first is mentioned in his biography written by Van and Tu. The pair mention his love for an American woman while he was studying in the United States in the late 1950s. An declined to extrapolate. The second girl was described by An to me as the daughter of a Cao Dai doctor who lived near Tay Ninh, The union was opposed by Viet Cong intelligence because her father was an ardent anti-Communist. The fact that there were no objections to An's marriage with Nhan indicated that she was not viewed as a threat.

Occasionally articles would surface in the Western press attempting to harness An's life, however, such stories—including a feature written by myself in 1992 and published by my then employer Australian Associated Press (AAP)—merely raised more questions than they answered. The most serious attempt to understand An was published by *The New Yorker* in May 2005 which was no less gushing in its praise than the politburo spin doctors who had resurrected An to the status of national hero. Entitled "The Spy Who Loved Us" *The New Yorker* told its readers, An "was a man of utter integrity, someone who lived a lie and always told the truth." Kind praise for a man who for more than half a century was master of the hoodwink, and there were no shortage of gullible players who abetted his work and ensured a Communist victory over South Vietnam.

CHAPTER NOTES

FOREWORD

The foreword is based on the author's first meeting with Pham Xuan An on February 17, 1992. The meeting was arranged through his old friend and colleague Pham Ngoc Dinh. At that point, security in Vietnam was far tighter than it was two decades later. An was under constant observation by the Communists and he asked me to smuggle a letter out of Vietnam and deliver it to Jan Smark Nilsson who was living in Melbourne, and I obliged. This incident, which was done despite the author being ordered out of the country, was also covered by Smark-Nilsson in her book *Walking the Tightrope*. The last interview with An was conducted at his home in Ho Chi Minh City on June 24, 2002. It should also be said that the Communist authorities in Vietnam did accommodate the author with interview requests and relations, while sometimes strained, were always cordial.

1. CHILDREN OF DIFFERENT GODS

Background to the childhoods of Pham Xuan An and Pham Ngoc Dinh was drawn from personal interviews conducted initially by telephone with Dinh in early 1989 when the author was researching An for an undergraduate thesis with Deakin University in Australia. Subsequent interviews were conducted at Dinh's Sydney home in 1991 which led to the initial trip to Vietnam in 1992. Information provided by An was enormously important, particularly during a series of visits to his home over March 1993. He also provided the author with access to his library and the original documents outlining the political structure of the Indochinese Communist Party and how it related to him as a member of the National Youth Association.

In regards to the early life of Ho Chi Minh, much of this is now open source where it was not when the author began writing this book. However, I did rely heavily on *Ho Chi Minh* by William Duiker, a telling and revealing book when released in 2000. Bernard Fall's *Ho Chi Minh on Revolution: Selected Writings, 1920-66* was also significant and equally important, particularly in regards to Cochin China, Annam and Tonkin, towards the end of World War II was *The First Vietnam War* by Peter Dunn. The Australian journalist, Denis Warner, a veteran of the era, provided insightful accounts from the period during a series of personal interviews in the mid-1990s. Works authored by Wilfred Burchett, in particular *Passport* and *Grasshoppers and Elephants,* were indeed insightful and helpful. Discussions with the American writer P.J. O'Rourke over the bar of the Foreign Correspondents Club, during the 1997 handover of Hong Kong sovereignty to China, also proved helpful.

2. END OF ANOTHER WAR

The First Vietnam War, authored by Peter Dunn was particularly helpful as was *The Two Vietnams: A Political and Military Analysis* by Bernard Fall. The immense knowledge accumulated by Denis Warner was, again, insightful as were the personal accounts of Pham Xuan An and his interpretation of events in Saigon at the end of World War II and how this accounted for his politics and the fighting he took part in, in Indochina, at that time. An liked to reminisce about his early days fighting for the Viet Minh, which lacked the political baggage that came with the following decades. An also recommended Dunn and Fall for their work as a 'matter of record' in regards to the history of Indochina at the end of the Second World War.

3. THE FIRST INDOCHINA WAR

On An's early life with the Communists, he initially gave off the record interviews into his recruitment. "Off the record" was to last until his death. However, much of this information was later verified in official accounts by Hoang Hai Van and Tan Tu in *Pham Xuan An, a General of the Secret Service*—released before An's death in 2006—and in Larry Berman's *Perfect Spy.* An knew Graham Greene, Robert Shaplen, Don Wise, Ngo Dinh Diem and Tran Kim Tuyen intimately and freely told stories about his associations with them. Tuyen, the former head of South Vietnamese intelligence operations, was interviewed over three days by the author at the family guest house he ran on Chesterton Road in Cambridge, England. He was interviewed on April 14 and 15 in 1994. Again the information was off the record until after his death. Tuyen would verify the information passed onto the author by An in regards to Pham

Ngoc Thao. A third source on this was Nguyen Ngoc Phach who worked under the pen name John Draw, and was interviewed in his Melbourne home on several occasions in the early 1990s. Further reading: Non-fiction, *The Quiet American* by Graham Greene.

4. PLEDGES OF ALLEGIANCE

In this chapter, Tran Kim Tuyen was again extremely helpful. He ordered many of the undercover incursions into North Vietnam and in the decades after the war he analysed what went wrong and why. He was particularly helpful, as was Pham Xuan An, on Le Duan and his escape to Hanoi. Equally important was Bui Tin, a Communist journalist who accepted the formal surrender of South Vietnam and later defected to the West. Tin verified accounts from Tuyen and An and told the author that An was responsible for Duan's escape which arguably precipitated the next phase of the war in Vietnam. Tin was interviewed by telephone from Paris while the author was in London on April 7, 1994. The death of An's father and his departure for the United States was relayed during initial interviews. Corruption regarding his visas and departures were also verified by Tuyen. It should also be noted that when interviewing An and Tuyen both had a habit for extreme detail. For example, a minor question about a political appointment in 1952 or 1962 would result in a sometimes frustrating response that began decades earlier with the family history of the people who made the appointment. Friends of An described this type of response as being 'old-school Vietnamese'.

5. CALIFORNIA DATELINE

Stories written by Pham Xuan An for the *Sacramento Bee* offered unprecedented insights into his thinking at the time. It also shaped his outlook. As the war escalated he realized the North Vietnamese and the Communists could not defeat the Americans on the battlefield in traditional warfare, hence his focus on defeating the U.S. in the political arena backed by asymmetrical warfare. An was also informative about those who helped in the United States while Earl Gustkey, a fellow student of An in California, remembered him well and was interviewed by telephone from his home in Los Angeles on March 31, 1994.

6. DOWN THE WIRE

Reuters correspondents Jim Pringle, Hugh Lunn, Peter Smark and Jan Smark Nilsson, Nick Turner along with Robin Strathdee of Australian Associated Press were primary sources of information about life for journalists as the war in South Vietnam began to unfold in the early 1960s. Others who knew Neil Davis—Tim Bowden, John McBeth, James Gerrand, Bob Davis and Tim Page—also contributed. McBeth's autobiography, *Reporter: Forty Years Covering Asia* provided personal insights at great detail. On April 13, 1994 the author interviewed Don Read who wrote *The Power of News: The History of Reuters* at Reuters headquarters in London. Reuters were generous and granted the author access to all relevant copy. Also present was David Chipp who initially hired Pham Xuan An, and was well versed about the office politics of the day. Further interviews were conducted on April 16 at Chipp's home in Eccleston Square, London.

7. INCIDENTS AND RUMORS

On the history of wires it is worth noting that the author spent 20 years working for wire services while Donald Read and David Chipp were insightful in regards to the internal operations of Reuters in the day. For further reading on Madame Nhu, Monique Brinson Demery's *Finding the Dragon Lady: The Mystery of Vietnam's Madame Nhu* is a more recent offering, published in 2013. Douglas Pike, a close confidante of Denis Warner, was interviewed by phone from Toronto (he was in San Fransisco) on March 27, 1994. Beverly Ann Deepe declined to be interviewed. *Newsweek* did not respond to requests for interviews or access to its files on the period. Jan Smark Nilsson and her former husband Peter, Wilf and Lucille Arthur, Laurie Crozier, Pham Xuan An, Bui Tin and Tran Kim Tuyen were tremendously helpful in regards to the kidnappings. Crozier's book *The Golden Land* offered further insights.

8. AP BAC, PLACE WITH A PLANT

A Bright Shining Lie by Neil Sheehan is an excellent account of the events at Ap Bac and its importance in the broader context of the war. The author also relied extensively on the personal accounts from the day, particularly from interviews with Pham Ngoc Dinh and Pham Xuan An. Dinh's eye for detail, particularly An's return from the battlefield and the in-house politics at Reuters was particularly helpful. Additionally, an official account entitled *Tran Ap Bac* published in Hanoi in 1992 provides further insights from the North Vietnamese perspective, including a photo of Ho Chi Minh examining a military map of Ap Bac at the time.

9. SHIFTING TIDES

This chapter, like much of Part Two, was derived through interviews conducted with primary sources. In terms of life and the changing times of Saigon it is difficult to escape the cultural influences that were pushed through Hollywood and Western-made movies and television programs in regards to war and Vietnam that were produced in the 1970s, 80s and beyond. Nick Turner confirmed the sacking of An but was coy about details which were enthusiastically filled in by Pham Ngoc Dinh while David Chipp also confirmed the reasons behind his removal. Frank McCulloch spoke readily about the changing dynamics in South Vietnam from the perspective of *Time* magazine and his final meeting with Robert "Blowtorch" Komer while Tim Page was sympathetic in his portrayal of Pham Xuan An. Gen. Tran Van Tra outlined the thinking of the day, confirming political objectives as taking priority over the military, although it should be added he was careful and deliberate in what he said.

10. TET – THE PUNJI TRAP

Journalists who covered the Tet Offensive in 1968, or were heavily involved with South Vietnam at that time, freely told their stories. In particular Jim Pringle, Hugh Lunn, Pham Ngoc Dinh and of course Pham Xuan An. Others included Tim Page, and Nick Turner. A special thanks to Bryan De Lacy, a veteran journalist with Australian Associated Press who was insightful in regards to Mike Birch and his final farewell, a family picnic, held near Melbourne before leaving for South Vietnam. There is no shortage of newspaper articles, magazine articles and books written about the Communist offensive; among them Hugh Lunn's. *A Reporter's War*. For a straight military perspective, a blow-by-blow account Jack Shulimson's *The Illustrated History of Tet-1968: The Vietnam War* proved worthy. From a North Vietnamese military perspective a *People's War People's Army: The Viet Cong Insurrection Manual for Underdeveloped Countries* by Gen. Vo Nguyen Giap was overbearing and loaded with Communist rhetoric, however, that in itself is useful in terms of the thinking in Hanoi ahead of the Tet offensive and Mini-Tet a few months later.

11. TET TWO, ENCORE

Frank Palmos, author of *Ridding the Devils*, and Pham Ngoc Dinh gave detailed first hand accounts of how the four Western journalists were killed during this battle while interviews with the political commissar Tran Bach Dang on March 5, 1992 and with Gen. Tran Van Tra were insightful and added confirmation and much needed context particularly when considered in light of Pham Xuan An's exploits. An was also enlightening, particularly in regards to the death of his close friend John Cantwell. Dinh provided context for the final days of his confidante Bruce Pigott. The importance of Operation Phoenix was underplayed by journalists, particularly those with left-wing leanings, covering the war and the editors who employed them. Pham Xuan An, Gen. Tran Van Tra, Tran Bach Dang, staff in the Vietnamese press offices in Hanoi and Ho Chi Minh City, Judy Stowe, Pham Lam Huong and Hung Le at the BBC all found it unfathomable that successes by the United States in that operation, which devastated the ranks of the Viet Cong, went largely ignored.

12. SUN SETS OVER SAIGON

Julio Jeldres was interviewed in Melbourne on September 8, 2017. Dutch photographer Hu van Es recounted his experiences and clarified misinterpretations of the pictures he took of the last U.S. military helicopter taking off and leaving Saigon. He was also a close friend of Bert Okuley, the bureau chief for United Press International. The author and Van Es, known as Vanes to his peers, sat on the board of the Foreign Correspondents Club (FCC) in Hong Kong, together in 2000 and 2001. Tim Bowden's *One Crowded Hour*, chronicling the life of combat cameraman Neil Davis, helped to provide much context on the final days of Saigon alongside personal interviews with the Viet Cong Gen. Tran Van Tra, Communist journalist Bui Tin, Pham Ngoc Dinh, and Pham Xuan An. Stanley Karnow's *Vietnam a History* is probably the most definitive account from that period, which he extrapolated upon during an interview on March 30, 1994, when the author was in New York. Oliver Todd's *Cruel April: The Fall of Saigon* also provided extensive background on the final days before the Communists invaded and finally defeated South Vietnam. Reports from *Time* magazine from the day were handy, particularly in providing a sense of immediacy. Those reports did not contain bylines, however, An told the author that he was responsible for much of the coverage published by *Time* following the fall of Saigon until the bureau was forced to close about a year later. Also helpful were the journalists Judy Stowe, Pham Lam Huong and Hung Le who were interviewed at the BBC on April 7, 1994, in London. Denis Warner was again helpful on Bob Shaplen's role, the kidnapping of Wilfred Arthur and how they left Saigon together, and of course his final conversation with Pham Xuan An. Agence France-Presse (AFP) supplied information in regards to its correspondents in Saigon during the closing days of the war in 1975. Additionally, in 2000, the New Zealand/Australian war correspondent Kate Webb wrote an excellent series of articles for AFP retracing the North Vietnamese 1975 march across the southern border to Saigon, to commemorate the 25th anniversary of the collapse of South Vietnam.

13. A PEOPLE'S LIBERATION

Life after the Communist takeover of Saigon, particularly the dismayed journalists who were used to working within a relatively free press environment, was evident during talks with Tran Cong Man, Vice Chairman of the Vietnam Press Association on March 3, 1993. On March 31, 1994 the author interviewed Morley Safer in New York, particularly in regards to his book *Flashbacks* and the chapter relating to Pham Xuan An, The Spy in Winter. An told the author he was of the understanding the interview with Safer in January 1989 was off the record and he was upset when it was published in Safer's memoirs. So was Hanoi where An's handlers bolstered surveillance on him. Safer was unrepentant arguing An more than anyone would have known the interview was on the record, it was assumed and that no off the record deal was ever struck. Bui Tin and Pham Ngoc Dinh also corroborated An's testimony that the North Vietnamese Communists had failed to live up to their expectations in the south and the ham-fisted approch by the incoming authorities had upset those who had supported Hanoi most.

14. MISSING LINKS

This chapter relied heavily on the recollections of three people: Pham Xuan An

Pham Ngoc Dinh and his wife Vy, particularly in regards to their final meeting. While it should be expected that Vy would support her husband, she was a determined, intelligent woman who knew her own mind. She verified their final meeting, the publication An produced with photographs of him with Ho Chi Minh, his breakdown and requests for help and a way out of Vietnam. It was subject matter that An was reluctant to discuss, however, he did not deny the meeting nor did he try to refute Dinh's account of their final meeting.

15. ENTRENCHED

After the Vietnam War, or Second Indochina War, concluded most of those involved moved on or returned home to lick their wounds and nurse their memories. Like the soldiers who fought the war many of the war correspondents endured shell shock or Post Traumatic Stress Syndrome. Some tried to forget while others became obsessed with the country that had defined their lives. Some felt betrayed and Pham Xuan An was the touchstone for that treachery as news of his duel life trickled out of Vietnam, which was by now locked-down. With that in mind interviews with Vietnamese— from the North and South—conducted as the Cold War concluded in the late 80s and early 90s laid the spade work for this book. Especially the author's meetings with Dr. Tran Kim Tuyen, Bui Tin, Nguyen Ngoc Phach and of course Pham Ngoc Dinh and his wife Vy.

16. TWO LIVES, ONE LEGACY

The author's conclusions are his own. The author first met the banker John Brinsden during an interview on February 13, 1992. At that point he ran Standard and Chartered's operations in Vietnam and he remained a contact for the next 25 years. Also interviewed on March 11, 1992, was another banker and former South Vietnamese prime minister Nguyen Xuan Oanh, considered by some to be the architect of Vietnam's Doi Moi reforms designed to open up the country's economy and initiated in 1986. Both men were incisive in off the record interviews regarding Vietnam and issues with a state-planned centrally run economy. Oanh also mentioned eight former United States military personnel who had deserted and were living with their Vietnamese wives in Danang. Pen Sovann, former prime minister of Cambodia, was jailed by the Vietnamese and spent 10 years in the Hanoi Hilton. Released in 1992 he was interviewed by the author and Cambodian journalist Hang Sokunthea in 2016, shortly before his death. He said about 10 U.S. military personnel were occupying neighboring cells during his incarceration. Excerpts of that interview were published by *The Diplomat* on November 8, 2016.

Life in the capital under communism could also be witnessed first hand with the first Westerners entering the country in the aftermath of the Cold War. Interviews with Le Van Ching who owned a Saigon bookshop, and outfits like the No. 5 Bar on the renamed Nguyen Thiep Street, a Viet Cong run girlie bar where staff proved able informers on a clientele made-up largely of military servicemen, added some color.

Of correspondents covering the Vietnam War, journalists were often divided between the left and right of politics with a healthy dose of those in the middle. Throughout the war soldiers on the ground would complain there were too many journalists, particularly from their own countries, who wanted to see them lose the war. There is much truth to this, Pham Xuan An played on that throughout his long and distinguished career in espionage.

A reunion of journalists at the Majestic Hotel in 2015 attended by the author and such luminaries as George Hamilton, the actor and friend of Sean Flynn, was at times a sombre affair. Also present was the Hollywood author Perry Deane Young and the usual array of independent journalists and photographers including Peter Arnett, Tim Page, Jim Pringle and Al Rockoff. Those who had passed away included Hu van Es and Kate Webb. It was noted then that the disappearance of South Vietnam meant that press freedom had been subjected to Communist controls for 40 years and that no journalists, including those present, were able to report on Vietnam as they had done before the war ended.

Notes on Second Print

This is a second print of the first edition of the *Punji Trap* and includes clarifications and an updated back cover. Page 104 clarifies that British journalist Donald Wise was working with the *Daily Mirror* as opposed to the *Rand Daily Mail* in Johannesburg where he was in fact working previously. Four typos were fixed, in the acknowledgments, the first and second block of maps and photos and on page 109. Names of *Time* magazine staffers should read Rademaekers and McCulloch throughout.

SOURCES

PRIMARY SOURCES

Australia: Wilfred Arthur, Lucille Arthur, Peter Barnett, Tim Bowden, Laurie Crozier, Bryan De Lacy, Evan Ham, John Hurst, Tan Nguyen Ha, Hugh Lunn, Dr. John Murphy, Julio Jeldres, Frank Palmos, Andrew Peacock, Nguyen Ngoc Phac (John Draw), Pham Ngoc Dinh, Pham Vy, Billy Powis, Alison Puchy, John Radovan, Carl Robinson, Peter Smark, Jan Smark Nilsson, Ross Smith, John Sorell, Denis Warner, Peg Warner. *Britain:* David Chipp, Pham Lam Huong, Hung Le, Clare McDermott, Tim Page, Don Read, Judy Stowe, Dr. Tran Kim Tuyen. *Cambodia:* James Gerrand, Philip Jones Griffiths, Sokunthea Hang, Pen Sovann. *Canada:* Bill Charney. *France:* Bill Rademaekers, Bruce Russell, Bui Tin. *Hong Kong:* Bob Davis, Annie van Es, Hu van Es, Clare Hollingworth, Don North, Kate Webb. *New Zealand:* Nick Turner. *Thailand*: John McBeth, Jim Pringle. *United States:* Earl Gustkey, Stanley Karnow, Germain Loch, Frank McCulloch, Douglas Pike, Morley Safer, Nguyen Thu. *Vietnam:* Bruce Aitken, Brig. Gen. Pham Xuan An, Peter Arnett, John Brinsden, Dr. Nguyen Xuan Oahn, Bill Rodgers, Yana Sisi, Tran Bach Dang, Maj. Gen. Tran Cong Man, Gen. Tran Van Tra.

NEWSPAPER, PERIODICALS AND AGENCY SOURCES

Agence France-Presse, *Asiaweek, Asian Business Review,* Associated Press, Australian Associated Press, BBC World Service, *Christian Science Monitor, Far East Economic Review, New York Herald Tribune,* Reuters, *Sacramento Bee, Sydney Morning Herald, The Diplomat, The Globe Mail, Time-Life, The Spectator, The Herald, The Age, Vietnam Investment Review, Tuoi Tre, The New York Times, The New Yorker.*

OTHER NOTES AND SOURCES

Australian Archives, Department of Administrative Services.
 —File Reference: A1992/60
 —Job reference: 193/208 & A93/209

Central Intelligence Agency (CIA) reference letter: F92—2325, November 16, 1992.

Neil Davis diaries, with thanks to Tim Bowden.

Access to tapes of Neil Davis' death, courtesy of Tim Page and Marianne Harris

Asia Foundation annual reports.

Report to the Committee on Foreign Relations, United States Senate, Senator Joseph S. Clark — Stalemate in Vietnam, 1968 (Unclassified).

Indo-China, Geographical Handbook Series, United States Naval Intelligence Division, December 1943.

First international conference on Defence and the Media in Time of Limited Conflict—Brisbane, April 4, 1991; General William Westmoreland, Accuracy in the Media.

Foreign Correspondents Club, Hong Kong.

HISTORYNET, an online resource, proved a useful source of corroboration.

Last Days in Vietnam, a documentary by Rory Kennedy, 2014.

PHOTOGRAPHS

1-6   Photos supplied by Jan Smark-Nilsson
7   Photo supplied by Pham Ngoc Dinh
8   Photo supplied by Jan Smark-Nilsson
9   Photo supplied by Jim Pringle
10   Photo by John McBeth
11-12   Author's photos
13   Photo supplied by Jim Pringle
14-15   Author's photos
16   Photo supplied by Jim Pringle
17-18   Author's photos
19   Photo supplied by Bui Tin
20-22   Author's photos
23   Photo supplied by Pham Xuan An
24-40   Author's photos

Author portrait by Steve Porte ©2017

SELECTED BIBLIOGRAPHY

Anson, Robert Sam. *War News*. Simon & Schuster, New York, 1989.

McBeth, John. *Reporter: Forty Years Covering Asia*. Talisman Publishing, Singapore, 2011.

Berman, Larry. *Perfect Spy—The Incredibly Double Life of Pham Xuan An*. Smithsonian Books, New York, 2007.

Bizot, Francois. *The Gate*. The Harvill Press London, 2003.

Bowden, Tim. *One Crowded Hour—Neil Davis Combat Cameraman 1934-1985*. Imprint Collins Publishers Australia, Sydney, 1987.

Burchett, Wilfred. *Passport, an Autobiography*. Thomas Nelson (Australia) Limited, Melbourne, 1969.

Burchett, Wilfred. *Grasshoppers & Elephants: Why Viet Nam Fell*. Outback Press, Collingwood, 1977.

Butler, David. *The Fall of Saigon*. Dell, 1986.

Crozier, L.A. *The Golden Land*. Griffith University, 1992.

Demery, Monique Brinson. *Finding the Dragon Lady: The Mystery of Vietnam's Madame Nhu*. Public Affairs, New York, 2013.

Duiker, William J. *Ho Chi Minh*. Hyperion, New York, 2000.

Dunn, Peter. *The First Vietnam War*. C. Hurst & Company, London, 1985.

Fall, Bernard. *The Two Vietnams: A Political and Military Analysis*. Frederick A. Praeger, Publisher, New York, 1963.

Fall, Bernard (Editor). *Ho Chi Minh on Revolution: Selected Writings, 1920-66*. A Signet Book published by The New American Library, New York, 1968.

Gaffen, Fred. *Canadians in the Vietnam War—Unknown Warriors.* Dundurn Press, Toronto, 1990.

Gettleman, Evan (Editor). *Vietnam: History, Documents and Opinions on a Major World Crisis.* Penguin Books, Ringwood, 1965.

Giap, Vo Nguyen. *People's War People's Army. The Viet Cong Insurrection Manual for Underdeveloped Countries.* Bantam, New York, 1968.

Giap, Vo Nguyen. *The General Headquarters in the Spring of Brilliant Victory.* The Gioi Publishers, Hanoi, 2013.

Graham, Andrew. *Interval in Indo-China.* Macmillan & Co Ltd, New York, 1956.

Griffiths, Philip Jones. *Vietnam Inc.* Phaidon Press Limited, New York, 2001.

Hendon, Bill and Stewart, Elizabeth A. *An Enormous Crime: The Definitive Account of American POWs Abandoned in Southeast Asia.* Thomas Dunne Books St Martin's Griffin, New York, 2008.

Herr, Michael. *Dispatches.* Picador, London, 1978.

Hudson, Miles and Stanier, John. *War and the Media.* Stroud: Sutton Publishing Ltd, Pheonix Mill, 1997.

Jeffrey, Keith. *MI6: The History of Secret Intelligence Service 1909-1949.* Bloomsbury, London, 2010.

Karnow, Stanley. *Vietnam—A History.* Penguin Books, Ringwood, 1983.

Kiernan, Ben. *The Pol Pot Regime.* Silkworm Books, Chiang Mai, 1999.

Kirk, Donald. *Tell it to the Dead—Stories of a War.* M.E. Sharp, New York, 1996.

Knightly, Phillip. *The First Casualty.* Harcourt, Brace Jovanovich, USA, 1975.

Lunn, Hugh. *A Reporter's War*. University of Queensland Press, St Lucia, 1985.

McNamara, Robert and Van DerMark, Brian. *In Retrospect: The Tragedy and Lessons of Vietnam*. First Vintage Books, New York, 1995.

Osborne, Milton. *Sihanouk, Prince of Light Prince of Darkness*. Allen & Unwin, Sydney, 1994.

Page, Tim. *Page After Page*. Atheneum, New York, 1989.

Palmos, Frank. *Ridding the Devils*. Bantom Books, Moorebank, 1990.

Quinn-Judge, Sophie. *Ho Chi Minh: The Missing Years, 1919-1941*. Hurst & Company, London, 2003.

Raskin, Marcus G, and Fall, Bernard B. *The Viet-Nam Reader*. Random House, New York, 1965.

Read, Donald. *The Power of News: The History of Reuters*. Oxford University Press, New York, 1992.

Rosie, George. *The British in Vietnam: How the Twenty-Five-Year War Began*. HarperCollins, 1970.

Safer, Morley. *Flashbacks: On Returning to Vietnam*. Random House, New York, 1990.

Shaplen, Robert. *The Lost Revolution: Vietnam 1945-65*. Deutsch; 1st Edition, 1966.

Shaplen, Robert. *Time out of Hand, Revolution and Reaction in Southeast Asia*. Andre Deutsch, London, 1969.

Sheehan, Neil. *A Bright Shining Lie*. Picador by Pan Books Ltd, London, 1990.

Shulimson, Jack. *The Illustrated History of Tet—1968: The Vietnam War*. Bantam Books, New York, 1988.

Smark Nilsson, Jan. *Walking the Tightrope*. Trinity Beach, Tereba Publishing, Queensland, 2012.

Terzani, Tiziano. *Giai Phong! The Liberation and Fall of Saigon*. St Martin's Press, London, 1972.

Tin, Bui. *Following Ho Chi Minh—Memoirs of a North Vietnamese Colonel*. University of Hawaii, 1995.

Todd, Oliver. *Cruel April: The Fall of Saigon*. W.W. Norton & Company, 1990.

Tra, Tran Van. Vietnam: History of the Bulwark B2 Theatre, Vol. 5: Concluding the 30 Years War. 1982, *JPRS Southeast Asia Report*, No. 1247 Foreign Broadcast Information Service, February 2, 1983.

Van, Hoang Hai and Tu, Tan. *Pham Xuan An, a General of the Secret Service*. NXB The Gioi, Hanoi, 2008.

Veith, George J. *Black April: The Fall of South Vietnam, 1973-75,* Encounter Books, New York, 2013.

Vickery, Michael. *Kampuchea—Politics, Economics and Society*. Pinter Publishers Limited, London, 1989.

Warbey, William. *Ho Chi Minh and the Struggle for an Independent Vietnam*. Merlin Press, London, 1972.

Warner, Denis. *Not Always on Horseback—An Australian Correspondent at War and Peace in Asia 1961-1993*. Allen & Unwin, St Leonards, 1997.

Webb, Kate. *On The Other Side: 23 Days with the Viet Cong*. Quadrangle Books, New York, 1972.

INDEX

ABOUT THE AUTHOR

LUKE HUNT began his career as a journalist on outback newspapers. He was editor of the student newspaper *Planet* while studying at Deakin University before undertaking a cadetship with Australian Associated Press. He then covered wars, international politics and economics for Agence France-Presse where he served as bureau chief for Afghanistan and then Cambodia and held roving reporting duties from his home in Hong Kong. Hunt has written for *The Age* in his native Melbourne, *The New York Times*, *The Times of London*, *The Economist* and writes a weekly column on Southeast Asia for *The Diplomat*. His broadcasts have appeared regularly on ABC in Australia and on Voice of America.

He has been honored with several awards, including a shared World Association of Newspapers, an Amnesty Human Rights Press Award and been personally commended by the U.N. Special Representative for Afghanistan, Lakhdar Brahimi, for his bureau-coverage of the Afghan conflict, prior to the September 11, 2001, attacks on New York and Washington.

He is a senior lecturer at Pannasastra University in Phnom Penh where he wrote the course War, Media and International Relations.